MR. SMITH GOES TO PRISON

MR. SMITH GOES TO PRISON

JEFF SMITH

What My Year Behind Bars Taught Me
About America's Prison Crisis

St. Martin's Press ≈ New York

www.stmartins.com

Designed by Omar Chapa

Library of Congress Cataloging-in-Publication Data

Smith, Jeff, 1973–
    Mr. Smith goes to prison : what my year behind bars taught me about America's prison crisis / Jeff Smith.—First edition.
        p. cm.
    ISBN 978-1-250-05840-9 (hardcover)
    ISBN 978-1-4668-6256-2 (e-book)
    1. Smith, Jeff, 1973– 2. Prisoners—United States—Biography.
3. Ex-legislators—United States—Biography.   4. Imprisonment—
United States.   5. Corrections—United States.   6. Criminal justice,
Administration of—United States.   I. Title.
HV9468.S655A3   2015
365'.6092—dc23
[B]
                                                              2015017831

Our books may be purchased in bulk for promotional, educational, or business use. Please contact your local bookseller or the Macmillan Corporate and Premium Sales Department at (800) 221-7945, extension 5442, or by e-mail at MacmillanSpecialMarkets@macmillan.com.

First Edition: September 2015

10   9   8   7   6   5   4   3   2   1

To my parents, for warning me to avoid politics.
To Teresa, for riding with me.
To the warehouse crew, for looking out.
And to everyone who wrote or came to visit.

CONTENTS

AUTHOR'S NOTE

Most of this book was originally written in shorthand on napkins, toilet paper, or in a pocket-sized spiral notebook and then transferred to larger pieces of paper and hidden in another prisoner's cell in a different unit before being mailed to a friend for safekeeping. Conversations were recorded contemporaneously and reported as close to verbatim as possible. Some language used may be offensive, most notably the use of racial epithets (especially "n——") by both black and white prisoners. This was a difficult decision to make, and I apologize for any resulting discomfort to readers. However, in order to maintain the authenticity and intent of the speaker, I have chosen to keep particular words and phrases in the text.

My former senate aide Kailey Burger and former New School student Justine Gonzalez assisted with transcription, logistics, and research. Any errors are mine and mine alone.

MR. SMITH GOES TO PRISON

INTRODUCTION

The first correctional officer had two visible teeth. I came in with a young black guy who mumbled and a Chinese man who spoke broken English, but at least I could decipher their words. The CO was harder to understand. Manchester, Kentucky, is tucked in an Appalachian mountain hollow, and he had apparently never left. When he sauntered into the austere holding room and asked the Chinese man his name, the man replied, "Shoi-ming Chung."

"Sesame Chicken?" replied the CO, laughing uproariously and then repeating it twice as if it were the funniest thing he'd ever heard.

He sent me to a heavyset nurse for a battery of questions.

"Height and weight?" she asked.

"Five feet, six inches, a hundred twenty pounds."

She examined my slight frame and frowned. "Education level?"

"Ph.D."

She shot me a skeptical look. "Last profession?"

"State senator."

She rolled her eyes. "Well, I'll put it down if ya want. If ya wanna play games, play games. You'll fit right in. We got ones who think they're Jesus Christ, too."

Another guard escorted me to a bathroom without a door. He was morbidly obese and spoke gruffly in a thick Kentucky drawl. "Stree-ip," he commanded. I did. "Tern 'round," he barked. I did.

"Open up yer prison wallet," he ordered.

I looked at him quizzically.

"Tern 'round and open up yer butt cheeks."

I did.

He manhandled me roughly. "All right, you'se good to go."

The last stop was in the office of the counselor, a wiry, compact, sandy-haired man named Mr. Sims with a light blue polo-style shirt and a wispy mustache. He flipped through the presentencing report, pausing briefly to absorb the case summary, and shook his head. "This is crazy," he said quietly, without looking at me. "You shouldn't be here. Complete waste of time. Money. Space."

A complete waste! Exactly!

Finally, someone agreed. But now it was too late.

Six months earlier, with a nervous spring in my step, I'd bounded onto the elevator up to my lawyer's office. Like most politicians, I had a uniform. Blue shirt, sleeves rolled-up, yellow print tie, slim-fitting khakis: the picture of a young, energetic state senator with a bright future. Five years earlier, I'd challenged the scion of Missouri's leading political dynasty; I came within 1,700 votes of toppling him and reaching Congress at age twenty-nine. An award-winning film chronicling my efforts titled *Can Mr. Smith*

Get to Washington Anymore? earned a cult-like following among young politicos around the country. And now, the vaguely familiar man in the elevator up to my lawyer's office smiled when he referenced the film. "Gonna run for Congress again, Mr. Smith? Or city hall?"

My heart pounded and I told the man in the elevator, "Right now, sir, I'm happy in the state senate." I knew I wouldn't be going to Capitol Hill or city hall any time soon.

When I left an hour later—having learned that (a) my political career was over, (b) my best friend had been taping our conversations for months, and (c) the contents of these tapes would be splashed across the front page of the newspaper—I realized I was going to prison.

Six months later, I was adrift in a sea of sharks—an academic-cum-politician-cum-felon forced to learn prison patois and the politics of survival. Instead of the quiet, uneventful post teaching GED courses I'd expected, I was assigned to unload food trucks at the warehouse. In prison I would be the student, not the teacher.

Mr. Smith Goes to Prison is the story of what I learned there—about my fellow prisoners, the guards and administrators, and the system in which we operated. My story is a cautionary tale of friendship and betrayal. It is a story of how politics prepared me for prison—and how prison prepared me for life. But more broadly, it is a scathing indictment of a system that teaches prisoners to be better criminals instead of better citizens. And finally, it is a prescription for how we can address our nation's prison crisis and harness the untapped potential of 7 million people now enmeshed in the criminal justice system, 2.3 million of whom are behind bars. I meld my own experience with research and interviews with scholars, policymakers, ex-offenders, and innovators who are rethinking prison to produce a blueprint to address our nation's mass incarceration problem through new programs that can transform the lives of offenders, make prisons safer, infuse our economy with entrepreneurial energy, and save taxpayers billions by slashing sky-high recidivism rates.

My research approach might be called "involuntary participant observation." The product suffers from all the flaws inherent in ethnographic work; the main flaw, of course, was my total lack of objectivity. In prison, despite simmering racial tension and petty disputes, there are really only two teams: the prisoners versus the prison. I never had any doubt about which team I was on.

Books such as Dwayne Betts's *A Question of Freedom*, Marie Gottschalk's *Caught,* and Michelle Alexander's *The New Jim Crow*; documentary films like Eugene Jarecki's *The House I Live In*; a recent PBS *Frontline* series on mass incarceration—all have used divergent approaches to illuminate the same problem: the U.S. prison population has grown eightfold since Ronald Reagan's inauguration at the beginning of 1981; one in three black men has been locked up, helping give America the largest (and most expensive) prison population of any nation in history.[1]

While I offer my own perspective on the problem of mass incarceration, I also focus on solutions. First, how do we improve the odds for millions of prisoners to successfully reenter society? Second—given the pervasive waste and debilitation, as opposed to rehabilitation, of people in prison—how do we change the mentality of a system that dehumanizes those within it? As an activist, a scholar, a former policymaker, and—regrettably—a felon, I have a unique perspective: when most other researchers, authors, and filmmakers have concluded their interviews and shot their B-roll, the prison gates clanged shut behind them, and they were able to go home.

1

"THE MISSILE'S ALREADY LEFT THE SILO"

How I Went to Prison Instead of Washington

I was twenty-nine when I decided to run for Congress. It was summer 2003, and President Bush had just invaded Iraq. I was incensed about the war and distressed about the Bush tax cuts given the looming expense of boomer retirement. But the issue that animated me was education reform and St. Louis's school-to-prison pipeline. To understand my passion, one must first understand my father's.

My dad dreamed that I'd play in the NBA. That he was five-foot-six and my mom was five-foot-two did not deter him. When I was three years old, my parents took me to the pediatrician, and my dad asked him about my chances at basketball stardom. "I've got good news and bad news," he said. "The good news is, your son's healthy. The bad news: he's in the third percentile in both height and weight."

"Well," replied my mom optimistically, "at least he's not in the first or second percentile."

"There's actually no such thing," said the doctor grimly.

But my dad didn't abandon his hoop dreams. Starting when I was about nine, he would take me to gyms and playgrounds in dilapidated parts of St. Louis where dusk brought with it the sound of gunfire, advising me to tell my mom that he had taken me to play golf. By my senior year of high school—then five-foot-three—I became a pretty good point guard and the only white starter on a team of mostly black kids bused out to our suburb via a special interdistrict program. Basketball was my lingua franca, my bridge to their world. At the preseason physical, I weighed ninety-three pounds. My coach looked at the trainer and shrugged. "Jesus Christ, we can't list him at that. Just put down one hundred."

I was probably the smallest person in every high school game I ever played, but on the court I never felt small; as point guard and captain, I called the plays and directed traffic. On defense, I was tenacious and got a lot of steals. But the opposing coach usually called plays to isolate me down on the blocks. Since my counterpart was often a hundred pounds heavier and a foot taller, I was forced to learn every defensive trick in the book; that grit would define me.

My senior year, we were ranked number one in the region. My teammates had become my closest friends. One told me, "People think we're stupid 'cause we come out on the bus. But this school is three, four years ahead of my old school. I can barely keep up." He was right: most county kids thought the city kids were dumb, and they didn't disguise it. Seeing the difference between our worlds—their crowded neighborhoods and ramshackle homes versus my own middle-class street with trees and lawns and actual space between the houses; their lousy education at city elementary schools versus our schooling in one of the state's top districts—opened my eyes to the inequities that persisted forty years after *Brown v. Board of Education* and made me want to fix them.

I attended the University of North Carolina at Chapel Hill, where I was one of two white students majoring in Black Studies, to the chagrin of my family and some of my professors. My dad, who'd done so much to expose me to black culture via basketball, advised me to be more practical. "If you want to be a doctor, do premed. If you want to be a lawyer, do prelaw. I hate to break it to you, Jeffrey, but you'll never be black."

When I returned to St. Louis after graduation, I wanted to teach black history in the city public schools, which had some of the state's lowest test scores and highest dropout rates. I applied but couldn't get hired without a teaching certificate. Instead, I was hired in part to evaluate and train certified teachers. I wish I could say that in my time there, I learned about the roots of the achievement gap or how best to address it. But those weren't my main takeaways.

Though well paid, the district's administrators generally performed without accountability or urgency. I could offer dozens of examples, but one stands out. I had just returned to the central office from a mid-November school visit at which I had encountered a teacher who told me that she still hadn't received the textbooks she'd ordered during the summer, and I went down to the department in charge of educational materials. When I explained the teacher's predicament, the man who appeared to be in charge eyed me wearily. "What kind of book?"

"Seventh-grade math."

"I'm not in charge of that," he said impassively.

"So . . . who is?"

"She won't be back till after Thanksgiving," he said with finality.

"So, who could help me now . . . or point me to the books?"

"Didn't I just tell you she's on vacation?"

That lack of urgency—two more weeks students would go without books and the guy was completely blasé!—was both ubiquitous and mystifying: the district had lost two-thirds of its students in the last thirty years, and it was about to lose state accreditation. Just one in every ten freshmen would attend a four-year college; half would fail to graduate. A stunning proportion of black male dropouts would end up in prison before age thirty-five. This was hardly unique: one Harvard study pegged the rate of incarceration nationally at 60 percent. The amount of money the nation wasted on this was mind-boggling: a joint Columbia-Princeton study estimated that society could save $209,000 in prison and other costs for every potential dropout who completed high school instead.[1] But absent drastic change, another generation of kids would be lost—in fact, multiple generations, because children of incarcerated men were far more likely than other children to end up in prison themselves.

That challenge would animate my next decade. After my frustrating tenure with a school district plagued by a sclerotic bureaucracy, I joined a woman who ran the city's interdistrict busing program to cofound a charter school that had more flexibility in its curriculum and personnel. Confluence Academy began with 250 kids whose parents gave us a chance; it now educates 3,500 students on five campuses.

While working for the public schools, I took a night job teaching ACT and SAT test-prep courses for Kaplan, but I soon realized that I didn't want to spend my life teaching rich kids how to beat a test. To make broad changes in public policy, I would need a graduate degree. I originally figured I'd continue with my primary major, African American Studies, and called one of my college professors to request a reference. "Jeff," he said, "I can't in good conscience write this rec. No white AF-AM Ph.D. will get a job these days." After hearing similar though slightly more diplomatic advice from another professor, I decided to pursue a doctorate in political science instead.

During grad school, I continued at Kaplan, where I taught a high school senior who was a top-flight Division I basketball recruit. He lived in the projects; his summer league team paid his Kaplan tuition. Despite his 3.0 high school GPA, his original ACT score was lower than the likely score of someone guessing randomly. Tutoring him at his apartment, I realized that he was illiterate. After we spent months reading *Sports Illustrated* together a word at a time, he earned a high enough score to attend a Big East school on a full scholarship and later play pro ball. Without a qualifying ACT score, he would've gone the junior college route, and the odds from there to pro ball were not much better than the lottery.

From this beginning, I created a tutoring program for disadvantaged high school athletes to help them earn scores above the threshold necessary for freshman eligibility, since failing to do so would cost them scholarship offers. I used Kaplan's copyrighted materials, telling myself that Kaplan was doing just fine, and anyway, these kids couldn't afford a $1,000 class. (I charged $50.) If they became NCAA Proposition 48 casualties and lost scholarship offers, I reasoned, many would quit high school; the statistics for black males were pretty clear from there: unemployment and likely brushes with the law. Here were some kids with the chance to escape, and since Kaplan wasn't losing business, no one was getting hurt. In five years I taught over a hundred athletes, many of whom went on to earn D-I scholarship offers. The ends justified the means, I thought. That view would come back to haunt me a decade later.

In 2000, I spent a year working in Iowa on Bill Bradley's presidential campaign. Then I went back to grad school, and one day after completing my doctoral exams, I got a call from a man named Steve Brown. He was thirty-five, recently remarried with a big new house and a plan to run for the Missouri House of Representatives. On the advice of a mutual friend, he called me to discuss the race. We met for lunch at Blueberry Hill, a diner famous for its burgers, antique jukeboxes, and the weekly Chuck Berry shows held in its basement concert venue, the Duck Room. I was a few minutes late.

As I walked in, a bear of a man—six-foot-two, 275, I guessed—approached from the bar. He was wearing an expensive suit, monogrammed cuff links, and a watch that cost more than I made in a year. (I soon learned that he owned five such watches.) He shook my hand firmly and led me to his table, where he was on his second Diet Coke. "If you're early, then you're on time," he said. "If you're on time, you're late. And if you're late, don't bother showing up. That's what Vince Lombardi used to say."

Steve inhaled his burger. I asked him why he was running for state rep. "Hell, I wanna be a United States senator, but you gotta start somewhere." He laughed. His family had resources that could be leveraged, he said—a billionaire uncle and a father worth $100 million. No one would outspend him; of that he would make sure. He talked about his college football days and vowed to destroy his primary foe like he used to destroy opponents at the line of scrimmage. I hesitated when he asked me to manage his campaign, and he promised I could hire whomever I wanted. "Money is no object," he said. I accepted.

Our opponent in the primary was Dr. Sam Page, a wealthy anesthesiologist and town councilman who also had the ability to self-fund. Unbeknown to Steve, Sam had quietly begun his campaign a year earlier, and he had already garnered the support of the Democratic establishment.

Lacking endorsements, we went directly to voters. I hired a bright, capable Washington University senior named Nick

Adams as my deputy, and other former students under him. We swarmed voters with enthusiastic young canvassers, using an Iowa caucus model. They learned, as I had, that every single voter mattered.

The only problem with our model was the candidate. I was used to doing 125 or 150 doors a night, but when we canvassed together, he'd often stop after 25 or 30 doors and ask to go home. He was too tired from playing squash that morning. It was too hot. He'd promised his wife they'd have dinner.

Yet I found Steve endearing. He was as loyal as anyone I'd known; he even defended me when his wife got angry that I demanded so much of his time. He was surprisingly athletic and always game for a contest, whether in tennis, basketball, golf, or squash. Generous to a fault, he'd take the staff out for wings and beer whenever the mood struck. He remembered everyone he met on the campaign trail. And for a guy with five Rolexes and three country club memberships, he could relate to voters; he knew they'd rather talk about the Cardinals than the state budget. He genuinely liked people. You just can't teach that.

Steve spent liberally from his family fortune, as did Sam Page. The difference? Page felt it; Steve didn't. In fact, when I asked if Steve could come up with another $10,000, he replied, "If I'm gonna call my uncle for money, it's easier to ask for a million than ten grand." In what was the most expensive house primary in state history, Steve lost by twenty-eight votes. Sometimes I wonder how things might have turned out differently had we convinced fifteen Page voters to pull the lever for Steve.

When House minority leader Dick Gephardt, arguably the most powerful member of Congress in Missouri history, decided in January 2003 to run for president and not seek reelection in 2004, a bevy of ambitious politicians lined up to succeed him.

By Labor Day, following declarations of candidacy by six others, I had been bitten by the bug.

I knew a congressional candidate needed three things to be successful: a resonant message, a strategy, and money. I figured I might have the first: I was pissed off at the war in Iraq and a tax structure that seemed tilted toward the rich and was causing deficits that would cripple future generations. As for the second, my experience with the Bradley campaign and Steve's nearly successful run had taught me how to run a grassroots campaign against the establishment. Number three was the problem. Not only did I lack money, but I knew very few people who had it—and those who did were mostly either apolitical or Republicans.

Instead of focusing on my doctoral thesis as my family had urged, I'd spent the summer coaching basketball camps. I was sitting on the deck at the home of my high school coach one Friday night, drinking beer and arguing about which kids at camp had D-I potential, which kid was the laziest, and which kid's mom was most attractive, when my phone buzzed.

It was Steve Brown. "Man, I'm getting impatient," he said. "I hate sitting on the sidelines. I think I'm gonna come in heavy for Claire." Claire McCaskill was Missouri's state auditor at the time. "That cocksucker Holden, the way he fucked me, he's gonna pay for that." Bob Holden, then Missouri's governor, had stayed neutral in Steve's house primary, despite Steve's family having been top fund-raisers for Holden. "Claire called me, she wants to have lunch. I like her style. She doesn't fuck around. She's gonna primary him, and I think she can take him. We're having lunch next week. Whaddaya think? Can she win?"

"Well, yeah, I think she can. The governor is weak enough with the base to make him vulnerable in a primary. As far as you jumping in big, well, I guess you don't have much to lose.

After the way you left things with the governor last year, I don't see him doing much for you any time soon."

"He'll never do shit for me. I'm gonna help Claire, but I'm not gonna do shit for anyone anymore without a hard and fast promise—except for you, because you're my friend, and I know you'll be there when I need you. From now on, though, I'm not lifting a fucking finger for anyone until I get an ironclad promise that they'll be with me in a primary—no ifs, ands, or buts."

"I understand, Steve."

"So I'm gonna help her. I don't wanna just sit on the sidelines all my life. I wanna play in some of this stuff."

"Well, there may be another race for you to play in," I blurted out.

"Huh?"

"Mine."

"What?!"

"Steve, I know it sounds crazy, but I'm thinking about running for Gephardt's open seat."

"Wow. That's a lot to bite off. Wow. I don't know what to say. I think maybe you can do it. Russ is weak. And Mark Smith? Come on," Steve scoffed. "He's assistant dean for something at the law school, he's a nobody, he's got no juice, trust me." Steve's father served on the board of trustees at the law school.

"Well, if I run, I don't want him in the race. Two Smiths isn't real promising against one Carnahan. Hell, one Smith isn't real promising against one Carnahan . . . although hopefully some distant cousin of his will get inspired and run, too."

"Good point." We laughed at the thought.

"Steve, I'm gonna need your help if I do this." This was an understatement. I would need him to get out every country club directory he had—and there were several—to make calls and introduce me to people.

"You know I'll be there for you. You went balls-out for me. I'll be there for you. We didn't quite pull it off for me, but we will next time. And in the meantime, you're gonna make some waves. You may not win, but you're gonna surprise people."

"I'm not running to surprise people. I'm only running if I think I can win. If I can't raise a hundred grand my first quarter in, I won't run." Probably too high a bar, I thought to myself, but it sounded good, ambitious, strong.

I set two benchmarks for myself, one concrete, the other less so. The concrete benchmark was the $100,000. The other was somewhat less scientific: one evening after teaching the following week, I walked across the street from Washington University and canvassed a neighborhood to see if people would take me seriously as a congressional candidate or if they thought I looked too young (I was a boyish twenty-nine, five feet, six inches tall, and 120 pounds soaking wet). I knocked on forty doors. A thirty-something woman answered the first door and asked me point-blank if I was pro-choice. I said, absolutely. She said she'd vote for me as long as I don't waver on that issue. I thought to myself, *Okay, there's one vote. At least I won't get shut out.* A few doors later an older man asked me if I supported stem-cell research. I said yes, and he said he was a researcher and would support me if I supported the right to unfettered scientific research. *Two for two. I can do this.* About twenty minutes later, I reached the door of a woman in her midforties. "Hi, my name's Jeff Smith, and I'm planning to run for Congress, but I just wanted to come by today and introduce myself."

She looked at me quizzically. "Where are you coming here from?"

"Uh, well, from campus, actually."

"Oh, yes, you must be looking for Janie. Hold on a second." She called up the stairs, "Janie, come on down, there's a young man here running for your student congress."

"Tell him I'm busy, Mom," came the disembodied voice of a college girl.

I was too embarrassed to explain myself. I said good-bye, walked back to campus, and resolved to keep my sense of humor for the next year.

I decided to broach the idea to my parents at Sunday dinner, a family tradition, but they thought it was a joke. Literally, they thought I was playing a practical joke at first.

"Hey, guys, I'm serious about this. I think I can win."

"Okay, Beavis," said my brother Andy, and everyone laughed at his imitation of the 1990s cartoon.

"C'mon, guys, seriously, I need your help. Can you each give me two thousand bucks?"

"Will that get me a personal dinner with the candidate?" asked Andy, and everyone laughed again.

I wasn't laughing. "Listen, I can win this thing. But I gotta raise a hundred grand in my first three months if I wanna be taken seriously. And I can't get there if you guys aren't all in for two thousand." I knew it sounded cold, but they could've each given me two thousand dollars without feeling it too much.

Andy turned serious. "Okay, if I give two grand now, can I get my money back as soon as other people put their money in?"

"No."

"That's ridiculous. There's no way I'm doing that, then."

My mom interjected. "Jeffrey, have you thought this through? The whole idea just seems preposterous. Why don't you finish your Ph.D.? Maybe you could try this after you get established."

"Mom, the seat's open. It hasn't been open for twenty-eight years, and it may not open up for another twenty-eight years if Carnahan wins."

"Well, I can promise you I won't be giving you any of my

money. And if I hear that you're asking any of our friends or relatives for money, I will be absolutely mortified."

"Seriously, Mom? Aunt Vivian has tons of money. She wouldn't even feel a thousand bucks."

"Yes, I'm dead serious. I will disown you if you call Aunt Vivian about this nonsense."

I shook my head. "How am I going to beat Carnahan if I can't ask our friends for money?"

"Carnahan?" asked my dad. "Didn't he die in a plane crash?"

"It's his son, Dad." I was losing patience. "Are you guys going to help or not?"

"Jeffrey," said my mom haltingly, "I feel like you're just running away from finishing your Ph.D. Always running, you never slow down. Running to ACT tutoring. To your charter school. And for what? When will the running stop?"

My dad chimed in to agree, invoking his best friend. "Sandy says the same thing. He says you gotta get focused. Whether it's academia or politics or TV commentary, he thinks you need to pick one—"

"I am picking! I'm running for Congress. Are you guys gonna help?"

Silence.

"Uh, if you, like, win and stuff, will you get Secret Cervix protection?" My big brother was imitating Beavis again. Everyone cracked up.

I got up from the table. "Okay, that's fine. I'll get the money from other people." I knew I sounded like a petulant teenager whose request for the car keys had been denied, but I couldn't help it.

Of course, my family's skepticism wasn't entirely unfounded. Every poll taken named state rep Russ Carnahan, heir to Missouri's most powerful political dynasty, the front-runner. As one political science professor said: "The Carnahan name is to Missouri what the Kennedy name is to Massachusetts." Carnahan's record was thin, his public speaking was weak, and his campaign was uninspired. But his family's deep ties provided him with key endorsements, fund-raising connections, and near-universal name recognition. His name ID in our first poll of likely primary voters was 99 percent. Mine was 3 percent, and as my press secretary liked to remind me, 2 percent of that 3 percent just knew *someone* named Jeff Smith—not me.

My pollster told me something he claimed he'd never told a client before: he couldn't see a path to victory. Carnahan's name ID was overwhelmingly positive: people didn't distinguish him from his family. Russ's father, a popular two-term governor who died tragically in a plane crash weeks *before* his election to the U.S. Senate, won from the grave, posthumously beating John Ashcroft. Russ's mother served in his stead. Older voters recalled his grandfather, a congressman and an ambassador. Women admired his mother's service in the Senate and were thrilled by his sister's candidacy for secretary of state. This all translated into a favorable image that no negatives we tested could touch—just as I'd been warned. "You might consider a different race," said my pollster. "A winnable one. How about Russ's seat in the statehouse?"

My formal announcement—a press release I sent to local media on October 1, 2003, from the Washington University Arts and Sciences computing lab since I had no computer and no office, but did not ever think to report as an in-kind contribution—was met with deafening silence from reporters, other campaigns, and voters, 99.9 percent of whom never learned of it. This was a harbinger of the year to come.

But all was not lost. As I struggled to get someone— anyone!—to notice me, I inadvertently drew the attention of the most important person in Third Congressional District politics.

I was teaching a Washington University course on the inter-
play between electoral politics and the policy process, and had
devoted a week to readings on the exercise of power in urban
politics. I assigned an article from the city's alternative weekly,
the *Riverfront Times*, about Gephardt's national political director,
Joyce Aboussie. As Gephardt's right-hand woman, she was the
most powerful behind-the-scenes figure in Missouri politics. I
sent the article, which described her hardball tactics and was
titled "Joyce Abusive," to my students, and within the hour my
cell phone rang. "Blocked Number" flashed the screen. I figured
it was a reporter calling to follow up on the press release.

"WHO IN THE FUCK DO YOU THINK YOU ARE?" demanded a woman.

"Uh, this is Jeff Smith."

"Yeah, I know who the fuck it is. What I wanna know is, who
the fuck do you think you are?"

"Joyce?" I asked, but I already knew the answer.

"You're goddamn right. And I wanna know why you're putting out that trash about me."

"Joyce, I don't think it's a bad article. And anyway, I didn't
write it—"

"No, you went one worse. You disseminated that SHIT all
over the country. You've really fucked yourself, do you realize
that?" I was standing in the political science graduate student
office, a few feet from students poring over journal articles and
statistics textbooks. I was getting a real lesson in politics. They
seemed oblivious, though I suspected they could hear her across
the room.

"Joyce, it only went out to thirty students, none of whom are
even from Missou—"

"Now you listen to me. I am NOT the person you want as
an enemy if you want to even THINK about having a chance to
win this congressional race, do you fucking understand that?"

"Yes, I'm sorry. I didn't know the article bothered you so much. I apologize."

I hung up in shock. She was right: if there was one person out of the 750,000 people in the Third Congressional District that I did not want to alienate, it was her. And on my first day in the race, I had done precisely that.

I called a friend who had worked for Gephardt to ask for advice. "Should I send chocolates?" I asked. "Roses?"

"No, none of that will work," he said. "Nothing phony or contrived. Your only chance here is a handwritten, hand-delivered apology. Dude, that article is her Kryptonite. You better get off the phone with me and get down to her office right now."

I wasn't sure why she hated the article so much; it showed her to be tough, savvy, and powerful. But I didn't quibble. I wrote the apology and drove to her office, a nondescript storefront at a nondescript strip mall in a nondescript suburb, where a receptionist greeted me. "Can I help you?"

"Yes, I hope so." I held up the letter. "I have something I'd like to give Ms. Aboussie."

"Let me check and see if she's available. What's your name?"

I told her. She returned a few minutes later, explained that Joyce was on a conference call, and asked if I would like to wait or leave the letter with her. "I'll wait," I said cheerfully.

Six hours later, I was still waiting. I had to teach that night, so finally I left.

I spent most of the month in the Washington University computer lab, where as a doctoral candidate without my own computer or campaign staff, I stayed up until 4:00 A.M. nearly every night researching different policy areas and drafting preliminary position papers for my campaign. I also researched strategy, examining voting history throughout the district. I knew there would be at least eight candidates, and with each candidate that entered, the race became that much more attractive to later candidates, because a smaller percentage of votes was needed to win. If Carnahan proved as weak as I anticipated he would be (based on a one-time meeting and the fact that he had won his first race by only sixty-four votes despite outspending his unknown opponent 20 to 1), I estimated that someone could win with just 25 percent of the vote. And with each new candidate who entered the race, that percentage went down even more, making the race even more appealing to me: The smaller the number of votes needed to win, the more important each vote would become. And the increased importance of each vote magnified the influence of a grassroots campaign relative to a money- and media-driven campaign.

But before I pulled the trigger, I needed to survey the district firsthand to get a sense of the types of people and neighborhoods in unfamiliar areas, so I took a bike ride through the entire district over several days. I lived in the northwest corner of the district; by happy coincidence, the northern third of the district was home to the candidate with the weakest geographic base and was also the most progressive and youngest part of the district—the two characteristics that best fit me. So the opportunity was there, but it would not be easy.

One of the first items of campaign business was to seek the support of my own state representative; there were approximately twenty-five state legislators with territory in the district, and while I realized that most would never consider supporting me, my best shot would be with my own representative. I called her three times and left messages, but got no answer. A few weeks later, in October, I approached her at a pro-choice event. "Hi, Representative Donnelly, I'm Jeff Smith, the guy running for Congress. I'm sorry we've had such a tough time connecting."

"I've been very busy," she replied coolly.

"Anyway, I was wondering if I might be able to take you for coffee sometime in the next few weeks before the holidays and get your advice on issues and on the race."

"I've got a very full schedule."

"Just twenty minutes or so would be great."

"How about sometime after session?" It was October, and she didn't have twenty minutes for me until the end of May.

"You know, Representative, I'm one of your constituents. I live at 7754 Kingsbury."

She pursed her lips. "Well, I have an awful lot of constituents."

And that was one of the most polite responses I got from an elected official.

Nick Adams, the thoughtful student of mine who had served as my deputy for Steve's first campaign, had moved to Chicago and was working as a temp, but he came back to St. Louis to be my first staffer. He and I believed in the same causes, and we believed in each other's ability. But reality being what it was, I paid him in room and board for the first three months. My first public speech as a candidate, on Nick's first day with the campaign, was an appearance before the Shaw Neighborhood Improvement Association. Shaw was one of the city's few integrated neighborhoods, then about 60–40 black and white. It was solid in the 1950s, went downhill in the 1960s, started to gentrify in the 1970s, and had been "in transition" for over thirty years. Its association had acquired a reputation for being opinionated. As I scanned the room, I saw mostly people in their fifties and sixties, many with the weary look of people who had expected the homes they'd bought for a song thirty years earlier to be worth ten times as much, only to be disappointed when the neighborhood kept taking one step forward, one step back.

I introduced myself and began my stump speech. "America

is facing historic challenges. We're embroiled in a quagmire in Iraq that is costing us billions of dollars and thousands of lives. This war of choice that George W.—"

"We don't want to hear your war crap. This is a neighborhood meeting!" screamed an unkempt, obese woman with black matted hair and pallid, blotchy skin.

The audience rustled but was otherwise silent, neither voicing agreement nor defending me. I decided to shift gears. "Closer to home, we face huge challenges in our public schools. When I came home from college, I took a job with St. Louis Public Schools. I learned a ton, but I was disturbed by much of what I saw. And so, a few years later, along with Dr. Susan Uchitelle, I cofounded a charter school called Confluence Academy. We've grown rapidly—"

"We don't want to hear about your charter schools either! They're destroying our city!" Her again. I scanned the room, looking for sympathy and finding only blank stares.

"Uh, okay, so the, uh, election is next August, and I just wanted to introduce myself. We'll put some literature on the table by the door if you'd like to learn more. Thanks for giving me the chance to talk." Nick and I dropped some policy papers on a table and skulked out. He nearly quit that night and moved back to Chicago. "Jeff," he asked, "are you sure you want to put yourself through this?"

"Nick, they won't all be like that," I reassured him. But I had no idea what they were going to be like. I was flying blind.

Fortunately, my friends responded differently than the Shaw crowd. I asked thirteen of them to serve as cohosts for my kickoff fund-raiser and agree to each raise $1,000 for me. Nearly all did, some even surpassing their goal, raising $15,000 in a single night. Thanks to dozens of coffees at people's homes, attended by anywhere from ten to fifty people, I was beginning to raise real money, $25, $50, and $100 at a time. Over the next couple of months, the coffees would help me sign up two hundred volunteers and raise approximately $80,000, and then I loaned my campaign a big chunk of my savings, about $20,000, in order to reach the magical $100,000 quarterly benchmark that national political reporters then seemed to agree signified a serious primary candidacy. Now that I had seed funding for office space, palm cards, and other campaign supplies, Nick and two other volunteers, Danny Kohn and Emily Fox, became actual paid staffers, and I cajoled a ragtag group of others into joining the campaign.

First was Clay Haynes, my campaign manager, who had been an A student in the very first class I ever taught—"Race and Ethnicity in American Politics"—back in 2000. He was politically savvy and perhaps the most likable of the hundreds of students I had taught. In September 2003, I met Clay on the street outside a laundromat where he was washing his clothes and told him that I was running for Congress and I wanted him to manage my campaign. "I just have absolutely no idea how to respond to that," he said.

"Just say yes." I felt like I was proposing.

"Let me think about it," he replied diplomatically.

It was not a no, I told myself. A few months later, after much prodding, Clay signed on, although he still didn't really believe we could win. He was twenty-three, hailed from Tennessee, and had the baritone voice of a radio deejay, the hair of a Benetton model, and the face of a teen idol. His winks, nods, smiles, and heartfelt thank-yous were ultimately responsible for the retention of a good portion of our female volunteers.

Next came Artie Harris, a recent Columbia grad who had worked as a researcher for a Washington political consulting firm. I met Artie in late 2003 after a Washington fund-raiser hosted by some friends from the Bradley campaign. What shocked me most at that first meeting was his appearance. I knew he was young—it came up that he had graduated from high school with a boy I once babysat—but with his paunch, receding hairline, glasses, and three-day beard (which took half a day to grow), he looked a good decade older than me. He hadn't had a haircut in a while, and his mop of curly hair made him look like a Jewish Muppet.

Artie had some rough edges. His profanity on the occasion of our first meeting would have been jarring at a bachelor party, let alone a job interview. And every time a young woman walked by, he ogled her briefly, letting his eyes wander as I talked or pausing in the middle of his own sentence. Each time I waited in vain for an apology. After the fourth or fifth time, Artie finally addressed the matter, obliquely. "God, I love this town," he said, shaking his head.

But I could tell he was very smart and I appreciated his mordant sense of humor, and so two months after that first meeting, once the campaign was on firmer footing, I offered him a job making $750 a month. He accepted, moved to St. Louis, and quickly anointed himself communications director, though I never gave him that title or even discussed it with him.

But he was brilliant, with a biting wit and keen insight into the mind-set of voters. Often volunteers would return to the office and complain that voters would say they would probably support Carnahan because they liked his parents. "You call them back right now and ask them if they'd have some guy they just met on the street operate on their kid's heart because the fuckin' guy's dad was a surgeon. When they say no, ask them why we should let idiots like Rusty run the country just because their dads were politicians." I often had to temper his advice, but the kernel of wisdom at the core of it was usually spot-on.

It didn't take long for the loose cannon to start shooting in the wrong direction. In Artie's first e-mail to our list, sent without anyone seeing a draft, he wrote that he had been hired to handle communications plus "local bartender/coed outreach." He later admitted that he had been drunk when he wrote it. Some of my most devoted volunteers demanded that I fire him and threatened to quit if I didn't. There were many things I'd rather do than waste an entire, very precious campaign day defending a guy I barely knew—three days on the job and drunk on the afternoon in question—to my staunchest supporters. But I never fired someone for one mistake, because I wanted my aides to take risks. And I was confident that Artie would hit more home runs than strikeouts.

I started with no money and no base, ignored by elected officials, voters, journalists, and my parents.* I called every elected official in the district, starting with every alderman and committeeperson—forty-five in all. A few were wrong numbers. I left messages for the rest. Several said they weren't interested, including St. Louis Democratic Party chairman Brian Wahby, who to his credit did not waste my time when I asked him if he'd sit down with me. "No. I'm with Russ. And I'm gettin' my hair cut. Later." Click.

Two of the forty-five officials agreed to meet me—an older couple, the Kirners. Dan, alderman of the twenty-fifth ward, had been a boxer and a cop; his neck was thicker than my thigh. His wife, Dorothy, the ward committeewoman, was a sturdy, gruff woman with a few unusually long gray hairs protruding from her chin. They called the meeting for 10:00 P.M. in a makeshift garage-cum-office with an alley entrance that took me a half hour to find—they clearly wanted to ensure that no one saw us together. I had no idea why they, unlike the others, took the meeting at all.

I entered the dark, grungy room and saw Dan seated behind a desk. He half nodded, half grunted toward a metal folding

---

* My parents would later contribute $4,000 to the effort.

chair. I seated myself and Dorothy reclined in an upholstered armchair. Dan asked a few questions: where was I from, who had I helped in city politics, what was my platform? Dan grimaced when I went through my platform. "Whaddaya runnin' as, a Democrat or a socialist?"

I asked if he'd give me names of others in the ward who might be more in line with me, and he stroked his chin and turned to Dorothy. She cackled and I forced a smile, though I didn't know what was funny. "Hell, outside-a Dorothy an' me," offered Dan, "I can't thinka nobody else in the ward who matters." And so it was, in St. Louis machine politics.

The Kirners wouldn't endorse me, but they were more cordial than any of their ward counterparts. Dorothy insisted I attend the ward Christmas party at an old banquet facility on a cramped residential street with tidy bungalows that had pink flamingos on the front lawns. It was $2 per ticket for all you could drink, Budweiser or water. I knew almost no one, but Dorothy helpfully introduced me to Missouri state representative Mike Vogt, who asked where I lived. "In Clayton, in an apartment," I replied. Clayton was a ritzy suburb. My apartment was a shithole, but that was hard to explain.

He shoved his plastic cup into my chest, spilling beer onto my tie. "Ya want my advice? Ya wanna win this race? First, take off your tie. Second, ya need to get some fuckin' hoosier in ya!"

I didn't have much hoosier—St. Louis jargon for "urban redneck"—but I had Steve Brown, who had become my closest friend. We talked every day, about politics, sports, women. No one did more than Steve to help me, both financially and by keeping my spirits up. "Fuck all these other people," he said, referring to the politicians who called him for money. (Steve was one of the state's top fund-raisers.) "I'm done with all of 'em, except you and Jay [Nixon, then the attorney general and aspiring governor]. You were the only two who were there for me."

Steve's Rolodex was golden, and he never hesitated to use it for me. It pained me to think of his narrow loss—I wished I'd somehow done just a little more to get him over the top! But that was the past, and we focused on the present—and the future. We knew he'd run again, and when he did (which turned out to be 2008), I'd do all I could to help him.

By midsummer 2004, our strategy to overcome my lack of name recognition and media interest by connecting directly with voters seemed to be working. Despite many setbacks and frustrations, we stuck to our plan: 93 coffees (our goal was 100), hiring 18 full-time interns, who helped recruit an army of 600 volunteers who planted 5,000 yard signs at homes of supporters across the district, nearly a half million dollars raised (average contribution: $62, with a handwritten thank-you to every donor). Much of our success at the grassroots level was due to our indefatigable twenty-year-old field director, a Harvard sophomore named Sam Simon whom I hired sight unseen based on references from his volunteer work with Howard Dean's presidential campaign. Sam directed our nightly canvassing efforts; I canvassed every day for ten months, hitting twenty-six thousand doors; the campaign in total hit a hundred thousand.

But the media stuck to its script, too: Carnahan had a million bucks, every endorsement, a thirty-point lead, and universal name ID. How could he lose?

This narrative frustrated us—and other candidates—to no end. If the candidate forums were any indication, Carnahan knew less about public policy than any of his ten competitors—or most of my undergrads. After a few poor performances in which he haltingly read each answer straight from index cards, Carnahan avoided nearly all public forums and debates. A close friend who was a labor union official said that during an endorsement interview, he had asked Carnahan's opinion on right-to-work, referring to labor laws reviled by unions that hinder a union's ability to organize. "Absolutely," Carnahan had confidently replied. "Everyone should have the right to work."

And yet many (though not all) labor unions still endorsed Carnahan. None of the city's major editorial pages endorsed me, either. The leading African American newspaper's decision to endorse Carnahan stung the most; I'd been a volunteer basketball coach and tutor at a Boys and Girls Club in the black community for a decade, and my platform emphasized issues like racial profiling that had resonated with black voters. The news pages of the newspaper tried to remain studiously evenhanded, which meant neglecting to compare the candidates' platforms (the issue section of our website contained one-page white papers on thirteen issue areas; Carnahan's had six sentences total covering four issues). It also meant refraining from editorial comments about the candidates' respective performances and mostly ignoring comparisons of the candidates' grassroots campaign efforts. Instead, reporters highlighted Carnahan's establishment support, fund-raising heft, and huge poll lead.

Frustrated by this story line, we leveraged a unique chance to circumvent it. In May, a local filmmaker had requested access to our campaign. We granted him conditional access: in exchange for giving him the right to use footage after the campaign, we'd be able to use it if we asked. So, in July, we cut a short video in an attempt to give voters substance instead of sound bites. While delivering the videos door-to-door, we discovered that tons of voters we tagged as undecided were actually supporters; many requested extra videos to share with others. They'd been trying to spread the word, and in the absence of media coverage, they were just waiting for the right vehicle. They never told us they were helping. They just did it. This was the culmination of all our efforts: regular people taking ownership of the campaign.

By June, we realized that we were closing quickly. Progressives were responding to our attacks on the Iraq War, strident opposition to Bush's debt-fueled tax cuts that largely benefited the rich, and nuanced discussion of urban education reforms. Attendance at rallies soared, and yard signs flew out the door faster than we could reorder them.

Still, we figured it wouldn't be enough unless we gave more people a reason to abandon the family they'd known and loved for decades. There was information to give people pause: Carnahan's attendance record in the recent state legislative session lagged behind that of 95 percent of his colleagues, and he'd missed many critical votes. And in contrast to his boasts, most legislation he sponsored went nowhere. For weeks, Artie fed this information to reporters, but none would write it. And in our frustration, in the campaign's waning days, I made a serious mistake.

One day during the homestretch, I was sitting in our call room trying to hit my daily quota of calling five hundred voters when Artie and Nick burst in. They had been approached again by a guy named Skip Ohlsen, a specialist in the political dark arts: opposition research and negative ads. He had an idea that he—and Artie as well—thought might just turn the election.

Skip's tentacles reached to the top of the state Democratic Party; he squired the lieutenant governor to events and had stayed at the governor's mansion. He had briefly pitched us months earlier, hoping to serve as a media consultant, but I'd found him shady and declined. Now he was back, proposing a mailer to highlight Carnahan's miserable attendance record. Artie made a passionate case for approving it. "The media won't print anything negative about the Carnahans," he said. "This is the only way to show people the difference between the dad and the idiot son. If we don't show them that, we lose: there's just not enough young liberals in this city." Artie pounded the table. "It's now or never—if we wait another day it won't go out in time." We'd come a long way—from zero to contender, picking up momentum every day in the last month of the campaign as yard signs spread like wildfire—but I agreed with Artie's basic logic: there just weren't enough like-minded voters hearing my message to get me over the top. We needed an extra push, and here—it almost seemed like fate—was someone offering to do it.

"Whatever you guys do," I said, "I don't wanna know any details. Understand?"

They nodded.

I didn't know the finer points of campaign finance law, but I was pretty sure it was illegal for campaign aides to work with an outside party who planned an expenditure to influence an election. I also figured it happened every day. I knew the game was largely rigged for people like Carnahan, that money and connections and name ID usually carried the day; that upstarts like me wouldn't be on anything close to equal footing without public campaign financing. And like the other candidates, I was appalled that the press hadn't challenged Carnahan on any issues or on his dismal attendance record. But none of that excuses my actions. At the end of the day, the buck stopped with me. My team wouldn't have gone ahead with the postcard if I had vetoed it.

I didn't know if the postcard would happen or not; we all figured Skip might pocket whatever money he raised. But in truth, I barely thought about it—I had a campaign to oversee: a half million bucks to raise, thousands of doors to canvass, hundreds of events to attend. Nick later told me that the decision weighed more heavily upon him than it did on me; he said that he felt conflicted, though I'd been too absorbed in the campaign to recognize it. On the one hand, my aides badly wanted to win, and they were young men susceptible to the idea that newbies cut their political teeth by playing the game like the big boys;

Artie in particular was adamant that we should encourage Skip to act. Steve Brown was also a strong advocate. "Look, Russ was born on third base and thinks he hit a triple," said Steve, a fan of sports metaphors. "Somebody's gotta whack him. And nobody else has the balls to do it."

On the other hand, Nick and Clay feared that the postcard's negativity would be discordant with our campaign's tone and might depress our volunteers' enthusiasm. But when I okayed it, we all agreed to move forward—and never to speak of the matter again to anyone, no matter what. My aides said they'd have Steve deal with Skip since Steve, who wasn't a campaign staffer, could legally do so—and Steve, who enjoyed political intrigue and loved to throw a punch, didn't object.

Yet, doubtful that Skip would actually follow through, we decided to call a press conference along with one of my opponents, Joan Barry, a pro-life state rep, to highlight precisely the material that Artie had given Skip—the publicly available information about Carnahan's dismal legislative attendance record. "Joan and I disagree on many things," I said. "But we agree that voters expect a leader who works as hard for this district as Congressman Gephardt has. And you can't do that if you don't show up." Joan echoed my comments; we agreed that Carnahan had not earned a promotion with his lackluster efforts in the state legislature.

The press ignored us.

"How is this not news?" Artie screamed to a local TV producer. "You have two candidates saying that another is totally unqualified to serve!"

"If that's how your candidate feels, he can buy some ads and say so," came the reply.

A few days later, Artie barreled into my call room. "The eagle has landed."

"What are you talking about?" I asked. It was less than a week before Election Day.

Artie took a postcard from his pocket. It was much smaller than I'd imagined it would be. Russ was pictured on a milk carton. MISSING: RUSS CARNAHAN, it read and in tiny print detailed his absenteeism. It was totally amateurish: three inches by five inches and shoddily designed. We laughed and shook our heads. This was what we'd hoped would be a game-changer.

About the only people who noticed the postcard were the people on the Carnahan team. They promptly filed a complaint with the Federal Election Commission alleging that my campaign and that of Joan Barry had illegally conspired with the producer of the anonymous postcard—an allegation facilitated by Skip Ohlsen's omission of the requisite "Paid For By" disclaimer.* Their complaint was lost in the same swirl of charges and countercharges that swamped the postcard.

The final week was a blur. At 4:00 A.M. on election night, we were down a thousand votes, with many votes still out. I'd won the Kirners' ward overwhelmingly, and most other city wards as well. I also won the St. Louis suburbs. But the southern third of the district consisted of exurban and rural areas with conservative views and houses far enough apart to preclude door-to-door canvassing. Residents in these areas had received anonymous flyers insinuating that I was gay because I opposed a constitutional amendment to ban gay marriage; the mailers had superimposed my face against the face of a flamboyant-seeming gay man. I was running about fifty points behind in that part of the district, which was keeping me out of the lead despite my being comfortably ahead everywhere else. I'd been too amused by the flyer to consider filing a complaint about it.

---

* Joan Barry's campaign had no involvement with the postcard.

I headed home at 5:00 A.M. Suddenly my phone awakened me. It was 7:00 A.M. The final tally was in; I finished second of ten, losing 21.3 percent to 22.9 percent.

The *St. Louis Business Journal* published a postmortem:

Smith didn't have a single endorsement. [Smith] worked like a maniac. He was tireless, and he was everywhere. He carried a yellow legal pad, an unending and growing list of folks to meet. His cell phone occupied any time between meetings. His . . . full-throttle energy bred and fed a contagion. . . . He didn't have any traditional forms of support. And yet Smith won the city. His campaign made endorsements look meaningless, and the machine look rusty. . . . [He] articulated an agenda that dared to move beyond the platitudes of common political rhetoric. It resonated, particularly with younger voters and new city residents disillusioned with the politics of dumpster maintenance. They had been waiting for a breath of fresh air. This was it.[2]

The morning after the campaign, I called Russ. "Congratulations, Congressman," I said with good humor and a dash of insouciance. We arranged to meet at his office, where I offered to endorse him and help him in the general election. "There is one more thing," I added. "I wonder if you'd consider dropping the FEC complaint you guys filed. I'd like to put it behind us. The help I'm offering doesn't hinge on your answer. I'm asking if you'd consider doing this as a gesture of goodwill."

Russ looked at his brother Tom, who had come in near the end to run his campaign. "I'm sorry." Tom grimaced. "But I'm afraid the missile's already left the silo."

That is, they wouldn't be withdrawing the complaint.

• • •

For the first couple of weeks after Election Day, I basked in the glow of a defeat that area politicos and journalists practically construed as a win. All of a sudden people who had thrown me forcibly out of meetings, such as St. Louis's Democratic Party chairman, Brian Wahby, wanted to have beers with me. Claire McCaskill, the Democratic gubernatorial nominee who had just toppled a sitting governor for the first time in state history, asked me to come work on her campaign to galvanize the youth vote statewide. Reporters called to ask how we came so close, and to apologize for not taking our campaign more seriously. And organizations that had snubbed me just weeks before were calling me for policy ideas and inviting me to keynote their next event. I lost, but it sure felt like I had a political future.

A couple of weeks after Election Day, we received an inquiry from the FEC, which wanted to ascertain whether our campaign had illegally coordinated with the producer of the postcard. The following week, my lawyer prepared a response—an affidavit with fifteen numbered statements that answered the questions posed by the FEC. Nearly all were true. One was not. "I don't know who designed, produced, printed, disseminated, or financed the postcard," it read. My lawyer didn't know my aides had met with Skip, and I didn't volunteer that they had. She handed me the affidavit.

I didn't know exactly who had done the first four things, though I figured Skip had some involvement, but I knew Steve had raised the money. And I knew my staff had given Skip information about Carnahan's attendance record. That the information was publicly available and possessed by other campaigns as well as journalists didn't matter: the exchange broke a law.

I also knew that—like jumping into icy water—if I waited too long to sign, I wouldn't do it.

My mind raced with reasons to sign it. I'd made a pact with Steve and my aides to deny any involvement with the mailer. I wanted to protect my aides from legal trouble. I wanted to avoid tarnishing our acclaimed campaign, and to escape a big fine after having just spent much of my savings on the campaign. I was exhausted and I just wanted to put the campaign behind me as I prepared to move to New Hampshire for a visiting professorship at Dartmouth College.

My lawyer handed me a pen; my mind was still whirring. *Didn't the FEC get thousands of these complaints every cycle and let them pile up for years? And why on earth would anybody spend time pursuing this one, since I lost and the candidate who filed it went on to win?*

I tried to clear all those thoughts from my head. I willed my hand toward the desk and signed, and with that, I closed the book on the 2004 campaign. Unfortunately, the Carnahans did not.

My successful run had raised my profile and drawn job offers. I accepted a one-year gig at Dartmouth, where I could finish my doctoral thesis, consider an academic career, and weigh future political options. After seriously considering a primary rematch against Carnahan (very risky) and moving to a district near Washington University with an open seat in the statehouse (pretty safe bet), I decided to run for an open, majority-black state senate seat covering half of St. Louis City.

As I was nearing a decision, Artie Harris, who had remained a close friend and adviser since our 2004 loss, called and strongly encouraged me to run for the state senate seat, arguing that I was better suited to representing a racially split district than a predominantly white one. Two hours after we spoke, an unsolicited e-mail from him arrived. It contained the guts of what would become my announcement e-mail and ultimately my senate campaign stump speech. "For too long, St. Louis politicians have pitted neighborhood against neighborhood, North against

South, black against white. These artificial walls, perpetuated by people who fiercely guard their fiefdoms and cling desperately to power, must be torn down. My campaign will do that. It will work to obliterate the racial demarcation line of Delmar Boulevard and help us become one city again, one St. Louis." This may not sound groundbreaking in 2015, but when Artie and I wrote it in 2005, it felt bold, even exhilarating. I hadn't seen any St. Louis politician lay bare the city's divisions as starkly, or call other pols on the carpet for maintaining them.

I did not look like the district I sought to represent. I was a thirty-two-year-old agnostic Jew with a Ph.D. The district was mostly black and 90 percent Protestant or Catholic; less than one-fifth of voters had college degrees; and the median age of voters was over sixty.

The city's most influential black politicos all endorsed the state representative Yaphett El-Amin, the leading black candidate. Upon returning from New Hampshire, I sat down at a local diner with a top aide to Congressman Lacy Clay, who represented most of St. Louis City and whose father had done so before him and whose congressional district encompassed most of the state senate district. The Clay aide, a former Ivy League basketball star, was Clay's go-to guy back in the district, and I intended to ask for his—and thereby the congressman's—consideration. But I was really just hoping to disarm him. I wanted to shoot the bull, stress our hoops bond, get to know him better.

"Look here, why don't you find another district to run in?" came his opening salvo.

"Because the seat's open, and I can win." Forget hoops, if he was gonna come at me like that. Forget that I felt uniquely qualified to represent a racially split district. Down to brass tacks.

We argued, him guaranteeing that I would ruin my reputation in the black community if I ran, me vowing to run a unifying campaign that would bridge the city's racial divide.

"You plannin' on doin' that grassroots shit you did last time?" he asked with disdain.

"Yeah, I'm gonna knock on tons of doors, north and south." White politicians did not canvass north of Delmar.

"If you come up in my ward, you best bring security. 'Cause it ain't gon' be pretty."

"C'mon, man." I laughed drily as I rose to leave. "I didn't know the Ivy League was so rough."

Organizationally speaking, 2006 was like 2004 on steroids. Thanks in large part to Sam Simon, who came back to St. Louis and became our campaign manager, we reengaged much of our volunteer base from 2004 and refocused on grassroots organizing. Led by Quinton Lucas, a brilliant Washington University graduate who would go on to succeed in his first run for the Kansas City Council, we added new layers in the black community. And Dan Herman, a St. Louis University track star who became my "body guy" and traveled with me everywhere, quietly earned respect for his strategic insight.

Dan also sat with me during fund-raising call time, which was quite unlike 2004. This time, most people actually took my call. The money flowed, and I filled out our $225,000 campaign budget early, enabling me to contact voters nonstop during the final month.

After a year of canvassing and church visits that built on my decade of basketball coaching and work with the Confluence Academy charter schools, we began making inroads in the black community.

My unique approach to North Side canvassing began as a lark. I was knocking on doors with an aide one day in the Penrose neighborhood a few blocks from the Boys and Girls Club where I had coached, and a group of middle school kids were playing pickup ball in the street. "Yo, Mr. White, you lost?" one of them called out, and the others laughed. Other than the odd utility worker or repairman, you didn't see many white people in Penrose.

I turned to my aide and said, "Gimme two minutes."

"C'mon, Jeff, they can't vote," he said.

"Two minutes," I repeated, and walked over to the game. Most were taller than me, but none over six feet, and the tallest one was overweight and wearing jeans. "All right, who wants a shot at five bucks?" I asked.

"Ain't none of us suckin' your dick, man," replied one, and the rest laughed.

"Actually, I was tryna see if one of y'all wanted to play one-on-one," I said.

They all pointed at one five-foot-ten-ish kid who stepped forward and sized up the thirtyish white guy in a blue button-down, khakis, and wing tips. "I ain't got five bucks, but I ain't gon' need it."

"No, you won't," I said, "'cause you get five bucks if you win, but if I win, you gotta hand these out on your block." I flashed a stack of literature that promoted my vow to stop racial profiling. DRIVING WHILE BLACK IS NOT A CRIME, it blared.

"We ain't gotta worry about those," he smiled and tossed the ball at me a little harder than I expected.

I caught it, removed my tie, and threw it on the ground. "Okay, I only got time to play to three, straight."*

"Fine," he said, practically licking his lips as he checked the ball back to me. I pump-faked, then went by him for a layup. One to zero. The dozen spectators hooted. Next possession I

---

* A pickup game can be played "straight"—that is, first one to the designated winning tally wins—or as a "deuce game" in which the victor must win by two.

tried a slick crossover dribble that usually works the first time I use it on someone and went in for another layup. Two to zero, more whooping. Third possession he got up close on me, and I blew by him to the left and hit a short jumper for the win.

At that point I didn't even need the kid to hand out my flyers; two other boys had already started running around the neighborhood, talking about the white dude with the handles,* and one of them had the lit. I slapped hands with the rest of the kids, grabbed my tie, and went back to canvassing. I didn't realize it at the time, but that would become a formula for the next six months of canvassing—I ended up challenging dozens of kids to pickup games and using them to create buzz in the community.

My chief opponent, Representative El-Amin, was a community activist and was not about to let my grassroots work go unchallenged. Soon, a massive truck equipped with a sound system started following me on my North Side canvasses, booming out her disembodied voice and drowning me out at the door. Overall it was tough to say if this helped or hurt me. On one hand, it told black voters that there was a black alternative and perhaps subtly reminded them that the district had a black majority. But the contrast of seeing me in the flesh, sweating in a torrid St. Louis summer and at their door asking for their vote in person versus seeing her pristine image on a truck, may have worked to my advantage.

In an effort to provide a positive outlet for young people— and to raise funds for health care and services for their parents— we hosted a 3-on-3 basketball tournament and community fair in a park in a high-crime area. During a canvass to promote the event, two of my white interns were greeted by a man who saw my picture on the flyer and told them, "When the Caucasians

---

* Ballhandling skills.

take over my city, it's gonna be a muthafuckin' bloodbath!" It was a harbinger of the simmering anger among black St. Louisans that the nation would see in 2014, the roots of which I describe elsewhere.[3]

The tournament drew two hundred people, plus a dozen protesters (one of whom later said that they had been paid $20 apiece by a supporter of one of my opponents) waving handmade signs with creative alliterations like NO BBQ, NO B-BALL, NO RACIST JEFF SMITH! I asked my former high school teammate and tournament cochair Dave Buckner if, as a white guy, I went too far by serving BBQ and watermelon at a North Side hoops tourney. He nodded to the food line snaking around a tree and snapped, "What the fuck you think these people want, mostaccioli?"

The same opponent whose supporter allegedly paid the protesters issued a press release attacking me as a "known Caucasian." And on the North Side, one of our canvassers found a flyer of unknown origin featuring a picture of me and a Star of David. "Who will he really represent in Jefferson City?" it asked. "North St. Louis or Israel?"

In addition to two black state representatives, a prominent ex-legislator of Italian descent also entered the race. Despite the district's demographics, Derio Gambaro's direct mail pictured whites under the slogan FROM THE NEIGHBORHOOD, FOR THE NEIGHBORHOOD. Gambaro sent several pieces of mail to the South Side's overwhelmingly white, conservative neighborhoods calling me a carpetbagger (true, since I grew up in St. Louis County, not the city) and featuring a snapshot of me throwing my blazer over my back but without the jacket visible, suggesting a stereotypically gay limp-wristed gesture. The caption read: "Jeff Smith won't be straight with us."

Soon voters received calls from people purporting to take a poll. After several questions about me, polltakers asked, "Would you be more or less likely to vote for a candidate if you knew that he was secretly gay but paid a woman to pose as his girlfriend?"

Then a new round of phone calls hit overwhelmingly white wards. A man speaking in an exaggerated black dialect intoned: "I wanna tell you about my man Jeff Smith. He may be a carpetbagger without any experience, but Jeff Smith majored in African American Studies. Jeff Smith coached basketball in North St. Louis. Jeff Smith started a charter school in North St. Louis. Jeff Smith *understands* the black community. . . ." All the calls lacked a "Paid For" disclaimer—just like Skip's postcard from 2004.

In 2004, our desperation led me to approve Skip's postcard, and I still felt the weight of that deception. So in 2006, we played it straight, responding to the above attacks with a midnight run—twenty of us sprinting house to house from midnight to 3:00 A.M. with flyers asking voters to ignore the negativity. Thanks in part to the timely premiere of *Can Mr. Smith Get to Washington Anymore*, the documentary about our near-miss 2004 campaign, just before Election Day, we won by double digits. The film received awards at several film festivals and made the short list of twelve for a 2006 Academy Award in the Best Documentary category. Life was good.

Looking out at the diverse crowd at my election night party, thinking about the arc of my life, I felt as if there was no one in the city better equipped to unify the diverse district. The *St. Louis Post-Dispatch* reporter at my election night party summed up the vibe: "Watching Jeff Smith's victory party, it was hard to tell whether he had won a race for the Legislature or for Student Council. College-age volunteers were drinking beer and chasing each other with water guns. A live band belted out 'Freebird.' And there was Smith playing the drums. St. Louis, meet your new senator."

Even Congressman Clay showed up, all smiles and well

wishes. "I knew you was gon' win all along, Jeff," he said in his
gravelly voice. This gave me some sort of epiphany. I huddled
four of my closest friends on the driveway and told them—almost
as a warning to myself—"You are my friends and I trust you;
everyone after tonight is suspect because they may want something from me. You are the only people I know I can trust."

My best friend Steve Brown was in that tight circle on the
driveway that night, telling me how proud he was of me and of
our effort. So it never occurred to me, three years later, that he
would be wearing a wire.

The year 2007 was a roller-coaster year for me. I loved the
senate—loved listening to floor debate, loved the nitty-gritty of
the legislative process, loved the camaraderie with other senators, and loved helping constituents one at a time.

But then a couple of months into my term, I got a phone call.
It was Artie calling from New York City, and he was distraught.
He'd struggled with depression for as long as I'd known him, and
during our campaign he self-medicated by drinking excessively—
often a dozen or more drinks, sometimes starting before noon.
Since our 2004 campaign, he'd cycled through several political
jobs. With each one he seemed to have become more downcast.
He'd disliked his bosses since 2004, with the exception of
New York's senator, Chuck Schumer, but he couldn't take the
stress of working for Schumer, whose micromanagement of his
press office is legendary. "Nothing's ever gonna be as much
fun as 2004," he said. "We had so little to lose compared to the
guys I work for now. Even when I was getting into drunken
fistfights with Nick, I felt alive. Everything since then is so
deadening."

He was having dating problems, and was miserable in his
new job and fed up with politics generally. "Look, most people in
politics can't write for shit," he observed. "I should be living

on the beach in LA writing screenplays and dating starlets." After the documentary film began to get traction and Artie appeared at film festivals, he hoped to be discovered as an actor-screenwriter. The notion wasn't crazy; Artie had the film's most memorable lines. Unfortunately, his hopes were dashed, and amidst the turmoil of a difficult breakup with a longtime girlfriend, he started drinking heavily again. After he drunk-dialed me a few nights in a row, I warned him that he was drinking too much and could get himself into trouble.

"You're wrong," he said. "When I drank on your campaign, I got wild and out of control. Now I drink and I just get depressed and wanna kill myself."

"Artie, do not ever fucking say that. You have so much talent, and so many people who love you. I don't ever want to hear you say that again, you understand me? Do you want me to come out to New York? I love you. I would come out on the next flight." I had no training or experience in this sort of thing, and I failed miserably. He said he'd be fine. A week later, he overdosed. At his mother's house afterward, she played the documentary on a loop for family and close friends; we laughed at his lines through our tears.

Six months after Artie died, I received a letter from the FEC. We were cleared. Home free, we thought. I called Steve. We agreed we'd never, ever take another risk like that.

Two years after that, soon after I came home from a productive third session in Jefferson City, Steve called me and explained that he needed to talk. In person.

Steve arrived at my house along with Nick Adams. "Remember Skip?" began Steve.

"Yeah, why?" I felt my muscles tighten, but I tried to keep my poise.

"Well, you're not going to believe this, but Skip's the chief suspect in a car bombing that almost killed a lawyer," Steve said. "And get this: they've already got him on cocaine distribution, illegal weapons possession, bank fraud, mortgage fraud, wife beating. I mean, this is serious, Jeff."

"Oh, fuck." It registered almost instantly. Skip was fucked. He wouldn't want to go away for twenty years. He'd be tempted to do what he needed to do and say what he needed to say to cut his time. He could easily give up Steve and me for the postcard.

Steve sighed heavily. "So what do you think we do here, guys?"

"I say we stick to our story," I replied. We'd made a pact back in 2004 to keep quiet, and I'd signed an affidavit reflecting that. It seemed too late to turn back: in for a dime, in for a dollar.

Nick agreed. "I don't think they have anything," said Nick. "And whatever they do have is coming from a convicted felon. Remember, this is the word of a state senator and Wash U Ph.D., a state rep and Wash U J.D., and a Wash U Ph.D. candidate against the word of a twice-convicted felon. That's not even close."

"So you guys wanna gamble," Steve said.

"I don't know what else I can do," I said. "I mean, I signed an affidavit five years ago."

"Agree," said Nick. "If we lie now, we *might* get caught. If we tell the truth now, they know we lied before and we *definitely* get caught."

It seemed logical. "I mean, let's be honest: we weren't fucking white knights here," I said. "None of us are going to get the fucking Nobel Peace Prize for our interaction with Skip."

Later Nick would lay it out clearly. "Listen, I hate to say this, but there were two people on the campaign who dealt with Skip. One is alive. The other's dead. So why don't we just put it all on Artie?"

I looked at Nick, then looked skyward and sighed. I loved

Artie and missed him dearly, and I smiled at the thought of him looking down on us right then. "You know, Artie would totally want us to throw him under the bus." Nick agreed. No one we knew had a darker sense of humor than Artie, and no one was more loyal. It was not a statement I am proud of. But it was true, in our eyes and in the eyes of most who knew him well.*

Though Steve seemed apprehensive, Nick and I resolved to keep our pact. I figured Steve would be fine, if it ever came to that. Then, a few days later, at 7:00 A.M., the morning after I'd broken two ribs in a basketball game, I was awakened from a Percocet-induced daze by a persistent rap on the door. I stumbled downstairs in boxers, thinking I might've dreamed the knock.

"Good morning, Mr. Smith," said a tall man with a pock-marked face and close-cropped hair. "We're with the FBI and we'd like to talk to you for just a minute. Do you mind if we come in?" He flashed a badge. This was no dream.

"About what?" I tried to shake off the Percocet, but everything was hazy and muffled, like I was underwater.

"Don't worry—this isn't about you—but we'd like to talk to you about a guy we think you might know, Skip Ohlsen." Their body language was confident. They were coming in.

"Okay." I didn't have to let them in. In a clear frame of mind, maybe I wouldn't have.

The questions started out easy and got harder. I acknowledged that I knew Skip and that he had met with our campaign early on to pitch his services as a media consultant, but when they asked if I knew anything about the postcard before it hit mailboxes, I lied and said no.

---

* "I do agree that Arthur would have said to blame him! I can hear him now," his mother wrote to me on the day I resigned and pleaded guilty.

When they left I called Steve. "Jesus Christ, the feds just came to my house."

"They came here, too, and left a card. Thank God I wasn't home. What'd you tell 'em?"

"Nothing. It could be five years in jail for what I just did, you think?" I was nervous.

"There could definitely be jail time, yes."

"Do you think I made a huge mistake today telling them I didn't know who did the mailer? If I called them back, would that change things?"

"I dunno, Jeff. I didn't do this stuff in the AGO. It's way above my pay grade." Steve had been chief deputy counsel to the attorney general. "So whaddaya tell 'em if they come back?"

"I'm going to tell them ninety percent of the truth. I'm assuming I broke the law by having knowledge of what Skip was going to do, but I don't know for sure—I mean, I didn't *know* he was going to do anything. I had an inkling, but how can they prove that?"

You might be wondering how I remembered all of those conversations from such a stressful time so well. I didn't have to— they were all on tape.

Within a few minutes of being recognized on the elevator to my lawyer's office, after my lawyer called the U.S. attorney's office and explained the situation to me, I realized that my face would soon be more recognizable than ever.

Steve had actually been home when the feds knocked on his door. And apparently he had quickly made a choice that would allow him to stay out of prison.

First, it's denial. They're bluffing. There's no *way* he wore a wire. He's my best friend. Loyalty is everything to him. He couldn't do it. Not capable of it.

Then anger. That motherfucker. After all the years we spent together, talking about politics, friendship, loyalty, trust? That motherfucker.

Then disbelief at the amazing confluence of bad decisions and bad luck. *Why didn't I tell Artie and Nick to avoid Skip? Why didn't Skip just put the fucking disclaimer on the postcard? Why didn't Russ withdraw the complaint after he won? Why did I sign that affidavit? Why did the feds spend five years and God knows how much money worrying about a postcard that cost ten grand and didn't change the outcome of a race? Why, oh why, did Skip have to car-bomb that lawyer? And if Steve was gonna flip, why didn't he just give 'em the goods and cut me off, instead of taping hours and hours of conversations where I said . . . Jesus . . . who knows what horrible shit I said?*

Once I contemplated the damage to my reputation if those tapes emerged, I moved past disbelief to shame. The shame of my colleagues, my supporters, my constituents. The shame of my parents.

They lived five minutes from my attorney's office. It was the longest five minutes of my life.

"Let's sit down," I said.

"Is everything okay?" they asked.

"Look, I made a mistake back in 2004. Remember that postcard that came out near the end of the campaign about Carnahan's attendance record? Artie and Nick had met with the guy who did it, and I okayed it and then lied about that on an affidavit."

"So you'll have to pay a big fine?" asked my dad.

"No, Dad, it's worse than that. I'll have to resign and probably go to prison."

My mom's lips quivered. "I knew it. I knew it. Knew it from the start. Knew you'd get mixed up in this side of politics. I tried to tell you. Tried to tell you what was going to happen."

"I'm sorry, Mom." She stared out the window and cried. "Mom, please don't cry. It's not the end of the world. I'll survive."

"You'll *survive*? What about us? You don't know what it's like to be a parent—you can't possibly understand!" She was hyperventilating.

My dad tried to keep the peace. "Okay, how can we help you keep from going to prison, Jeffrey? How do they even know you lied?"

"Steve's been wearing a wire for the last couple of months."

"That son of a bitch," said my dad.

"I told you he was no good," said my mom. "But you wouldn't listen."

I breathed deeply.

"Jeffrey, do you have money for a lawyer?" Dad, always practical.

"I have my savings—what's left after the campaign."

"Do you have a decent lawyer?"

"I think so. I'm headed downtown now to meet with him. I am so sorry about all of this." They looked much older and grayer than I'd remembered.

I hugged them and left to meet my new lawyers. They greeted me with looks of grim resignation and showed me the sentencing guidelines. I was looking at two to three years.

We began a dance with the assistant U.S. attorney, Hal Goldsmith, a twitchy, anxious career prosecutor who refused to shake my outstretched hand when we met. The dance began with a lengthy session with Goldsmith, another attorney, and the two investigators who had visited my home, during which we heard the highlights of Steve's tapes. It wasn't easy listening to myself wistfully agree with Nick that we lay the blame on the now-deceased Artie, who had urged us to approve the postcard. It was harder still to imagine that these tapes could become public.

I left the courthouse. "What'd you guys think?" I asked my lawyers.

"The audio quality—it's the best I've ever heard," said one of them.

"Okay, overall what'd you think? Scale of one to ten, ten being the worst?" I asked my other lawyer, himself an ex-prosecutor.

"Maybe 2.5," he said, squinting. "It's some good buddies talkin', ya know? Nobody's talking about what to do with the bodies in the trunk. You're a likable guy—it's possible you could hang a jury. But they've probably got enough to get you. And if you hang it, they'll come right back and do it again—and it'll cost you a million bucks each time."

We soon came to the consensus that I would plead guilty. After that, the main question was whether I would be able to reach a cooperation agreement. In the parlance of the feds, "cooperation" didn't mean "being cooperative" or "explaining all the details of my crime." It meant helping them nab someone higher up the food chain—a mayor, attorney general, congressman, or U.S. senator. The best I could do was to tell Hal about a retired former colleague who'd once told me she opposed a bill because its beneficiary, a major real estate developer, "didn't give me a dime." But Hal wasn't interested in a minnow; he wanted a whale. He twitched and huffed at me, then addressed my lawyer. "Clearly, your client has no interest in cooperating," he said, affecting his best *Law & Order* tone. "I think we're done here." And that was that.

A few weeks later I submitted my resignation, sent a mass e-mail to my constituents apologizing for letting them down, walked past the cameras outside my house, and drove to the courthouse in downtown St. Louis. The courtroom was packed with media, friends, and supporters. When my turn came, I read an apology I'd prepared. Then I walked out and read a statement.

I was catatonic, but I remember who came to support me. My numbness would be interrupted only by a persistent legislative aide who called, texted, and e-mailed to request a formal letter awarding her a raise in my final hour as a senator.

Excerpts from the tape flooded the airwaves; despite my pre-indictment agreement to plead guilty, the prosecutor fed the most salacious excerpts—namely, my comments referencing Artie—to the press. The city's FBI head trembled with fury as he condemned the "textbook case of corruption," as though I'd taken bribes or stolen public money. "I loved the chase," he added, describing his work. "[It] was fantastic. It was me against them. And the smarter they were . . . the more I enjoyed catching them." (He was later promoted to head of the FBI's Miami bureau.)

I came home to reporters and three thousand replies to the mass e-mail I had sent with my letter of resignation. All except eight expressed support; most urged me to reconsider resigning. Of course, they didn't understand: I was now a felon, prohibited from serving.

A lawyer friend soon found out who my sentencing judge would be. "She's a black Republican," he said.

"Well, one out of two ain't bad," I said hopefully.

"I think her political worldview is more 'Republican' than 'black,'" my friend replied. "She's the harshest judge in the circuit." *When it rains, it pours,* I thought.

In a memo to the court, I requested an unorthodox sentence: two years of home confinement and full-time community service during which I would be allowed to leave my house only to teach civics and coach basketball at the charter school I'd cofounded. It would've saved taxpayers about $175,000: two years of a teacher's salary, plus the cost of housing a federal prisoner; I would've paid for my electronic monitoring. Hundreds of people—from the state's attorney general, lieutenant governor, and auditor to my ex-girlfriend's mom and the impoverished kids I'd coached and tutored—wrote impassioned letters to the judge requesting mercy, for which I was extremely grateful.

Nick and Steve were at the courthouse with their families, and though we sat just a few feet from one another, none of us spoke. Nick, not yet thirty, received probation at Hal's recommendation. Hal then called Steve—approximately six feet, two inches and 300 pounds to my five-foot-six 120-pound frame—the most heroic informant Hal had seen since he had sent a Miami drug dealer to Colombia to make a huge buy from a kingpin as armed thugs pointed rifles at him. At his urging, Steve also received probation. When my turn came, Hal argued for a harsh sentence, and I got a year and a day. Despite the fact that there was a similar facility about a hundred miles away, the Bureau of Prisons assigned me to Federal Correctional Institution Manchester in rural Kentucky, which was 501 miles away from my house and contained a medium- and a minimum-security facility. I would be confined in the latter. Official BOP policy was to place offenders within 500 miles of their home, but at this point, I thought it wise to cut my losses.

2

"HAVE SOME RESPECT, MR. 90210!"

A Crash Course in Prison Life

I remember leaving for college with some clothes stuffed into a suitcase and a Cardinals trash can after a last-minute change of plans meant that I would be flying instead of driving down with my family. The Raleigh-Durham airport had none of the Southern charm I'd heard about. I'd never actually been to North Carolina and didn't know anyone there except an orientation counselor who had written me a welcome letter. For the first time in my life, I felt alone. I was eighteen then, and I don't recall feeling alone for another eighteen years, when Teresa dropped me off in Manchester, Kentucky, on January 5, 2010.

I'd met Teresa, a newly minted Washington University MSW-MBA, about a year earlier, and we'd quickly fallen in love. I'd visited her at work that fateful day on the way from my parents' house to meet my lawyer. She had moved into my house two days earlier.

"Listen, baby, I have some bad news," I'd begun. "I don't have time to go into the details, but I'm going to resign from the senate. And I'm probably going to prison. And it's going to be all over the news soon, and so everyone at your office and your friends and your family—"

"What happened? Why? What's going on? Are you serious?"

"It's a long story. But right now I gotta go see a lawyer. I just wanted to tell you that I'm not coming home tonight. I want to give you a chance to move your stuff back out without me around. Or if you want, I can help. But maybe it's easier for you if I don't? And if you want to be friends . . . but I mean . . . prison . . . you didn't sign up for this."

Her eyes moistened. An eternity passed. "Come home tonight," she said. "I'm not going anywhere." But the next month had been tough; she fell into despair and returned home to Texas, and I doubted she would return.

Now, outside the barbed-wire fence of the intake building, I looked at her one last time and waved good-bye. I'd heard the stories of guys who went in with wives and then the next thing they heard from them was a letter from a divorce attorney. Unlike some of those guys, I had only a year and a day. Still, her friends thought she was crazy for staying with me. I hoped we'd make it, but I wasn't sure that I'd see her again.

Issues of crime and prison weren't completely foreign to me. As a senator, I was able to do a dozen all-night police ride-alongs during which I saw crime up close. This gave me a bit of insight into the city's high crime rate.

Because of the stagnant economy, a sky-high dropout rate that left many unprepared for jobs and lacking networks to find them, the widespread availability of handguns, and the nihilism of some young men who saw far too much violence and didn't expect to see thirty, the crime rate rose sharply in summer 2009. The neighborhoods that experienced the most murders in the city lay within my senate district.

I wanted to understand what the city was doing to address the rash of violence and how we could improve our efforts. So one night I asked an officer if I could join him on his beat, and he agreed. At the outset I asked him if there were any ground rules. He asked if I'd signed the waiver releasing the department from liability if I was injured or killed.

"Yep," I replied.

"Then do whatever you want," he said. I laughed uneasily.

Almost immediately, the wire crackled, and we responded to a succession of stabbings, robberies, car thefts, prostitution, drug dealing, and gunshots fired. The dispatcher's description did not always resemble what was actually happening at the scene, fueling the mix of adrenaline and anxiety upon arriving. Police did their best to comfort victims, listen to witnesses, and deal fairly with suspects. Particularly challenging were the victims and witnesses who painted vivid portraits of a crime but refused to name the offender, some terrified of potential retribution, others simply because they neither liked nor trusted the police.

I accompanied officers nearly every night for two weeks. At 4:00 A.M. on my last night, a woman reported that her nephew had stolen a $20 tax rebate check and a bag of marijuana from her safe; she wanted the police to return them to their rightful owner. We arrived at a chaotic scene; children streamed out of a first-floor unit and scurried in all directions. Two women—sisters, we gathered—berated each other, one accusing the other's son of thievery. The cops interviewed several witnesses, who offered varying accounts of what had transpired. A woman who seemed to be the grandmother circled the periphery in a sort of fugue state, loudly bemoaning her family's strife. Several children snuggled in the backseat of a car, confused. I thought about how scared I'd have been if my family's house had been surrounded by cops at 4:00 A.M. I asked one of the kids if he was okay. He looked at me, numb to the screaming, the uniforms, the squad cars' mesmerizing lights. "I just wanna go back to sleep," he said.

I also began to receive invitations to dramatic performances put on by a local nonprofit called Prison Performing Arts, which produced theatrical performances by prisoners, and I invited the rest of the senate to join me. None actually did, but it seemed important for prisoners working to better themselves to know that elected officials saw them as people with potential, not just costs on a ledger.

There was always a post-performance social hour, often more compelling than the play, where we got to meet the actors and hear about their pre-prison lives, their mistakes, and how the theater program had finally given them something "to live for." They were strikingly reflective about their lives and their mistakes; many expressed what appeared to be genuine remorse for their crimes, with one crying as he spoke of the children of a man he had killed decades earlier. They seemed at peace with the sins for which they had atoned and believed that even if they died in prison, life was worth living if they could nurture their minds and souls through theater. The juxtaposition of the chaos I saw on the midnight patrols and the humility and peace I saw in prison obsessed me.

Now, six months later, I wasn't riding along with cops looking for criminals. I was about to live with them for a year, but not in the way that I had once briefly lived on food stamps to make a point about poverty and nutrition. No, this wasn't a social experiment.

• • •

I walked into the dank intake center wearing a gray T-shirt, mesh shorts, white ankle socks, and tennis shoes. A guard with what seemed to be twenty pounds worth of keys ordered our eclectic group of three—black, white, and Chinese—to sit in a concrete-slab holding cell that smelled vaguely of urine. A few minutes later, I was ordered to strip down for a search. As described earlier, I passed only after revealing my empty "prison wallet."

Teresa had read the guidelines online, and prisoners were allowed to bring in a soft-cover religious text, a religious pendant such as a cross, dentures, eyeglasses, a plain wedding ring, and relevant legal paperwork. Not in possession of any of these things, I held only a driver's license in my hand, which was held at the desk to await my release in a year and a day—ten and a half months if I earned "good time" by avoiding serious infractions.

After the strip search, the prison counselor, Mr. Sims, looked over my case file. When he told me point-blank that my incarceration was a complete waste, my hopes rose; it would be months before I taught myself to block such thoughts. Although I took care not to betray it, I was practically giddy. *This was all just a big mistake! Maybe they'd come to their senses and send me back on the first bus home in the morning for a year of home confinement and teaching!*

My hopes were dashed a few minutes later when two overweight correctional officers led me and the other men in the holding cell out into the yard, unlocked three layers of gates, and motioned for us to pile into a pickup truck that would carry us to the compound. But during the ride I remained optimistic. I had intermittent visions of Mr. Sims, who was obviously more educated and civilized than the regular COs who had handled me, recruiting me to teach college-style public policy courses to other inmates or even to help the prison administration analyze policy issues with which they grappled. It had taken only a five-minute conversation for me to see that he understood the ridiculousness of my sentence, the value I could bring to the prison, the many ways in which I was *different* from the other men I came in with. . . .

"WAKE UP AND GET OUT, INMATE!" screamed the CO, who was now waiting behind the truck for me to jump down, jarring me out of my reverie. Mr. Sims wasn't going to save me. In fact, he'd probably already forgotten about me.

We sat in silence for an hour until two COs ambled in and walked us out of the intake center toward a truck that drove us about a half mile past the shooting range to our new home on the other side of a huge hill.

In a few minutes we reached the facility, which sat snugly in a hollow, framed by cliffs and rocky inclines that seemed to substitute for an actual fence. We got out of the truck, and a CO brought us around the front of a nondescript one-story building toward a side door—no prisoner, I would learn, was ever allowed to enter the front door of the administration building. The CO opened the side door, leading us into a caged laundry room that reminded me of the liquor stores and chop suey joints in my old senate district, the ones with glass windows or bars between the customer and the cashier. A prisoner who was working behind the cage nodded at me. "First we'll do your jacket, then your greens," he said. Obviously the public associates prison with orange jumpsuits, but the two prisons at Manchester outfitted residents in khaki and green. "You want a large or an extra large?" That was a question no one had ever asked me, but I understood why prisoners didn't favor formfitting clothes.

Once we picked out our greens, two COs and a veteran prisoner escorted us up the compound. A few dozen prisoners working

out on free weights and another dozen or so doing push-ups on a
sidewalk spotted us and begin circling, drawing a larger crowd
of men, who started hollering at us, just as I'd seen in the movies. "Yo, Popcorn!" yelled someone in a long line of men waiting
outside a low-rise building, and an overweight guy walking next
to me with a plastic hair pick protruding from his uncombed
Afro nodded back and pounded his chest.

"My nigga!" he replied.

Amid all the inmates hollering, one massive, mustached
white guy stood out. "'Sup oh-seven-six!" he kept shouting at
someone in my group. I later learned that the incoming inmate
receiving the shout-out was from Memphis: the final three digits in the inmate number of anyone convicted in the Western
District of Tennessee were zero-seven-six.

One of the saddest things about prison hit me within minutes of arriving. It's the way in which new prisoners—most of
them newly transferred from other prisons—treat their introduction onto the compound not unlike people on the outside
might treat a high school reunion, greeting old friends from other
prisons or from their hometown, updating one another on the
time they had remaining. It strikes a neophyte as incongruous,
but placed within a context in which two-thirds of inmates reoffend, it begins to make sense. Very few of these men had ever
attended a high school graduation, and many have spent the
majority of their lives locked up. For most, this was as close as
they would get to a reunion.

Some sociological research has described a "normalization"
of the prison experience among some subgroups, suggesting that
relentless police harassment (see, for instance, the 2015 Department of Justice report on Ferguson, Missouri) and ubiquitous
surveillance in black neighborhoods conditions residents for
incarceration.[1] But in rural Kentucky, this normalization wasn't
limited to blacks. One white inmate named JT, who came in

shortly after me for dealing oxycodone, seemed to know every-thing about the way prison worked and even talked to the guards as if they were old friends. He'd been locked up at some point every year for seventeen years on a dizzying array of charges, and bragged about it as if it were Joe DiMaggio's fifty-six-game hitting streak.

We continued up the compound on a narrow strip of side-walk, walking past the weight pile toward the housing units. I noticed that all the prisoners crowded onto the sidewalk, despite the large swath of exquisitely manicured grass nearby. I would soon learn that the grass was "out of bounds"—forbidden terri-tory that prisoners cultivated, mowed, and then received disci-plinary sanctions for walking on in the presence of a CO.

I kept moving toward a passel of men in a semicircle near the back of the line who were occupying the entirety of the side-walk. "Excuse me," I said. Most ignored me. Two glowered at me. None moved. I met their eyes and nodded at them.

"Self-surrender," said one.

I was confused.

"Yo! I'm talkin' to you, white boy! You self-surrender?"

I nodded.

"Have some respect, Mr. 90210!" he said with finality, and they all broke up laughing. In some ways prisoners were on the leading edge of pop culture, pioneering saggy pants and slang terms. And yet in other ways, as the allusion to the 1990s tele-vision show suggested, they were twenty years behind. I was just hoping the nickname wouldn't stick.

I needed to change the vibe. "What's the line for?" I asked a black guy walking with me, less out of curiosity than a vain at-tempt to appear to the crowd as if I actually knew someone.

"Chow," he said, as if I were ignorant.

I wasn't sure what meal people were eating at 4:15 P.M., but as we continued up the compound toward the unit where we were assigned, I vowed to myself that I wouldn't ask any more questions. The three of us had merged with four other new inductees, and with the exception of the Chinese guy, the inductees continued to catch up with the crowd, providing updates on guys at other facilities. I was surprised at the genuine warmth among prisoners—they treated one another almost like family. Since I had no friends, no family, and no clue what to do, I kept my mouth shut.

The largest "families" in prison are, of course, racial ones. There are blacks, whites, and "Spanish" or "Mexicans," which are the catchall terms for anyone of Latino descent. Gang affiliation, hometown, and cell block matter, too, but race is predominant. Black inmates in particular doubted the fairness of the criminal justice system, which isn't surprising. According to the American Civil Liberties Union, blacks constitute 74 percent of those imprisoned for drug possession despite being outnumbered five to one by whites and reporting nearly equal usage rates.[2] At Manchester FCI, black inmates' racial resentment was likely magnified by the fact that all the prison administrators and COs were white and many of the COs were openly racist; they would often joke with veteran white prisoners but were generally all business with black ones. All of this likely reinforced or exacerbated extant divisions between the various racial families.

Part of being family means that you protect your kin and the elders mentor the youngsters under their wing and teach them the codes. The racial codes are strictest in maximum-security prisons and get slightly more lenient with each drop in security level. Even at lower security levels in which codes are both less elaborate and less brutally enforced, they inform nearly every aspect of prison life. For instance, as David Arenberg observed in an essay on race and prison, people of different races attend church together as there is often only one Sunday service, but with the exception of Muslims, they do not pray together outside of church.[3] People of different races routinely join the same softball teams but rarely the same basketball teams, and they definitely do not lift weights together; the people you lift with—those "in your car," per prison lingo—are considered your closest allies, the people who would shank somebody for you.

Somewhat paradoxically, the apartheid-like rules actually work to reduce the likelihood of major racial fights. Violations of protocol earn a reprimand from the "shot-callers," who are themselves exempt from most rules, despite the fact that they often earn leadership positions by distinguishing themselves in battles against other racial groups.[4] Interestingly enough, as I would soon learn, breaches involving food can be among the most serious of all.

Each of us new prisoners was taken to his bunk, but by the time it was my turn, there were no more bunks available in all but one of the units. I was taken to a unit that had been opened the prior week to accommodate an influx of inmates from other prisons.

I was steered to the second cell on the right-hand side of the unit. A forty-something-year-old guy in a black do-rag was leaning up against the bunk, talking about his culinary skills and the money he'd earned through his cooking hustle at his last spot; he'd apparently just been transferred from someplace in Florida, where he had a CO smuggling spices and other ingredients to him.

As the only white guy on my cell block, I immediately became a source of curiosity. My cellie sized me up, then curled his upper lip. "White collar?" he asked, with a mix of disdain and bemusement.

"Yup." I didn't know quite what to make of him. He definitely had some attitude, but I wasn't about to start the relationship off by giving him any of it back.

"Whatchu done did?"

"Lied to the feds."

"Damn, how dey gintchu?" asked a guy in the next cell with dreadlocks, a Rasta cap, and a Jamaican accent.

"My best friend was wired."

A chorus of "Day-um," "Sheeeet," and "Bitch-ass nigga" rained down.

Then somebody said, "That nigga need to get chalked."*

A chorus of "Mmm-hmms."

Less than thirty seconds, and there was unanimous agreement in my cell block that someone should kill Steve Brown. I made a mental note not to get on these guys' bad side.

"So what they give you?" asked my cellie, whose freckles gave him a striking resemblance to Morgan Freeman; sure enough, guys called him "Red" after Freeman's *Shawshank Redemption* character.

"Year and a day."

"Man, I done did more time in this place on the toilet than you got time." He laughed.

"Really?" I asked. "How long you got?"

"Shit, I'm gettin' out on Friday if my halfway house come through." I would soon learn this was common: everybody was getting out Friday, if only their halfway house came through as staff "promised," if only their conviction was overturned as their lawyer promised, if only . . .

The Jamaican guy with headphones on started singing a reggae song, and my cellie rolled his eyes. "He sing that shit all day."

_____

* Slang referring to the chalk outline around dead bodies at crime scenes.

Not wanting to risk a value judgment, I changed the subject. "How long you been down?" I asked, having overheard that expression on the march up.

"This time, 'bout seven years."

"All here?"

"Hell, naw. I been at Butner, Edgefield, Coleman . . . this place ain't shit. 'Specially next to the USP, where I done did my first bid." USP, the U.S. Penitentiary—maximum security. In a low- or minimum-security prison, that was impressive: anyone who had done time at a USP commanded respect.

"Really?"

"Hell, yes."

The Jamaican guy stopped singing. "How yo' mattress?" he asked.

"Pretty thin," I replied.

My cellie looked at me and deadpanned, "What you think, you had a year and a day at the Ritz?" Everyone broke up laughing.

My cellie, who was six feet and two hundred pounds of equal parts muscle and paunch, had been locked up for most of the past thirty years on a variety of charges, most involving crack. Since turning eighteen, he'd done state time, fed time, and—the worst time according to him—about three years cumulative in county lockup, where he claimed to have been in a holding cell with one toilet and thirty-five other men for over a week without a shower.

Like Freeman's character, Red was often wise, always wary. He advised me and other newbies how to tie our bedsheets to minimize dirt accumulation, how to dress so as to avoid scrutiny from COs, how to stay out of fights, and most important, how to avoid getting a "shot." A shot was an infraction that led to denial of privileges. Low-level violations, such as removing food from the cafeteria, resulted in the loss of phone privileges, recreation, commissary, or visits; higher-level violations such as possessing steroids, a cell phone, or a woman's panties earned inmates ninety days in "the hole"—solitary confinement—transfer to a higher-security facility, and a delayed release date due to revocation of "good time"—the time off for good behavior at the end of a sentence. Outside of disciplinary violations, one surefire way to irritate prison staff was to file formal complaints against them using forms called BP-9s or BP-10s. If a warden or a captain (the number two position in the prison hierarchy) was so inclined—and they usually were when faced with inmates who lodged frequent complaints—he might make a prisoner's transfer especially miserable via "diesel therapy." That meant sending a prisoner on a six-month multicity tour of squalid county jails and holding facilities, thereby rendering contact with loved ones impossible and forcing the prisoner to adjust to new settings and new threats every week or so. Traveling around in buses, handcuffed and chained to a line of other prisoners, is no way to see the country.

Red knew more about criminal statutes and sentencing guidelines than most legislators whose job it was to write them. He enjoyed showing off his knowledge, especially to someone who had once been on the other side. And he gave me the lowdown on many of our fellow inmates—what they did, where they'd done time, how long they had left, and most important, whether they were "miked up" or "hot" (that is, known snitches). Red knew the sentencing guidelines so well and had connections at so many other prisons that he always seemed to be able to tell when new guys came in if they'd snitched on their suppliers. Anyone who snitched had an unusually short sentence, so they sometimes lied about the length of time they'd served at their prior spot. Red would check with his sources and often found their stories to be exaggerated. As the eldest on our cell block, Red was the informal enforcer of a no-snitch policy through which he demanded to see every newbie's "papers." Within a week or so the new neighbor would receive his belongings from his last prison, including the paperwork from his case, and Red would examine it to see if the guy had cooperated with prosecutors and to what extent. If the guy refused to show his papers, Red sent the word out loud and clear: "Do NOT fuck wit' dis new nigga," he once warned me about a guy who'd just moved in, "he so muthafuckin' hot he put halfa Memphis in the feds."

It was bad enough to be known as someone who had ratted out a close associate, friend, or relative to finagle a reduced sentence on the way in, but far worse to be a known snitch inside prison walls, once the teams (prisoners vs. the prison) were firmly established. Those were the prisoners who would send an anonymous note (called "dropping a kite") to a CO informing on a fellow prisoner's violation or illegal hustle. Except for suspected child molesters, who face the constant threat of beatings, snitches occupy the lowest rung on the prison hierarchy. (Most child molesters were housed in separate wings of correctional facilities, but there was constant scuttlebutt about certain men having slipped through the cracks of the system, or having dual sentences for drugs and child pornography, etc.) Suspected pedophiles were beaten and extorted, and faced other humiliations, such as having their cells or belongings sprayed with urine. Snitches sometimes faced similar threats but were mostly treated as lepers.

Above those groups, there was a generally understood hierarchy that moved upward from "inmate" to "camper" to "prisoner" to "convict." "Inmate" is a very derisive term inside prison because it is the term that COs typically use to address prisoners. Inmates are prisoners who identify as much (if not more) with the institution as with their fellow prisoners. Inmates feel superior to other prisoners; they don't deserve to be incarcerated, especially not with these other hardened criminals. They follow rules and express concern when others break them. An inmate might inquire about the CO's family, prior job, or hometown or casually joke with the CO about something; once other prisoners leave the vicinity, an inmate might allude to a fellow prisoner's messy cell, laziness on the job, or questionable activity. This is called "dry snitching": not directly ratting someone out, but offering self-aggrandizing information, especially through invidious comparison, that could cause extra scrutiny of others. An inmate would never "buck," or resist direction from prison staff. Inmates value their proximity to prison staff, and even if they aren't snitching, COs rest assured that inmates will help them maintain order. In return, COs might provide inmates with small perks—a second helping of meatloaf, help getting a favorable prison job placement, a superficial search after the inmate receives a visitor.

A "camper" is not nearly as insidious as an inmate, but is considered soft by "convicts." Campers are generally incarcerated in low- or minimum-security facilities and are typically first-time offenders with relatively light sentences. Campers might "eyefuck" strangers (that is, look at them for more than a fleeting moment) or even greet them, something a true convict would never do. Campers back down from possible confrontations, especially those with convicts. During the evening leisure time, a camper might quietly watch a softball game or enjoy a sudoku puzzle sent in by a relative. Campers are neither actively liked nor disliked by convicts, though they are pitied for their vulnerability to convicts' schemes and bullying. Campers just want to go home and may whine about being locked up.

Inside prison, "prisoner" is probably the least used of these terms, precisely because it is the most neutral; it indicates neither derision nor reverence. Prisoners simply put their heads down and do their time without bitching, which was my objective. They don't antagonize other prisoners, though they disdain snitches; they don't instigate fights, though they are quick to respond to provocation. They might speak briefly to COs, but never with the obsequiousness that an inmate would use or the bravado used by so-called convicts.

"Convicts" are the people who in some ways run the prison, or at least the prison's underground economy. Convicts, who have typically served long terms and are accustomed to prison life, adhere strictly to what is called the "convict code," which is very intricate but founded on a few simple truths: might makes right, weakness deserves predation, snitches get stitches, and prison staff are the enemy and must be defied when they try to encroach on prisoners' already-constricted zone of freedom. A convict rarely speaks when other means of communication will suffice; when he passes a fellow convict on the compound he might silently bump fists, but he ignores pretty much everyone below him on the spectrum. He would never shoot the bull with a CO or speak at length to one, unless he was either cursing the CO or conspiring with him to smuggle contraband. Any prisoner who forgets that prison staffers perform full-cavity searches, arbitrarily tear up people's belongings in search of contraband, and generally view prisoners as subhuman is just as deserving of bile as the COs themselves. COs may see convicts as truculent but maintain some level of respect for them—a respect they don't have for inmates, whom COs leverage to get information about various illegalities happening out of their view.

COs usually steer clear of convicts, understanding that they have far more to lose than long-term prisoners, and they are usually judicious in their use of overwhelming force. On the street, the fear of prison keeps most people in check, but once someone is locked up—and this is especially true of convicts— the only real consequence of inciting violence is solitary confinement. COs often form tacit détentes with convicts whereby convicts are allowed more leeway to commit small infractions than other prisoners in return for maintaining relative peace on the yard. They are aware that in the event of a riot they are woefully outnumbered and could easily die before reinforcements arrive.

Nearly all convicts started out in maximum- or high-security prisons, where the so-called convict code is strictly enforced. There are subtle distinctions as one travels down each security level, from maximum to high to medium to low to minimum. Perhaps the biggest difference is that in low- and minimum-security facilities, prisoners have more general freedom of movement and are rarely cuffed when moved from place to place, except after fights. This freedom allows for more potential violations of the code.

According to several prisoners who'd started out long sentences in high-security facilities, the mix of people at Manchester FCI actually made it more conflict-prone than a typical medium-security facility, because a lot of those who'd never been to prison were ignorant of or even flouted the code. Most of the prisoners started out in higher-security facilities before coming to Manchester after their Bureau of Prisons—calculated "threat level" had fallen based on age and time served without a major incident. As these prisoners mixed with the minority who were either coming from county jail and couldn't make bail or had originally been sentenced to Manchester, the prison was like a road on which some people are driving thirty miles per hour, some fifty-five miles per hour, and others eighty miles per hour. Indeed, one of the most vicious fights I observed began with an old-head veteran of high-security facilities telling a newbie, "You ain't no convict. You a camper. Go roast some motherfuckin' marshmallows." As you might imagine, the youngster on the other end of that comment did not respond well and ended up bashing the older man's head with a slock—a padlock or jagged rock wrapped in a sock.

* * *

During my first week, I spent a lot of time watching and learning. Since I had no official job, I was temporarily put to work cleaning the unit alongside Red, who showed me how to make the floors shine and gave me a crash course in prison culture. It seemed as if, after two decades on the inside, he knew it all. I felt lucky to have someone with so much experience showing me the ropes.

One of the first things Red explained was the prohibition on asking people about their case. (Apparently the fact that I was short and slight mitigated people's apprehension about asking me this question.) Of course, he grilled new inductees, because select old heads like him and the shot-callers asserted rights that few others had. (Nobody except the newest guys full of bravado even used the word "gang" because they understood that gang association would get you thrown in the SHU—the Special Housing Unit, i.e., solitary.)

As Red noted, nearly everyone at Manchester was convicted for dealing drugs—approximately two-thirds for coke, one-third for methamphetamine or oxycodone. This was not unique. According to the Department of Justice, the federal prison population has increased tenfold since 1980. And even though half of the drug-trafficking offenders were in the lowest criminal history category, their average sentence in 2010 was 45 percent longer than the average sentence for other offenders: seventy-eight months versus fifty-four months.[5]

All had been caught with enough of their chosen drug to receive a mandatory minimum sentence of five or, in most cases, ten years. Most of them also had a gun on their case, leading to a five-year enhancement. That left them with fifteen-year bids, where they typically started at high-security institutions (depending on their age) before transferring to successively lower security levels and ultimately reaching the Promised Land of the federal prison system, minimum security. Even after a decade without Internet access, they avidly followed pending legislation that could ameliorate their plight. Most knew by heart the relationship between crimes and their corresponding offense levels according to federal guidelines (along with the additional point values of various "enhancements" sought by prosecutors), as well as the exact sentencing range for each offense level.

Contrary to popular belief, very few prisoners actually claim innocence. However, most refer to "catching" their case as if they had caught the flu ("I was in Georgia with my old lady when I caught my case"). This, of course, serves to shift agency away from themselves and toward the system. Surely, some were caught up in circumstances beyond their control; many made mistakes that were compounded by the actions of others. And guilt and innocence come in many shades of gray. The government pursues certain cases but not others: young black men who sell crack are targeted more aggressively than Hollywood heiresses who share blow with their friends, and prominent elected officials (see Edwards, John) are prosecuted more tenaciously than others guilty of similar crimes. U.S. attorneys want to please their bosses in Washington, who want high numbers and high-value scalps. This works overwhelmingly to the detriment of racial and ethnic minorities and those who can't afford private legal representation—and sometimes public officials.

Despite an interest in the law, of course, few of my fellow prisoners claimed to be pristine. Red, for instance, had been in and out of federal, state, and county incarceration on a dizzying array of charges, from drugs to assault to robbery. When the conversation turned to taxes, he gazed out the window. "Shit, I been locked up so long I don't know when the last time was I filed taxes," he said wistfully. "They don't give you no muthafuckin' W-2 when you slingin' dope."

In addition to being my cellie, Red was my teacher and protector, against other prisoners and the prison staff. He explained what types of provocations would be shrugged off and what types would get me shanked; what kinds of infractions would get me a wrist slap and what kinds would earn me a year in the SHU. He pointed out which showers had hot water. And fortunately for me, in addition to his encyclopedic knowledge of the system, Red was one of Manchester FCI's better chefs. He taught me how to make a "nacho" (a prison delicacy made in a bowl with rice, chips, beef jerky, cheese, beans, and vegetables smuggled from the warehouse).

On my third day, as others languished in the long lunch line, he suddenly pulled me aside and whispered that I should follow him. As we snaked through the line I was a bit irritated at having lost my place. But then we arrived at a small storage room. He slid a slim metal object into the lock and winked at me. Inside was a pile of mattresses slightly less shitty than the paper-thin one I had inherited; this small act of kindness would make it significantly easier to survive my bid.

One of the first prison codes I learned from Red involved dining etiquette. There were only eight of us in the cell block, which had the capacity to hold about seventy. Since we lived in a newly occupied unit on the compound, we were the last to be counted during afternoon count, which meant that we had to wait in line together for nearly forty-five minutes as all the inmates from other blocks dug into their dinner. By the time we started eating, most of the other inmates had finished, and the chow hall was filing out. On my first full day, I proceeded through the line, and since the guys on my cell block were the only people I knew other than the guys with whom I'd gone through processing, I sat down to eat with them. Immediately a couple of guys at the table glanced at each other. Red put down his fork and fixed his eyes on me. "Listen, cellie, is you tryna start a muthafuckin' riot on yo' first day?"

"Huh?" I was confused.

"Look around, cellie. What you see?" he asked.

I shrugged.

He shook his head. "How many white folks you see eatin' with the kinfolk?"

"None."

"Thaz right. Thaz cuz if you do, you gon' hear 'bout it from yo' people. They *might* give you a break cuz you ain't never been down. But you pull this shit at the USP, you wouldn't see day 2, man. They be callin' yo' old lady, 'Yo, Miz Senator, they done put the senator in the ICU!'"

The table had a good laugh at that, but Red had made his point. "Ain't nobody jumpin' in to save yo' nigga-lovin' ass neither." More laughter from everyone except Red, who scowled derisively at my naïveté.

As I walked back to the unit alone, a beefy white guy with a red goatee and a shaved head approached. He had a thick Southern drawl and a chest completely covered in tattoos. "Listen heah, boy, is yew some kinda nigguh-lovuh?" he demanded. Apparently the guys from my cell block weren't the only ones to notice my break with form.

"No," I said, figuring it wasn't an opportune time to reveal my African American Studies major.

"Then sit wit' y'own kind tomorrow at chow."

"Okay, my bad, see, that was my cellie. I just got here today."

"Huh. They putja wit' a nigguh?"

"Uh, yeah."

"Why they do that?"

"I dunno."

"Well, look here, ya need to see Lamorie and fix that. They oughta know not to do that."

"Who's Lamorie?"

"Don't worry, I'll fix it. I'm Cornbread. Y'holla y'need sum'n, y'hear?"

"Yep."

"Lemme find out yew'se eatin wit' the nigguhs again," he concluded with a sneer.

I'd gotten off easy. As others have noted, violating this fundamental rule of prison life could lead to harsh consequences. Eating with members of another race could get you hurt; eating from the same tray as someone from another race could lead to a hospital visit; eating from the same actual food item as someone from another race could get you killed.[6]

When Cornbread walked away, I flashed back six months to a meeting I'd had while preparing for my reelection campaign with a few white politicos—guys who weren't with me in my first race but were with me now that I was a senator. One of them asked if I was planning on doing my signature 3-on-3 tournament again. Of course, I replied—every year.

"Look, Jeff, have you thought about maybe doing a soccer tournament on the South Side?" he asked. That was the whitest third of my district.

"Um, nah, that wouldn't really be me."

"I thought you played soccer in high school."

"I did, but still . . . you know, those kids' parents sign them up for leagues, and you know, it just doesn't seem necessary."

He looked at the other guy and then back at me. "Maybe not for them, but it might be necessary to get you reelected. Look, whether you like it or not, you can't ignore your base. Man, politics in this town is like prison—there's two teams, and the free agents don't survive very long. So before you spend too much time on the North Side, if I were you, I'd lock down the South Side and make sure you don't get a primary from there." A white primary opponent to split the white vote combined with a single strong black opponent would complicate my reelection in the majority-black district.

Cornbread was essentially repeating what I'd heard six months earlier in a very different context—the consequences were now more severe than an election loss, but the basic racial dynamics remained the same.

Other than the lack of freedom, race was probably the most salient factor shaping life at Manchester. A slight majority of the prisoners were black, about a third were white, and the rest were Latino or Asian. Blacks seemed to complain far less about being incarcerated than whites; I heard many more blacks than whites claim that they could "do an elbow" (a life sentence) with no problem.

I heard far more whites express disbelief that they were locked up with "people like this." Take, for example, Kyle, who was in for burning crosses outside black churches and became a sort of lone wolf on the compound. I met him shortly after he arrived; he beefed with a black guy before seeking support from whites with Aryan Brotherhood affiliations and was largely abandoned by veteran whites who didn't want to be dragged into racial warfare without cause. Kyle's saving grace was that he was the compound's only white barber—a practice too intimate to be performed interracially. Accordingly, I traded him two beef logs for a haircut. But as soon as he started talking, I regretted it. "Guys like us shouldn't be here," he told me. Other than our whiteness I didn't see much commonality between a cross-burner and a Black History major, but I didn't respond. Kyle alternately claimed that he was tight with the Klan; that the cross burning was just a prank; and that he had nothing to do with it but just happened to be in the car when the "actual" cross-burner was apprehended.

White prison veterans could parade around with giant KKK

tattoos and share jokes with black guys, but a young white newbie like Kyle—all of twenty years old—with no ability to navigate prison would have a different experience. He was soon
roughed up by a black prisoner and threatened with more. A
certain level of ethnic identification within prison was understood as necessary for protection, but for someone to have
proactively targeted blacks on the street was gratuitous and
offensive. Sensing that a beating was coming, Kyle soon requested a transfer into protective custody, which, in Manchester at least, meant solitary confinement. Few actions brought
more disrespect than the act of requesting PC. (Conversely,
some said that few actions brought more respect than a highly
regarded convict checking himself into the SHU after recogniz-
ing that he would likely kill or maim a CO and wanting to avoid
an elbow.)

Perhaps because of continuing societal inequalities—that is,
comparative white power and privilege—whites seemed to have
more trouble than blacks handling prison's daily humiliations.
Red, conversely, claimed to be at home in prison. He often reflected about the similarities between prison and his old life on
the street. "Other than pussy, shit ain't that different in here,"
he sneered. "That yard jus' like my stoop. I run shit in here
jus' like I did out there." While this sentiment comported with
criminologist Leo Carroll's early theory that black street life,
with its emphasis on cunning, toughness, and racial solidarity,
bears some cultural similarities to incarceration, it was certainly
not true for other black prisoners, and later research reveals far
more nuance. Kevin Wright, for instance, studied New York
State inmates and reported the following findings.[7]

1. Blacks and whites had exactly the same average
   number of assaults on staff and other inmates.
2. Inmates of both races ranked financial support as

their highest need and emotional feedback as their
second highest.

3. Inmates of both races who had gone beyond high
   school and had less experience "in the streets" (aka
   "lambs") were more likely to be hurt.

4. Unemployed inmates were shown to be more aggressive than inmates who were employed previously,
   suggesting that economic marginality regardless of
   race influences prison adjustment.

5. Race plays a small role in determining adjustment
   to prison, but it is less important than prior incarceration and "street" experience.

Though opposing images of the "typical" black prisoner
emerge in ethnographies—the aggressor who physically and psychologically dominates others versus the "chill" guy who hones
"a defensive, vigilant posture . . . conceal[ing] feelings behind a
façade" of serenity[8]—the folly of ascribing a prisoner's traits to
his race became quickly apparent. Indeed, I would soon see Red's
posture toward me swing wildly from one pole to the other.

Prisons are but a microcosm of society, so no one should expect them to be a postracial paradise. Our nation's prisons bear
the scars of more than a century of racially tinged drug law
enforcement often rooted in the white American male's deep-
seated fear of race mixing. The country's first antidrug law was
an 1875 San Francisco law banning opium, which many believed
Chinese men were using to lure white women into opium dens
for sex. When Congress passed a similar law decades later,
racial inequities remained: the law carved out an exception for
drinks with traces of opiates then popular among affluent
whites.[9] Soon came a 1914 law prohibiting cocaine use, catalyzed
by media accounts linking cocaine to black violence,[10] while the
Literary Digest blamed the "cocaine-crazed Negro brain" for

"most" sexual attacks against Southern women.[11] Similar dynamics facilitated marijuana crackdowns, with Mexicans as the original scapegoats, and later blacks, as data from New York, Chicago, and California show.[12] Blacks and whites use drugs at similar rates, and whites use cocaine more than blacks.[13] Yet arrest rates for blacks were 3.5 to 5.5 times higher than white arrest rates every year from 1983 to 2007.[14] Once arrested, blacks are more likely to be prosecuted than whites and to receive much longer sentences for similar crimes, thanks to the disparity in mandatory minimum sentences applied to crack cocaine and powder. Powder is the drug of choice for most whites, whereas crack is used predominantly by blacks; the two are simply different forms of the same drug, yet a defendant must possess eighteen times as much powder as crack in order to receive a comparable sentence. (The ratio was 100:1 until August 3, 2010, a day of jubilee in federal prison.) Even as research illuminates these inequities, they have actually worsened in recent years.[15]

It would be folly to think that somehow black prisoners leave all of this at the prison door when they walk in. Adding insult to injury is differential treatment blacks receive once they arrive at their destination. Historically, prisons were racially segregated by state law and this carried over into job assignments as well.[16] Just as on the outside—where black unemployment rates have typically hovered around twice that of white unemployment rates—white inmates are more likely to hold a job and are able to enjoy the benefits of working while in prison, namely, wages that afford them a slightly easier lifestyle via purchases at the prison canteen.[17] White inmates have also typically been awarded higher status and higher-paying jobs within prisons, a hierarchy that certainly existed at Manchester FCI. And as others have described, prison staff endorse this racial hierarchy by ensuring that white participants navigate the system more easily.[18] Although I clearly had a lot of advantages over most black prisoners—most notably, enough money to buy what I needed from the canteen* and stay in touch with loved ones—I would soon learn that the standard prison racial hierarchy wouldn't always apply to me.

---

* Another word for commissary.

3

"THE SENATOR BE EMBEZZLING . . . HE A REGULAR CONVICT NOW!"

Inside the Bowels of the Prison-Industrial Complex

Fairground Park—a green expanse surrounded by the dilapidated neighborhoods of my old senate district, and the former site of my annual 3-on-3 tournament—is picturesque only to a basketball junkie. The rims were bent from too many post-dunk chin-ups, and no one remembered the last time nets stayed up more than a day or two. Nearly thirty years have passed, but as I step onto the court to warm up the morning of my tournament, I have the same feeling I'd had since I was a nine-year-old kid. I see them licking their chops, wondering, "Fuck this white boy think he doin'?" Eight or nine dudes crowd under the rim playing Tips, an every-man-for-himself basketball game in which a single offensive player attempts to score against anywhere from two to twenty defenders.* While the guys in the paint wait for a tip-in,

---

* Some know this game as Tips or Bucket or 21, though it is actually played to 32, not 21, in St. Louis.

I hide near the free-throw line, since three-point shots tend to produce long rebounds. I get the carom off the back rim and some dude comes out to guard me. I've got about three original moves. They're good moves, heavy on the razzle-dazzle— behind the back and through the legs, head fake and body fake and all kinds of misdirection—and by the time I stop dancing and start penetrating, I've got a step on my defender. And I need it, because a bump from a dude with a hundred pounds on me means I'm off, so I've got to accelerate quick. But the trick isn't so much in the move as in the sight gag. The pale, scrawny runt knifing through the air for the layup. "Boy, you got shook like a bag of dope!" yells someone, mocking my defender, and it's on. I now have seven new fans, plus a cheering section of kids watching the game, talking about how Pistol Pete (when I was a kid) and then Stockton (my twenties) and later Nash (my thirties) broke some dude's ankle. Of course, I also acquire one new sworn enemy who is out for blood the rest of that day.

I'd continued hosting the 3-on-3 basketball tournament and community fair that I'd started years earlier, and by 2009 the event was drawing several thousand people, many of them ex-offenders. I found the same rhythms and patterns repeated themselves, even if I had a little less stamina each year, one less inch to my vertical, a split second less hang time. In basketball, politics—wherever—nothing beats being underestimated.

Between games we'd suck down Gatorade and get to talking about our lives. Many of the men, it turned out, had been in and out of prison multiple times. The main culprits were drugs, robberies, and failure to pay child support. Some of them had worked at an auto manufacturing plant outside of town and had been laid off when plants closed or shifts were reduced. St. Louis was once the largest car manufacturing center outside Detroit and employed thousands of people who made military planes—not to mention becoming a center for tool and die shops that supplied Ford, Chrysler, General Motors, and McDonnell Douglas (later bought by Boeing)—but the region had shed most of these jobs as manufacturing moved offshore or to the right-to-work South. It sometimes took these newly unemployed or underemployed men as long as two or three years to get child support orders modified, and during this time, a failure to make a full child support payment six times in any twelve-month span made a felony conviction and jail time possible.

I already knew from studying the state budget that an insane amount of our budget was eaten up by our staggering 67 percent recidivism rate. When I asked a Missouri Department of Corrections official why so many returned, I got a vague reply along with a "we're working on that."

Anybody who robbed somebody probably needed to go away for a little while. And while I found the drug war ridiculous, the real problem was at the federal level, with harsh mandatory minimums. So I started thinking about child support—and the thousands of men with felony convictions when they failed to pay it consistently—as an area where I might make a positive impact. I'd long supported a nonprofit called the Fathers Support Center on small projects, but now, in late summer of 2008, I told them that I'd like to work with them on legislation to change many criminal nonsupport convictions from felonies to misdemeanors and provide alternative sentencing instead of jail time. At first they were skeptical; a veteran African American legislator had long sponsored similar legislation and it had gone nowhere. But they put their faith in me.

From my perspective, the status quo seemed like a loser for everyone involved. Jailing nonviolent men who had lost jobs and the ability to support their children seemed little different from debtor's prison to me. Taxpayers paid millions to incarcerate and monitor nonviolent men because they were broke. If they had a job when they were prosecuted, they almost always lost the job permanently once imprisoned. (Assembly-line jobs aren't like professorships—you don't get sabbaticals.) In prison with meager wages, they fell further behind on payments. Many became further alienated from children and partners while they were in jail or on parole.[1] And of course, upon release they had to check "yes" on the deadly job application question, killing their employment prospects and perpetuating the vicious cycle of prison and poverty. Field research has shown that even attractive, articulate, and capable ex-offenders receive less than half the callbacks of equally qualified applicants without criminal backgrounds, with black men paying a particularly high price: just 5 percent received callbacks in a landmark Milwaukee study.[2] This helps explain why so many ex-offenders find themselves trapped in the vicious cycle of poverty, underground employment, and crime that led them to prison in the first place.

While there needed to be consequences for men who failed to meet their obligations, prison made no sense, and research showed that the most effective way to get men to support their families was to help them secure steady employment. It didn't take an economist to see that the law with regard to child-support violations was counterproductive. So I crafted legislation that changed most criminal nonsupport violations from felonies into misdemeanors and allowed alternative sentences requiring job training, substance abuse treatment, parenting courses, counseling, and other services instead of prison.

Among the first people I approached with what was dubbed my "deadbeat dads" bill was a Republican senate colleague. He had become a close friend during negotiations on an immigration bill into which he had allowed me to quietly insert a five-word clause that would delay some of the bill's adverse impact for over a decade. He asked how I planned to get the child support through an overwhelmingly Republican senate. To my surprise, he agreed with the bill's rationale but suggested that I reframe it in a way that focused on violators' potential to be devout fathers. I followed this strategy precisely, opening my judiciary committee presentation as follows: "Dan Quayle was right. You'll probably never hear me say that again. But he was right—two parents in a child's life are usually better than one. Now, we may disagree on their gender. But his belief underlies this bill." I added a fiscal argument, noting the millions Missouri would save on probation versus incarceration. Ultimately, the bill passed the state senate 33–0 and the house 154–1 before being signed into law, and the Fathers Support Center invited me to give the keynote address at their graduation ceremony, where I mingled with dozens of ex-offenders and tried to learn from them.

Six months after that bill passed and just a few days into my sentence, I concentrated more on survival than on what I might learn. I was focused on learning how to shower as quickly as possible while being prepared with steel-toed boots in case anyone got any ideas.

But it soon became clear that doing time would answer some of the questions that had seemed so impenetrable from the perspective of a policymaker. Indeed, I got my first clue one morning during my first week in prison when the loudspeaker awakened me at 6:00 A.M., booming out my name and summoning me to the admin building.

At first I was excited. This was my first "call-out." It was also the first time I realized that most of the slang I heard on the playgrounds of my senate district originated in prison. "Boy, you got called out," guys used to say to one another in a game of Tips when I would stand at the top of the key with the ball and cockily nod to a defender who talked shit when I entered the game. In prison, getting called out was much less fun: it meant you were either placed on the daily call-out sheet or simply called down to the admin building unexpectedly.

I thought my call-out either meant that my request to teach GED courses had been granted or, even better, that I'd received mail requiring my signature. About the only glimmer of good news on the way into prison had been an e-mail from a literary agent interested in working with me. I'd semi-spammed some agencies months earlier with a query and finally received a reply at 10:00 P.M. on the night before my surrender. The agent had said she was very interested in reading my book proposal. I'd sent her a copy and asked her to write me in prison and enclose a contract for me to peruse if she was so inclined.

But Red, who I'd thought was still asleep, caught the spring in my step as I prepared to leave. "They ain't call you down at 6:00 A.M. to sign no mail," he said assuredly. "And they sho' as shit ain't do it to tell you you gon' be teachin' no convicts." In fact, as I would learn, a call-out was almost never good. That's not because the administration took pleasure in calling people in to deliver bad news. It's because in prison, there's only one piece of good news—your out date—and that's almost never an upside surprise.

It was still pitch black when I got outside. I hurried past the weight pile, where a few dozen guys had already begun their predawn workout, and waited by the back door of the administration building until being motioned in by a CO. Another CO sat behind his desk in a small office talking into the phone. I peered into the office through a narrow glass strip. He shook his head and waved me off, so I waited.

I waited outside the office over an hour listening to the CO's frequent laughter during his personal phone call. As another prisoner would later note, when a prison staffer says that he'll take care of something for you "tomorrow," it doesn't actually mean tomorrow. It just means not today.

At last the CO motioned me inside and then led me back outside into a large, barren room with two vending machines and nothing on the walls. There, a stocky man with a shaved head, goatee, and brown shirt and tie combo identified himself as the prison captain—if prison were private school, the captain would be the dean of discipline—and then launched into a circuitous yet predictable line of questioning as I stood facing him.

"So, Inmate Smeeth," he sneered, slouching in his chair. "How long yew was in politics?"

"Off and on for about a decade."

"Hmm . . . well, then, yew prolly know more about politics than I do, dontcha think?" Though he wasn't smiling, he was clearly enjoying himself.

"Probably."

"Yeah. Prolly so." He paused to savor the tobacco plug against his lip. "And how long yew been in prison?"

"About a week."

"Hmm. Well, Ah been workin' in prisons fer eighteen years now. So who yew think knows more 'bout prison?" He'd hit his stride.

"Probably you," I said, trying not to smirk, feeling like I had felt in the principal's office after a junior high spelling bee when I'd been asked to spell "mountainous" and had instead spelled out "K-I-M-M-E-E M-O-R-G-A-N," the best-developed girl in the sixth grade.

"Yeah, probably so. And bein' as Ah know a little sum'n about prison, Ah got a little advice fer yew. Yew know what blendin' is? Cuz yew ain't blendin' so good. This book yew'se writin' ain't helpin', know what Ah'm sayin'?"

"Yessir."

"Maybe it ain't such a good idea after all, huh?"

"Well, sir, I hope to make the most of my time and finish it while I'm here."

"Mmm. Yew know it's rules against conductin' a bidness outta here. We been re-viewin' some things and we think yer 'negotiations' with this agent maght be 'ginst the rules."

So they were monitoring my e-mails. "I read the rules. They said inmates can't operate a business. The way I interpreted that, I'm not operating a business—like selling cigarettes or pornography or tattoos. I won't receive a penny while I'm locked up. So it doesn't seem like I'm breaking a rule."

"That how yew *interpret* it? See, Inmate Smeeth, thing is, this ain't no senate. This ain't no Supreme Court. This the B-O-P. Round here, ain't no such thing as 'beyond a reasonable doubt.' If Ah think yew'se conductin' a bidness, then yew'se prolly conductin' a bidness. And if y'ain't, ya might find yerself in the SHU for six months while we figger it out."

At that instant I hated him more than I had ever hated anyone, and had a vision of myself knocking every tooth out of his mouth until his awful drawl was nothing more than a desperate gurgle. But I just nodded, turned, and walked away feeling like a eunuch.

The next afternoon the call-out sheet was published, notifying everyone of their new work assignments or other daily requirements. I would be working on the loading dock, which I'd been warned was the prison's most grueling job. Several prisoners had also said that, contrary to popular myth, high-profile prisoners are often singled out for poor treatment, lest prison officials be accused of favoritism. My placement in southeast Kentucky was the first sign of this. I wondered if my work assignment was another. Why have a guy with a decade of teaching experience teach when he could move tens of thousands of pounds of food into and out of industrial freezers every day?

Sure, it seemed counterintuitive. But once I realized how little most Manchester FCI administrators and staff cared about the betterment of inmates—indeed, many seemed to enjoy antagonizing them—it made perfect sense. As I would learn, my experience was not uncommon. Dozens of guys approached me with stories of requests for educational materials or training that had been repeatedly ignored. (After my five written requests to teach different courses were ignored, I found their complaints believable.) Many states (and the federal government) advertise an array of educational and vocational programs.[3] Yet prison administrators' interest in programmatic success varies widely, leading to uneven implementation, according to my interviews with prisoners and ex-offenders from a variety of facilities.[4] It did not appear that authorities at Manchester had any interest in rehabilitating offenders or helping prepare them for the outside. And since several COs bid good-bye to departing prisoners with encomia like "See you next year, dipshit," the frontline staff didn't seem any more encouraging.

Now, a year after my inquiries as a state senator, I was beginning to answer the question about prison costs and return rates that had seemed to stump the Missouri Department of Corrections official. Regardless of what top-level bureaucrats might have wanted, it must have been extremely difficult to get wardens and frontline staff to care much about recidivism. As Upton Sinclair once said, "It is difficult to get a man to understand something when his salary depends upon his not understanding it."[5]

Since I thought that, given my grounding in black history, political experience, and love of teaching, I might be able to do some good if allowed to teach, I was disappointed when I received my warehouse placement. Of course, the idea of a year of hard labor contributed to my apprehension. But the assignment turned out to be the best thing the captain could've possibly done for me.

Prison labor has existed for centuries, at least since Britain's private jail owners leased inmates out daily as a profit-making enterprise.[6] In the crude criminal justice regime of early America, offenders received fines, public beatings, or execution, depending on the severity of the crime. The idealistic Quakers were perhaps the first to believe that offenders could actually be rehabilitated—through rigorous labor and the consequent development of morality and self-worth. They were concerned that prisons had merely become breeding grounds for better-trained thieves and killers—warehouses of torture no more civilized than the chain gangs and public gallows that preceded them—so in the late eighteenth century they built the Walnut Street Jail in Philadelphia to test their new philosophy, putting prisoners to work making handicrafts. Unfortunately, this experiment failed, and during the ensuing century, American prisons sacrificed rehabilitation to focus on punishment and security.

But after the Civil War, mobilized by muckrakers' revelations of a brutally oppressive prison system, a nation infused with the spirit of Reconstruction sought to reform its prisons. And not unlike the present day, reformers united with fiscally minded administrators to lease convict labor out, helping the bottom lines of businesses that paid below-market wages and benefiting governments, which expropriated those meager sums. The wages of prison labor allowed Southern states in particular to remain almost criminally undertaxed; nearly three-quarters of Alabama's 1878 revenue came from prison labor.[7] As the labor movement gained steam after the turn of the century, its increased clout helped gradually end private-sector prison labor that dramatically undercut and eroded market wages. Since then, prison labor has focused on the public sector—making license plates is a prime example—and other than crews that clean public spaces or fight forest fires in western states, most prison labor is performed on the inside.

But that doesn't mean private interests don't continue to benefit from prison labor.

I'd been at Manchester for just over a week when I started at the warehouse, which was located up the hill from the facility at the medium-security institution. I walked in on my first day with two other relatively new prisoners: Big Dog, a 350-pound black guy with braids and a complex about his weight, and Delgado, a stocky Mexican who tried to steal anything not tied down. Just as I left the bus that ferried prisoners who worked off the compound to their jobs, I spotted the captain. He sauntered up to the loading dock and smirked at me as he watched me jump out of the back of the truck. I wondered if my work assignment was more than a coincidence.

Working in the warehouse gave me a close-up view deep into the bowels of the prison-industrial complex. Having worked as a deliveryman for an extract company during grad school, I was familiar with the scope of a typical megastore's shipping and receiving area. But the prison operation dwarfed anything I'd seen. The enormous amounts of food required to feed the prison complex—not just the 2,500 or more inmates but the administrative staff and COs as well—ensured a hefty (and steady) stream of revenue for food supply companies, trucking firms, and, indirectly, farmers. Of course, the warehouse stored more than just food: it housed huge inventories of paper, appliances, furniture, and everything else required by a massive facility. The food we were forced to send onto the compound often had expiration dates of 2006 or 2007. It was 2010. I wondered whether the food had been sitting there for years, or if companies had been dumping excess, rotten food onto the prison. The prison bore at least some responsibility either way. At least, given our unique position, we knew exactly when to skip meals.

I worked with six other inmates, unloading approximately 35,000 to 40,000 pounds of food every day. Loads of meat varied in weight, coming in at anywhere from 20 to 80 pounds. Vegetables, fruit, seasonings, and condiments usually came in lighter containers, between 20 and 40 pounds. Rice, sugar, beans, and flour arrived in 100-pound bags. For most shipments, we lined up about five feet away from one another and tossed the packages to the next guy in the line. Four of my colleagues were twice my size, while the other two were approximately three times my weight. They got a kick out of throwing me those bags or, especially, dropping them to me from the top of a fifteen-foot rack, as the momentum added to their force. They roared when the bag knocked me back on my heels.

I went home with every muscle aching from hours of working in the freezer, where I was situated for most of the day. The next morning, we would start all over again.

Our crew leader was nicknamed KY. After having worked in the warehouse for years, KY had been promoted to "inmate supervisor," which meant he could, sort of, direct the rest of us. We listened to him, both because we liked him and respected him and because he worked harder than anyone. He had the body to show for it: six-foot-five, 230 pounds, all sinew. KY was a charming, handsome crack dealer from Owensboro, Kentucky, who could've passed for a Wall Street exec or a young Barack Obama if you put him in a business suit. But in greens, he was just another number, and a relentless (though usually good-humored) tormentor of others.

KY bestowed nicknames upon each of us, originally adhering to the compound's verdict for me ("Senator"). But one Monday after I'd shaved for a weekend visit, KY presciently warned with a laugh, "Big C gon' loooove that smooth-ass Booty-face." Big C was a massive, gregarious redneck who'd done four separate bids over the previous twenty years, whose prison boyfriend had just gone home, and who was rumored to be on the prowl. I would meet him soon enough.

The other members of the warehouse crew had little in common but size and strength. Ville (short for Louisville, where he'd been arrested) looked like someone you wouldn't want to encounter in a dark alley: six-foot-two, 315 pounds, cornrows that protruded wildly from his head like offshoots from a sparkler. He had six kids by three women and was probably the biggest personality at Manchester FCI. Ville entertained for hours on end in sunny times with his raps—usually Tupac, but sometimes original and improvised—and often by simply "bidding," or relentlessly mocking others. He was mercurial, though, and when dark moods struck, he scowled and resisted work. Though he struggled with his weight and was far from toned, he was one of the most feared guys on the compound; on the rare occasions that he hit the bench press, he effortlessly repped 405 eight times. He said he'd been a rap producer, and of all the stories I heard about people's pre-prison lives, it was one of the most believable, given his perfect pitch and his ability to free-style rap. He'd also been a male exotic dancer under the stage name Diamond and claimed he'd made several thousand dollars per night dancing in all-male revues and birthday parties where he would supplement his income with private dances. But since the one guy who tried calling him Diamond ended up bloodied, we stuck to Ville.

There were five others besides KY, Ville, and me. Wheelin' was a white Kentucky oxycodone dealer, six-foot-two and 260 pounds of muscle, facing nine more years; this was his second bid. As one of the leading contraband smugglers on the compound, he was always wheeling and dealing, thus his nickname.

Big Dog, also called Big Nasty, a young black guy who was six-foot-three and 375 pounds when he came in (he lost about fifty after six months of warehouse work), was a gentle giant who was always quick with a joke to lighten the mood when things got tense between two crew members. He earned his moniker by carrying around with him everywhere a picture of a naked woman whose measurements were listed as 36-24-48. Delgado (aka Amigo) was a doughy, thuggish Mexican, six feet tall and 240 pounds, who somehow had just two years on a dope charge, suggesting he'd given up somebody big since the feds rarely pick up drug cases unless the amount involved exceeds the threshold for a five-year mandatory minimum sentence. The crew mocked Amigo for his rancid breath and for being "thirsty"—no plunder was ever enough for him, and we often caught him surreptitiously hiding chunks of our collective bounty throughout the warehouse like Hansel or Gretel to get an extra bit for himself. Big E, a quiet, muscular, six-foot, two-inch, 230-pound guy with braids and an amazing work ethic, was my age but had been locked up most of his adult life and felt decades wiser. Charmin, the final addition to the crew, was a nearly illiterate, six-foot, two-inch, 270-pound white dude in for selling meth and oxycodone. He earned his nickname on his first day of work after complaining incessantly about the velocity with which hundred-pound bags of beans were tossed at him in the line we formed. "You country-ass motherfucker, you soft as cotton candy," said Ville to much laughter. KY chimed in: "Nah, man, he soft as Charmin." And so it was.*

We worked from seven in the morning until three in the afternoon, with a thirty-minute break for lunch midway unless

---

* Charmin's nickname stuck at the warehouse, but his cell block gave him a different name, HUD, because he was so crude that people tagged him as a product of public housing.

things were extremely busy. At first I thought it would be hard getting used to eating chili mac at 10:00 A.M., but after a few days' work I was so hungry I didn't mind. Our boss, Miss Horton, a hard-nosed veteran administrator with spiky gray hair, a wrestler's build, and a sailor's mouth, occasionally fed us extras from the warehouse, special treats you didn't get at the chow hall, like chocolate milk or Hostess cakes. I usually wasn't able to eat much because it vanished so quickly, since none of us knew when we'd get decent food again. Since you have no idea if or when you'll get decent food again, the rules of scarcity demand that you eat all you can as quickly as you can, and so when she'd toss stuff out to us it was like watching a pack of wolves feed. Plus I didn't want to be mocked the way Charmin was. "Prison saved you!" KY used to tell Charmin whenever Charmin stuffed his face. "This the best you ever ate, man!"

The work was difficult at first, since some of the items weighed nearly as much as I did and no one wanted to break their routine to throw a bag or box more gently if I was next in line. I knew I needed to get stronger. The strain was making me sweat profusely, but since we spent the majority of many days inside freezers, the sweat immediately froze, and this was making me prone to colds. These were new concerns for a former politician-professor. For my entire adult life, I'd showered before going to work. But since no one cared what I looked like in the morning, I joined the ranks of the nation's manual laborers who showered after work. I needed a shower to relieve muscle pain and get the stench off.

My pay for a forty-hour week started at $5.25 a month, which came out to approximately three cents an hour. But despite the low pay and aching back, I tried to focus on the silver lining: given my size, it was nice to be buddies with the biggest guys on the compound. I earned a measure of respect from them early in my tenure when Miss Horton ordered the head of the dry goods warehouse (the other half of the warehouse, which received clothes, mattresses, chairs, etc.) to "sweep and mop" the whole loading dock. Doss, a white Georgian oxycodone dealer who was the second-in-charge inmate in the dry goods division, immediately turned to me. "Smith, sweep and mop."

I looked at him quizzically. "Hey, what's that on your shirt? Right above your name?" Doss looked down, confused.

"Yeah, that's right," I said. "It's a number, just like mine. So do it yourself."

Doss muttered, "I should beat your ass, Smith, don't you ever try* me," but instead he trudged over to the cleaning supplies room and filled up a bucket with soapy water. "Yeah, tell that cracker-ass motherfucker what time it is," said Ville, and with that, they seemed to hold me in a new light: I'd made it clear to anyone testing me that I wouldn't roll over. It's not that everyone feared Doss. But the fact that I didn't, either—as a scrawny first-time prisoner fresh off the street—seemed to garner some respect. After that, I often played basketball and worked out with a few of the warehouse guys; in prison lingo, I "rode in their car," eating lunch with them[†] and spending most of the day with them, which likely helped discourage potential predators.

During my first week in the warehouse, I was reminded of something I'd learned in grad school: the prisoner's dilemma. Miss Horton told us on our first day that if we didn't steal any food, she would feed us adequately, and we wouldn't have any trouble.

---

* To "try" someone was to step to him, or speak to him in a manner likely to provoke a confrontation.

[†] As the only people on the compound responsible to outside parties—the corporate food truck drivers—we were allowed to cut the hour-long lunch line and eat together so that we could get immediately back to the warehouse. This exempted us, at least at lunchtime, from typical prohibitions on racially integrated dining.

Both of my first-day colleagues, Big Dog and Delgado, left that day with a dozen frozen chicken patties and several tomatoes. All the warehouse veterans did the same, Saran-wrapping food around their chests and stuffing produce into every available pocket and orifice to be sold upon our return to the compound. Sometimes, with particularly risky items or during crackdowns, crew members would intentionally leave a portion of food inside a larger box when unloading it, and then discard the box in the bottom of a Dumpster, where conspiring inmates who worked in trash collection would retrieve them and secretly lug them to the compound during the course of their workday. I often wondered how much demand would fall if customers knew the conditions of transit.

Bodybuilding was central to Manchester's culture, and nutrition was a big problem for serious weightlifters, given our steady diet of noodles, rice, enchiladas, potatoes, and bread. Guys looking to build lean muscle needed an alternative, and the warehouse crew was the key, siphoning off bags of raw meat while throwing them from man to man. The crew would wait for Miss Horton to turn in the other direction, and then almost instantly the second-to-last man in line, positioned to partially shield himself behind the freezer door, would take a blade, rip the tape off the box, snatch a twenty-pound bag of meat or patties out, stuff it inside his freezer jacket, and toss the box inside the freezer, where the final man would bury the box under others; we could return to reseal it later before leaving for the day. Amazingly this whole process caused only a four- or five-second delay.

I'd vowed to Teresa, my family, and myself that I wouldn't break any rules, but after a week, a prisoner who worked at the supplies warehouse next door approached me and told me that I'd better start stealing that afternoon because if I didn't, one of my warehouse colleagues was going to plant raw meat in my coat the next day. (Since I wasn't stealing, they feared I would rat them out.) I didn't know whether to trust him or not.

There were four levels of violations, or "shots," in federal prison. Series 4 shots were the prison equivalent of jaywalking—possession of more than four books in a cell, for instance. A breach might result in the denial of phone or visiting privileges for ninety days. Series 3 violations were slightly more serious—smoking, gambling, or mouthing off at a CO. These could result in a brief trip to the SHU. Series 2 infractions—such as fighting, attempting to bribe a CO, or having manual intercourse during visitation (yes, I saw this happen)—would earn you several months in the SHU or a transfer to a higher-security facility. Most serious were series 1 shots: killing another inmate, attacking a CO, inciting a riot, etc. Because of *E. coli* fears, theft of raw meat could potentially be treated as series 1, which would lead to new felony charges and an additional sentence in a high-security prison.

The SHU—dubbed "administrative segregation" or "ad seg" by prison officials and "the hole" by prisoners—was the administration's most effective behavior modification tool, save for the threat of "good time" revocation. ("Good time" is the 15 percent of a federal sentence that can disappear for prisoners who make it through their sentence without serious infractions.) Though few would admit it, most prisoners dreaded the hole, as evidenced by the mixture of fear and reverence with which they spoke of guys recently released from the SHU. "Check out that dude doin the Thorazine shuffle," lamented my warehouse colleague Ellis (Big E), shaking his head, when a prisoner emerged from six months in the SHU walking slowly with his head tilted at an angle. That aptly described the SHU's human destruction: it drove people crazy, and then they were sedated with psychotropic drugs.

Of course, the more direct indication of prisoners' fear came when prisoners were threatened with the SHU in real time: they grumbled, but usually stopped doing whatever it was they were doing. They got off their bed and stood for count or stopped shoving another prisoner after a rough foul on the basketball court. No matter how tough they talked ("Shit, I done two years in the SHU, I could do my whole bid there" was a frequent sample of bravado), their actions suggested otherwise. Only the baddest convicts "bucked"—continued disobedience in the face of grave consequences like a long-term stay in the SHU.

Solitary confinement was another of the Quakers' prison reforms. Inmates in the Walnut Street Jail were sometimes isolated in the "penitentiary house" not just as punishment but as a means to afford them the space and solitude to seek God's forgiveness. But this progressive experiment—then seen as a humane attempt to reform a squalid, overcrowded penal system—didn't bring penitence. It drove people crazy.[8]

Nearly two centuries later, however, solitary confinement made an unlikely comeback. One of the first attempts to confine a subgroup within a larger institution came in 1972 when the federal penitentiary in Marion, Illinois, isolated a group of sixty prisoners deemed very dangerous in a "management control unit." In 1990, the federal government built the first "supermax"—short for super-maximum-security prison. By 2002, fully 2 percent of U.S. prisoners lived in supermaxes, confined in tiny, continuously lighted cells for twenty-three or twenty-four hours a day, with no education or therapeutic programming, no visits or phone calls, and only occasional (and censored) reading material.[9]

Within twenty-five years, nearly every state had built similar units, some stand-alone and others within larger facilities. Since wardens rather than courts determine which prisoners are confined in these units, courts do not recognize solitary prisoners' constitutional rights.[10] According to Human Rights Watch, prisoners subjected to prolonged isolation may experience depression, rage, claustrophobia, hallucinations, and severe psychosis; many reported self-mutilation "just so they could feel something."[11] Many psychiatrists agree, arguing that prolonged isolation leads to a very specific type of psychiatric disorder that can lead to random violence or suicide.[12] The lack of interaction, mental stimulus, and exposure to nature may, to quote one federal judge, "press the outer bounds of what most humans can psychologically tolerate"—in other words, it's slow-motion torture.[13] As one prisoner isolated in a Maine SHU told a PBS documentarian: "Monsters. This is what they make in here, monsters. And then they drop you out in society and tell you, 'Be a good boy.' You can't conduct yourself like a human being when they treat you like an animal."[14]

People typically emerged from solitary confinement exhibiting symptoms similar to those of combat soldiers. Some of the Manchester prisoners who appeared most troubled reported having experienced solitary confinement as juvenile offenders—when they were, of course, even less psychologically prepared than adults to handle such harsh conditions.[15]

Given broad consensus on these points among psychiatric experts, why did U.S. policymakers tolerate the runaway growth of solitary over the last few decades? Not surprisingly, money is at the root of it. Though it is more expensive to build maximum-security units in the short term—and therefore lucrative for government contractors and useful for politicians looking to hand out goodies to major donors—management control units were believed to save money over the long term because fewer guards are required to oversee large numbers of prisoners. As the number of prisoners skyrocketed in the 1980s and 1990s in response to the tough-on-crime ethos that dominated American politics, policymakers believed management control units would be an effective way to handle the huge increases in the incarcerated population. Unfortunately, they were wrong: management control units ended up being more, not less, expensive to operate. But policymakers, bureaucrats, and wardens were undeterred, and the growth of solitary continued unabated throughout the 2000s.

At Manchester, there were five types of people in the SHU: those with severe mental illness or handicaps; those who "bucked" or refused to obey COs (often overlapping with those in the first category); those who had allegedly been in gang-related fights; those caught with more serious contraband, such as steroids or other drugs; and those who asked to go there. It was very rare that anyone would request the SHU, but I saw it happen a few times. Once, a guy with just a few months left checked himself in, afraid that a simmering rivalry with another prisoner would cause him to lose his cool and get into a violent confrontation that could cost him his accumulated eighteen months of good time. A second guy had ratted out a fellow prisoner but was mistakenly sent to the same prison—typically, informants are sent far away from those they've informed on, for obvious reasons—and was a marked man from the minute he arrived. Both of those requests were granted. Kyle—the young white cross-burner who feared a beating by black prisoners—had his request denied, as did a couple of men who were rumored to have been pedophiles and so feared for their lives.

The other reasons for being in the SHU were far more common. Since many prisoners with mental illness struggle to handle the omnipresent tension of prison and following stringent prison rules to a T (having your bed made with precise military corners, for instance), they are most likely to receive disciplinary "shots" and be sent to the SHU—where, of course, they tend to be most susceptible to mental breakdown and even suicide.[16] In the wake of deinstitutionalization, prisons have become America's "new asylums," with ten times more mentally ill Americans now incarcerated than hospitalized—and the SHU is how we house the most severe cases. In essence, we are placing those most in need of a caring, nurturing, calming environment into one that is practically designed to make even the most sane person lose his mind—and one that is generally considered to be a form of torture under international law.

One morning, the voice came over the loudspeaker at 5:30. "WORK CALL CANCELED." *Yes!* I thought. *A day off!* I'd tossed and turned all night because of a guy with sleep apnea snoring, wheezing, and gasping for air in the next cell, and a morning of rest was just what I needed. I rolled over and closed my eyes. "FOOD SERVICE WAREHOUSE WORKERS RE-PORT TO DUTY ASAP," boomed the voice over the loudspeaker. Damn.

I got up, put my greens on, and rushed down to the compound to be at our pickup spot by 5:45 A.M. Miss Horton wordlessly herded all the warehouse workers to her van. I pushed the door open and perhaps out of unconscious chivalry stepped aside to allow her to pass ahead of me. "Not today, Smith," she growled, pushing me ahead of her. "I ain't lettin' no prisoner behind me today."

I was confused until she explained that three men were stabbed the night before, and the entire facility was on lockdown. During a lockdown, every cell was searched, every trash and Dumpster, every bathroom and closet, every inch of every build-ing, and every prisoner—often every orifice. Prisoners are noto-rious pack rats; because they never know when they'll have access to, say, ketchup or mustard again, they'll store it in the fingers of makeshift plastic gloves back in their cell. They will store slices of bread, utensils, and other seemingly harmless but for-bidden items. But on a lockdown, COs confiscate all these accu-mulated goodies—the kind of things that anyone on the street would discard as rubbish but that are prized in prison because of their scarcity on the compound.

No one likes lockdowns. Prisoners hate them for a multitude of reasons: their privacy is violated; their belongings are often ransacked, trashed, and seized; their hustles and the markets that enable them dry up; and the daily routines that help them pass the time are disrupted—they can't work out with weights or even shower. Most, though not all, COs dislike them because they create a tense atmosphere that increases the likelihood of prisoners "bucking," especially amid the intrusive and invasive searches that COs are directed to initiate. Prison staff—counselors, housing unit managers, and others, some of whom started out as COs—dislike them because they are forced out of their relatively cushy roles to act as COs up in the units, searching cells and prisoners. And wardens dislike them because they are complicated and expensive: many prison staff are working out of their natural roles, which can lead to confusion and conflict, and most prison staff are working overtime. But despite all of that, lockdowns serve at least three important functions from the prison's perspective. First, they punish prisoners en masse for whatever alleged violation has occurred in hopes that they will discourage similar breaches in the future. Second, they eliminate large amounts of contraband through CO cell sweeps. The third purpose is far less concrete: they reinforce the prison's absolute control over prisoners' bodies.

And so from 6:00 A.M. to 8:00 A.M., we departed from our typical regimen to take out enough food for 2,500 prisoners. During a lockdown, we (and a few kitchen workers) were the only prisoners required to work, since food deliveries still needed to be unloaded, and someone needed to make bologna sandwiches for prisoners. But before making sandwiches, we were ordered to dig out the frozen sandwiches left over from the last lockdown. No one seemed to remember when that had occurred, and the bags of chips and bologna sandwiches were literally frozen together inside of paper bags. But we dutifully excavated the meals and piled them onto pallets to take to men at both the medium- and minimum-security facilities, since the lockdown covered all of Manchester FCI.

This would be my sole visit to the SHU—to deliver food to prisoners there during the lockdown. Some prisoners have compared living in the SHU to a tomb,[17] but that wasn't my impression at all. It was deafeningly loud, difficult to decipher any words above the cacophony of screaming. "CO, I NEED SOME GODDAMN TOILET PAPER!" one guy shouted repeatedly. "GET ME SOME GODDAMN TOILET PAPER 'FO I FLOOD THIS MUTHAFUCKA AGAIN!" His threats went unheeded. This prisoner had apparently repeatedly flooded his cell with dirty toilet water to antagonize the guards. Anyone willing to endure that kind of misery in order to inflict just a bit of it on others—the COs, of course, simply forced other prisoners to clean it up—was not psychologically healthy, and probably wouldn't be for a long, long time, if ever. I quickly realized that the SHU was not where I wanted to spend my year.

And yet now, just two weeks into my bid, the possibility of the SHU had instantly become real. If I didn't start stealing food from the warehouse, some unnamed colleague was going to plant raw meat in my freezer jacket and I was going to end up in the SHU—and possibly even with a fresh charge and more time. This was my first prison dilemma. Should I trust the guy who had warned me that my colleagues thought I was a rat? Or was he just trying to trap me into stealing so that he could then rat me out? I did a quick analysis of the situation: if I got caught stealing fruits and vegetables, I'd probably end up with a low-level shot, likely leading to a loss of visiting and phone privileges and time in the SHU. But if I got caught with raw meat—even if the evidence was only circumstantial, since I didn't have much faith in the presumption of innocence behind bars—then I could end up with years added to my sentence, transferred to a high-security 23-1 facility where I'd be confined all but one hour of the day and doing time with murderers. I'd already decided that while it wouldn't be easy, I could get through a year at Manchester. But could I get through five years at a high-security prison? I didn't want to find out. So I waited for Miss Horton to take her smoking break about twenty feet away but obscured by a door, drifted backward a few steps, dug into a box of green peppers, and frantically stuffed one in each sock and another in each pocket.

I turned back to the group discreetly and Ville let out a guffaw. "Y'all get a load of the Senator. He think he slick!" KY just shook his head. "Senator, take them peppers out yo' pocket," he ordered. He explained that because I hadn't thought to ask for prison greens a size too big, the outline of my bounty was easily apparent through my bulging pants pockets. I was chastened, but quietly proud that no one had noticed the peppers in my socks—which I only showed the group after work that day as we walked back up the compound after Delgado complained that he hadn't been able to steal any vegetables to put into the homemade nachos he planned to cook that night. "Damn!" exclaimed Ville. "The Senator be em-BEZZ-ling some shit! He a regular convict now!"

There was no higher praise. To anoint someone a convict was the prison equivalent of endowing a professorship. Even if I'd been so labeled only in jest, it gave me a hint of pride. Maybe I could fit in, even gain respect across the compound. What I didn't yet realize was that my first foray into prison hustling did more than just temporarily keep me out of trouble. It introduced me to a defining feature of prison culture.

4

"PRISON'S JUST LIKE THE STREET—WITH A DIFFERENT COLOR OF CHIPS"

Hustling: The Vibrant World of Prison Entrepreneurship

In my third week, I began to settle into a routine—as Red had counseled me, routine was the key to surviving decades of incarceration. In prison, every day centers around workout time; for me, that was 3:00 P.M. After lifting weights for 45 minutes I returned to my cell to get things in order for the formal 4:00 P.M. standing count, the most serious one of the day except in the rare case of census counts that occur when the first count comes up short and officials fear a possible escape. Once the count cleared, my cellie and I would walk down to dinner with our Rastafarian neighbor Dred, where I usually sat with whites but occasionally with blacks, in defiance of Cornbread's edict and without his further notice, since I usually ate at the tail end of chow time once the chow hall had emptied out. Evening recreation followed dinner; this meant an organized game of either basketball, football, or softball with other prisoners acting as umpires and referees, followed by a shower. Then, if the line at the phones was under an hour long, I might make a quick call to Teresa before hitting my bunk to read or write until midnight, at which time I'd try to sleep. The 10:00 P.M. count enforced quiet, and other counts at midnight, 3:00, and 5:00 A.M. tried to minimize nighttime chicanery.

We would wake up at 6:00 A.M. and go to the chow hall for breakfast at 6:15; Red would head back to our "house" to nap, and I would trudge out to the bus at 6:45 to be at the food warehouse by 7:00 A.M. Eight hours of loading and unloading were interrupted only by a fifteen-minute lunch and a few minutes of reading or writing. I began to know the day by the delivery: milk on Mondays and Thursdays, bread on Tuesday and Fridays, meat on Mondays and Wednesdays. Produce came irregularly. At around 2:30 we slowed up on work to focus on what we could steal, and at 3:00 Miss Horton loaded us into the van, sometimes frisking us on the way out, sometimes not. She took a sensibly practical approach to discouraging petty pilfering. If you were a hard worker and she caught you stealing, she scolded you and told you she better not catch you again. If you were lazy and she caught you stealing, she wrote you up and made damn sure you paid the price. Miss Horton was determined to snuff out the stubborn laws of capitalism that operated inside prison—except insofar as it affected her ability to operate an efficient food warehouse. From the minute I awoke each morning, the prison economy whirred with activity. Guys up out of bed cooking breakfast burritos in the unit microwave, preparing to sell them to men on their way out to their jobs. Other guys up at 6:00 A.M. for prework appointments with one of the two leading prison barbers—fresh haircuts were a necessity for men expecting female visitors on the weekend. And Chino, the compound's preeminent tattoo artist, was hard at work sterilizing needles and positioning his lookouts so that he could get started on his new client, who wanted a labor-intensive full sleeve. Were he alive

to see the hustle and bustle of activity, capitalist philosopher
Adam Smith would have been proud.

I was struck by the ingenuity I saw. Whether it was the
elaborate procurement and cooking methods that produced surprisingly tasty meals or the less benign efforts of prison drug
dealers, prison hustlers succeeded despite significant constraints.
And indeed, much research links criminality to some of our
prized cultural values, most especially entrepreneurship.

In his 1937 book *The Professional Thief,* Edwin Sutherland
depicted the professional thief as an entrepreneur.[1] And in his
influential 1938 article "Social Structure and Anomie," Robert
Merton argued that criminality resulted not from inherent
human defects but rather from the "acute disjunction" between
cultural goals (such as the American Dream) and the legitimate
means available for reaching them.[2] In other words, the disadvantaged are forced to choose deviant paths to try and achieve
financial success, so public policies to reduce criminality would
ideally increase legitimate opportunities to disadvantaged young
people.[3] After finding links between constrained opportunities
and the rise of criminal ventures,[4] as well as links between
illicit prison economies and free-market economies,[5] scholars
have proposed that those who have managed criminal enterprises be trained to run legitimate businesses. Research identified offenders' strong entrepreneurial instincts,[6] risk tolerance,[7]
personal motivation,[8] and desire for autonomy[9] as indications
that such training programs could succeed.[10]

That broad similarity in worldview, along with prisoners'
acquired ingenuity, suggests that entrepreneurship is a great
option for ex-offenders. In one study of motivational factors
associated with entrepreneurial success, inmates scored higher
than managerial professionals, scientists, and even legitimate
businessmen.[11] Another found that drug dealing in youth increased the probability of adult self-employment.[12] Prisoners and

entrepreneurs share certain traits, including free-spiritedness, nonconformism, risk tolerance, confidence, and ambition; entrepreneurship appears to provide criminals with an alternate legitimacy. Certain learning difficulties, such as dyslexia, may be more common among both prisoners and entrepreneurs than in the general population: half of all inmate respondents in one study tested positive for dyslexia, a condition five times as likely to plague entrepreneurs as average citizens.[13] Notably, nearly all dyslexic entrepreneurs studied had middle-class backgrounds while most prisoners grew up in poverty, suggesting that remedial literacy work among poor children could turn potential offenders into legitimate entrepreneurs.

Of course, no such grand thoughts crossed my mind as I stuffed green peppers—that I would barter for reading material and other items upon returning to the compound—into my pants. Something that began as a signal to colleagues that I wouldn't rat them out quickly became a useful habit. When I stepped into prison, I hadn't stolen anything since sixth grade, when I ripped off a tin of Skoal chewing tobacco from a local Walgreens. Now I was stuffing bananas in my socks, concealing onions in my pockets, Saran-wrapping peppers to my chest, and burying cellophane-covered food in Dumpsters to be ferried back to the compound by conspiring inmates. I was doing things I never would have contemplated on the outside in order to stay safe and relatively free. Sure, it was nice to have extra bananas to snack on at night, since dinner was served at 4:15, and it was helpful to strategically distribute produce in order to build alliances with some of the compound's most feared men. But I didn't think of these as moral choices so much as survival decisions rooted in my concern about being framed and ending up in the SHU.

But that rationale went out the window by the end of my first month. By then I'd been stealing regularly and had begun to gain the trust of my colleagues as a fellow thief and a stand-up guy, once people learned the circumstances of my case and my plea. So I developed new ways to justify my theft. If I stopped stealing, I might lose the trust of my colleagues and put myself back into danger of being set up. I didn't really think this would happen—at this point, we had established something of a bond and I'd handled myself well enough in other venues, such as the basketball court, to have been accepted—but I couldn't be sure. Hell, if my best friend of a decade had betrayed me, how could I trust a lifelong drug dealer I'd just met?

My second justification for theft was that I never sold anything back on the compound—I either ate the food myself, traded it for reading material, gave it away to build strategic alliances, or contributed items to community meals that a friend might cook for a group. With a direct line to all incoming food, I was eating better than most on the compound. Unlike most of my fellow prisoners who sold stolen food in exchange for "stickies" (prison lingo for stamps, which along with mackerel served as currency), I'd been able to set money aside from my savings before coming in; Teresa wired me $290 each month, which I mostly spent to communicate with friends and family. Many other inmates weren't nearly so fortunate. Even inside prison, I was privileged and aware of it. Of course, I wasn't as privileged as was commonly assumed. Fellow prisoners frequently asked me for stickies, bags of mackerel, or items at commissary. Unless it was a friend or an ally, I declined. One prisoner was particularly pushy. "C'mon, Senator, lemme get a ice cream, I know you got that long paper," he pressed, using prison lingo for wealth.

"Naw, man, I really don't," I replied.

"How many million you get off 'em?"

"Wasn't like that, man. I just lied to the feds about something stupid. I didn't steal money."

"How the fuck is you in here and didn't even get no money?" He laughed. "Fuck is wrong witchu, man?"

My third rationalization for stealing food was simpler. I fucking hated the prison, and this was a passive-aggressive way of getting a small revenge. I hated the captain, most of the COs, the 40 to 50 percent markup for every commissary item, and the dollar-a-minute they charged for phone calls after paying us $5.25 a month for full-time work. So it didn't bother me much to rip off an onion or two every day. Of course, whenever that justification crossed my mind, I could hear my mom saying, "That's exactly the kind of attitude that got you here!" But I didn't care.

Inmates have an underdog mentality. Most have operated in the shadows for much of their adult life, maneuvering, hustling, working angles. It didn't surprise me, then, that they continued to hustle in prison when opportunities presented themselves. In a pitched battle where everything is you versus the Man—the same Man who put a wire on one of your underlings, got your cousin to rat you out, withheld potentially exculpatory evidence, assigned you a public defender who didn't have time to read your case, and then took you from your family for trying to make enough money so your kids could have a better life than you did in a neighborhood where jobs were scarce—the minute they order you to open your "wallet" or "suitcase" during intake, the message is clear: the battle has resumed. And so you look for every possible opportunity to get over, to quietly subvert the system. Not the best training for a law-abiding life back on the street, of course. But both sides reinforce the us-versus-them mentality, and it will take a massive cultural shift in state and federal corrections systems to change that and establish the type of open respectful relationship between guards and guarded that could facilitate successful reentry.

Miss Horton and I actually had a decent relationship—better than I had with any other prison employee. She didn't catch me stealing for the first two months, until the March day I got sloppy and tried to make off with six bananas at once: one in each sock, one in each pants pocket, and one in each coat pocket. I had my cartoonishly bulky winter coat, which concealed the four in my coat and pants, and my pants did an adequate job of covering the ones in my socks as long as I remained upright. Miss Horton motioned that we were done for the day and I casually walked toward the van. We were all pretty loaded up that day, and since the weather had warmed up, we must have seemed suspicious in our thick coats. Suddenly when she was about to open the back of the van for us, Miss Horton stopped cold and swiveled. She looked at me, lingering in the middle of the pack to avoid detection, gnashed her teeth, and glared at the warehouse veterans. "Where in the hell did Smith learn to put bananas in his pants?" she barked, and my face reddened. Everyone seemed cowed for a minute until Ville, ever the cutup, broke the silence: "Senator *wish* he had a banana in his pants!"

The crew broke up laughing, but Miss Horton wasn't having it. "He ain't no senator," she growled. "He's a convict. Ain't no different than the rest of ya. And if I hear anyone call him that again, I'll write you both up."

That's when I realized that Miss Horton knew a thing or two about behavior modification. She didn't expel me from the warehouse or write me up or even take the bananas. She just wanted to let me know I wasn't nearly as slick as I thought. And it worked: in warehouse parlance, I "pumped the brakes," reining in my stealing for the next month.

Soon, though, I was tempted to go back to stealing, since the others were all taking a bounty on a daily basis and doing so with impunity. Near the end of one workday, a massive shipment of meat arrived, and I assumed my frequent place at the end of the line where my size best equipped me to navigate the freezer's nooks and crannies. Miss Horton stepped away for a quick smoke, and I plopped a box down and turned to catch the next one, only to receive it from Ville instead of Delgado, who had quietly slipped out of the line. I glanced to my left ever so slightly, taking care not to look away and get hit with eighty pounds of meat, and saw Delgado sawing his way into a box of tortillas. He stuffed several packs of them into his pockets and then reburied the box and eased back into the line. (Miss Horton kept count of the boxes but not the contents of each.) Once we finished unloading, Delgado stuffed a pack of twelve tortillas into his jacket and handed me one. I tried stuffing it into my jacket but it protruded, and Big E hissed, "Put the shit in your pants." So I did. A few minutes later we all piled into the back of the van, and after we felt it turn into the parking lot back at the compound, Miss Horton screeched to an unexpected stop. The dozen tortilla shells I'd hurriedly stuffed in my pants against my belt tumbled down my leg as Miss Horton slammed the door and made her way around to the back of the van. Everybody just about died laughing as I frantically tried to solidify the tortilla pack, which kept falling down my leg and out of my pants. Just as Miss Horton opened the back door, I clumsily gathered the tortillas under my freezer jacket, tucked them into my belt, and leapt out of the truck. "What the hell is so damn funny?" she snarled, and since everyone but me was laughing, she knew I was the butt of the joke. She shook her head at me mercifully. "Smith, you the saddest excuse for a convict I ever saw," she said. "Don't let those boys turn you into a real one."

One day in March Miss Horton called me back into her office. I figured I was in trouble for something. "You any good at math, Smith?" I figured this was a setup for a line like, "Yesterday there were x bunches of bananas, and today there were x minus eight bunches, blah blah."

"I'm okay, not great," I said.

"Well, you got a high school degree, right?"

"Yep."

"Well, that's probably more than anybody else around here." That wasn't the case—Ellis had attended junior college—but it was never smart to correct prison staff. "I want you to handle the paperwork around here from now on. So when the deliveries come in, you count 'em and check 'em off and do the math on the prices if they don't bring the amount on the invoice and then figure the difference and write it up and I'll sign for it. Understand?"

I didn't understand at all. "Yep," I said. "No problem." I figured I could learn as I went—and that the new role would give me information about how much food we received, the huge amounts we paid for it, and whether we actually needed it or not.

In addition to the food warehouse, there was a separate warehouse for dry goods. That warehouse generally received fewer and lighter goods, yet the workers there made more money and were all white, whereas five of our seven workers were black or Latino. The inmate in charge at the dry goods warehouse was Cowboy, a former meth dealer and addict who walked around muttering, clutching his dentures, and counting his remaining teeth with his tongue. He was said to be hilarious; I couldn't say since I could scarcely understand him. The first time he spoke to me at the warehouse came immediately following the first milk shipment on which I'd taken the lead, about six weeks into my tenure. The lead warehouse worker had to duck into the truck to lift hundreds of crates full of milk cartons and twist around repeatedly to toss the shipment back through the human line toward the refrigerator. We always eagerly anticipated deliveries of what we called "the fresh moo"; in addition to the possibility of receiving chocolate milk from Chester the Flav-O-Rich man, which we would ravenously swig, we had an informal competition to see which lead man could complete the milk shipment fastest. KY held the lead at nine minutes, forty-five seconds. I busted my ass in that first attempt but couldn't break eleven minutes, and afterward Cowboy caught me leaning against a wall, drenched with sweat. "Ain't pushin' that pencil no more, huh?" he scoffed, alluding to my white-collar background. But now I was pushing the pencil—in addition to unloading the trucks.

Now, forty thousand pounds of food per day may seem like a lot to feed just a few thousand men; indeed, prisoners and prison staff did not eat that much every day. But because lockdowns were always possible, the prison kept months' worth of food on hand. So we'd unload a delivery of, say, one hundred boxes of beef patties in eighty-pound boxes, pile it onto the warehouse floor, and then go into the freezer to remove months of deliveries of other food to pull out the beef patties buried deep in the back. We would then throw the newly delivered beef patties along the line to the back of the freezer, and complete the ritual by stacking the older beef patties close to the door.

Prisoners frequently alluded to the massive amounts of money made by private prison companies, construction firms, and the myriad of vendors whose trucks rattled up and down the narrow prison road into our Kentucky hollow. It was an open secret—actually prison staff didn't even try to pretend otherwise—that all commissary items were marked up 30 to 50 percent despite being of low quality. When I was young, my family used to joke that I thought my last name was "Irregular" since it was stamped on the labels of all my clothes. Those same types of terms were affixed to the boxes of many incoming prison items: FOR INSTITUTIONAL USE ONLY was the most common one, reminding us that we were not getting the choicest cuts of meat. One of the warehouse COs claimed that the food had improved tremendously. We were lucky, he assured us; some of the fish patties years ago were labeled NOT FOR HUMAN CONSUMPTION. Some members of the prison staff, of course, were in on the hustle,

taking home entire boxes of food and other products for themselves, and winking at us while they did so. "The fuck yew lookin'
at?" thundered one CO when I happened to catch him putting a
crate of Hostess cakes into his trunk. Another time a CO caught
my colleague Delgado burying a bag of fresh, just unloaded
onions at the bottom of a trash can, where they would be smuggled back to the compound by another prisoner who worked as a
trash hauler. "I know you gonna cut me in," he sneered. "Put half
them outside 'round the corner. And don't be putting this out on
inmate-dot-com neither."* Delgado discreetly split the contents
into two bags, placed one around the corner of the building, and
nodded at the CO as he came back inside. Moments like these
all added to our sense that we were pawns in a larger game of
private profiteering.

Nearly every evening we were reminded of the most egregious aspects of private profiteering: that moment when you try
to make a phone call and you hear a robotic voice tell your counterpart, "You have a call from Manchester Federal Correctional
Institution. Do you choose to accept this call? By doing so, you
agree that your conversation may be monitored and recorded."
The calls were five times as expensive as standard long-distance
calls for me, but far worse for many other prisoners forced to call
collect and pay well over a dollar a minute; indeed, a recent study
of phone rates for ten prison phone companies found rates of $15
to $19 for a fifteen-minute call, including many undisclosed
charges.[14]

As *The Nation* has reported, telecommunications companies make billions exploiting the families of incarcerated people
in part by offering substantial kickbacks to the prisons they
serve; the "commission" is based on a percentage of the revenue
generated by prisoners' calls and heavily influences the prison

---

* That is, don't gossip about it.

administrators who select firms.[15] Ergo, the companies most will-ing to charge rapacious rates are most likely to win contracts. While privatization advocates bill such outsourcing as efficient, cost-cutting measures, they frequently do so by diverting mas-sive, hidden costs away from government and onto inmates and their families—even as windfall profits often flow to private firms that make generous political contributions. This encour-ages policymakers to support policies such as mandatory min-imum sentences that not only exacerbate mass incarceration but provide shoddy services to inmates.

After all, neither prisoners nor most recent offenders can vote, and their families tend to be politically feeble: no one has ever lost an election by being too tough on crime or too hard on in-mates. Exacerbating this political weakness of minority of-fenders in particular is the fact that most urban offenders are removed from their voting district and transferred to some other voting district—usually whiter, more rural, and more sparsely populated—where their bodies are counted when states apportion legislative representation despite their inability to actually vote. It's akin to a modern-day Three-Fifths compromise, except that these offenders are five-fifths of a person in determining repre-sentation but zero-fifths when it comes time to actually vote. And many states even disenfranchise parolees and probationers, fur-ther impairing the ability of prisoners and civil rights advocates to effect policy change, even in situations where their arguments might garner strong support. The denial of regular contact be-tween 2.7 million children and their incarcerated parents, which increases the likelihood of both youth dysfunction[16] and adult recidivism,[17] is a good example of such a policy.

In fact, many prisons are moving to deny all physical con-tact between prisoners and their families by replacing in-person visits with video chats—which, not coincidentally, provide yet another substantial new revenue opportunity for prisons. In theory and at least in certain cases, the advent of video chats might help connect some prisoners to families who live far away and might otherwise not be able to make the trip. But only a naif would believe that rationale for videoconferencing— especially since the faraway families who might benefit most from it are often least able to afford it.[18] A more likely motive is profit: after hitting designated traffic goals, prisons reap 10 to 30 percent of profits from remote "visits" and also save additional money for prison by reducing visiting room staffing needs, since reduction or elimination of traditional visits typically follows the introduction of videoconferencing.[19] As prison phone companies face the threat of Federal Communications Commission action to cap their rates,[20] videoconferencing can preserve fat margins until the bureaucracy catches up in a decade or so. Some firms have even crafted an innovative pitch to security-conscious reluctant corrections officials: they tout behavior analysis of video chats as a "new investigative opportunity . . . fully admissible in court."[21] "What's . . . billed as a curb on recidivism," one observer wryly noted, "could also keep the jails full."[22]

Even more troubling is government's penny-wise, pound-foolish approach to such outsourcing regimes. Academic studies show that prisoners who maintain healthy relationships with family members are much more likely to obtain employment and less likely to recidivate.[23] Increasing the expense of such contact and thereby decreasing its likelihood and frequency is both callous and ultimately detrimental to public safety, given the expected increase in recidivism. My up-close look at the pain and frustration of men who kept getting phone calls to loved ones unceremoniously truncated because they could afford only a one- or two-minute call confirmed this: the expense of staying in touch severely strained familial relations, especially when mothers were already angry that male providers weren't present to provide financial or emotional support to their children. And thus not only does the transfer of urban minority offenders to rural counties provide immediate political benefits for conservatives, but it also increases the likelihood of recidivism—leading to future economic and political benefits for conservative rural counties—by making it more difficult for prisoners to remain in contact with loved ones. Indeed, upon closer inspection one might say that mass incarceration isn't the product of a system that is broken but rather the result of a well-oiled machine.

The government, vendors, and prison staff weren't the only ones who figured out how to make a profit from the prison system. Money, or more accurately the lack thereof, preoccupied many of my fellow inmates. Most inmates were skilled hustlers, and prison didn't change them. Except for those who had a sugar daddy on the inside or a sugar mama on the outside, inmates focused on how to make money to buy hygiene products, writing materials, stamps, haircuts, and snacks; and how to make a living on the outside, since for most, this was the final stop on a multifacility tour.

All of this confirmed my intuitions after getting an up-close look at the breadth of prison enterprises. Some hustles were perfectly legal: the guys who worked in the laundry room who ironed other prisoners' jumpsuits before a visit or the jailhouse lawyers who ghost-wrote legal briefs and cop-outs—standardized forms prisoners fill out to make requests of prison staff, since verbal requests are not considered. (Of course, neither are most cop-outs.) Others, such as the one-man barbershops or the in-cell stores reselling food items from the commissary, were technically illegal, but the COs looked the other way. On the next level of the continuum came the tattoo artists, poker dealers, and bookies, whose businesses were frowned upon and sometimes, though not always, busted up by COs.

The very riskiest enterprises, and the most profitable, of course—prison walls don't change the rules of risk versus reward—were smuggling operations: cigarettes, steroids, pornographic movies, and cell phones came in via a variety of vehicles. Sometimes they were dropped in giant duffel bags at a site over a rocky ridge to be retrieved by prisoners able to scale the ridge, since, like most minimum-security facilities, we were surrounded only by natural barriers. Other times contraband was smuggled in by visitors and temporarily stored in prisoners' "suitcases."

Most services, such as artwork, tattoos, haircuts, and cornrows, were much cheaper than they were on the street; you could get a decent haircut for around $2, a quality portrait for $5, and an intricate tattoo for $20. Tattoos were somewhat more expensive in part because they were illegal and customers had to find a lookout during the process. Early in my bid, I served as a lookout and asked what to do if a CO approached. The tattoo artist shook his head at me. "Boy, you green as a pool table and twice as square," he said. Because many prisoners had nothing *but* time, the time it took them to provide the service had little value, despite the often high quality of that service. But forbidden items were far more expensive than they would be on the street, mostly because of the premium associated with the costs and risks of transit and storage.

Of course, in the same way Wall Street has figured out how to ship liabilities offshore, many prisoners surreptitiously "outsource" the risks of contraband storage. I saw this process in action nearly every night, since I stayed up later than anyone in my cell block and had a top bunk. Just after the midnight count, I often saw an incredibly muscular and frequently threatening ex-Arena football player known as AK plant his cell phone deep in his cellmate's belongings. This he deemed necessary because COs often arbitrarily ransacked cells for contraband. This was a dangerous move on AK's part and went against many unspoken prison rules. He probably figured his bodybuilder's physique would scare off anyone who ever tried him, especially his much weaker bunkie.

COs come in all shapes and sizes. Most seek to project strength even while avoiding direct confrontations. Like parents of wayward children, they must display strength without constantly resorting to brute force, especially since they are outnumbered by a lot of men with little to lose. But just as many schools have found it effective to have one administrator whose severity discourages general misbehavior, Manchester had Al "Tuck" Williams.

Tuck was about five-foot-eight, his 350 or so pounds concentrated around his midsection. Bald but for a few unruly strands of gray hair circling his head, he was better known for his unique facial hair, a scraggly white goatee woven into a braid that cascaded past his sternum. The bottom of the braid was adorned with a pair of gold handcuffs; it was the first time I'd ever seen a bejeweled beard.

Tuck asserted his authority by tossing cells in search of contraband. He would stride up the compound on his forays to our unit quaking with anticipation, like a six-year-old boy on Christmas morning. Usually dour, Tuck would positively light up when he discovered a cell phone or cigarettes or a shank while rummaging through the nooks and crannies of a cell. "Everybody in your cells, on your feet, and shut your mouths!" he'd boom as he burst into a unit, keychain clanging into the ensuing silence. One time he entered my cell, opened up the locker, and with a quick and violent stroke of his arm swept the books, papers, and foodstuffs onto the floor. "No more'n three books is allowed," he said gruffly, grabbing two of them. I wasn't familiar with that rule—I later confirmed that up to five library books were allowed—but I didn't raise the issue. Back-talking Tuck while he tossed your cell was a good way to end up in the SHU for a month. "I'll be back to write you up," he said, then he grunted something unintelligible on his way out and left without giving me a shot.

That said, Tuck was frustrated more often than not. The cell phones, the drugs, the lucrative stuff was almost never stashed in cells; it was almost always placed in common areas. Guys had slowly loosened plaster tiles behind toilets where they'd store phones; or they'd hoisted one another high enough to lift a ceiling tile and stash drugs inside. That way, of course, even if someone ratted them out, it would be nigh impossible to make a new charge against them stick unless the prison conducted fingerprint analysis, which was rightly thought by prisoners to be more hassle and expense than the prison was willing to incur.

In spite of his sporadic success, Tuck almost singlehandedly affected the cost of contraband—the price went up when he was on duty and dropped during his week off. And there were many other ways in which the prison market obeyed basic laws of supply and demand. When cigarette prices briefly spiked to approximately $50 a pack after a mass raid in which COs tossed every cell on the compound, a new player entered the market to capitalize on the excess profits available. Soon a war between the new rival factions developed, and the price dropped again until the two main players colluded and arrived at a price of five books of stamps per pack ($30), and three books per pack for rerolled cigarettes produced by prisoners who worked in proximity to prison staff and surreptitiously collected their discarded butts ($18). Of course, most prisoners could afford to buy cigarettes only one at a time, so the "kingpins" charged higher unit prices for smaller quantities. With cigarettes going for $3 and $4 apiece and certain types of pornography for up to $1,000, the business "owners" became quite wealthy by prison standards. In the parlance of Manchester FCI, they were dubbed "entrepre-niggaz."

• • •

BJ was one of many fellow inmates with entrepreneurial drive. His twin obsessions—sports cars and redheads—had, he told us, been readily available to him in his previous life as a cocaine kingpin. He regaled us with stories of elaborate threesomes, spectacularly developed women, and other tales of sexual prowess. But now BJ vowed to put those days behind him. He was done with the dope game; when he got out, he intended to fly straight. He'd recently purchased a porn website targeted at men with a fetish for women having sex on top of or inside luxury cars, with a special focus that explained his nickname. For just $10,000, he'd purchased the domain name, the site design, and all of the necessary back-end work enabling financial transactions.

Prison was teeming with ambitious, street-smart men, some of whom possessed business instincts not unlike those of the CEOs who had wined and dined me six months before. Using somewhat different jargon than you might hear at Wharton, they discussed business concepts such as promotional incentives ("I don't never charge no first-time user"); quality control and new product launches ("you try anything new, you better have some longtime crackhead test your new shit"); risk management ("I knew I could make mo' money in lil'-ass Owensboro and not worry 'bout nobody than go up to Louisville and fuck wit' them crazy-ass thugs"); territorial expansion ("Once Dude on the East Side got chalked, I had my dopeboys out on his corners fo' that muthafucka's body was cold"); supply chain management ("You always got to stock up a few days before Santa Claus come");* and barriers to entry ("Any muthafucka wanna do bidness on the West Side know me and my boys ain't scurred to cap his ass").

There was a lot of money floating around the prison,

---

* "Santa Claus" refers to public assistance checks.

although most of it was in 37- and 39-cent stamps (which, incidentally, were worth exactly as much as 44-cent ones). Books of stamps went for a discount—$6 instead of $8.80—and before going home, inmates who had accumulated hundreds of books of stamps sold them to other inmates, whose relatives on the street would wire money to the account of the seller. Prison, as Red once noted, "is just like the street, except with a different color of chips." Another hustler named Jesse, a fellow St. Louisan and ex-Arena football player who always seemed to be hatching entrepreneurial (and occasionally criminal) ideas, liked to say, "If it don't make dollars, then it don't make sense."

The black market and the entrepreneurial drive of those who operated within it fascinated me. Want an old flip phone? In prison it's called a "jack" and costs $250 to $300, due to the revenue stream it afforded its owner, who sold or traded minutes to other inmates. Want dirty pictures? The price depended on the woman's measurements and how brazenly she displayed them. But one issue of the right magazine could fetch anywhere from $200 to $1,000, due to the recurring revenue stream possible from copying the pictures and selling them individually, and from renting the magazine by the hour after laminating it in plastic.

How did the contraband arrive? Sometimes things were passed during visits, as there were some COs who didn't perform the full strip search after visits, or some prisoners were trusted enough by COs that they could potentially serve as mules. And according to the veterans, there were always COs who would help for the right price. But that wasn't always necessary at our facility, since we were surrounded only by natural barriers that were navigable depending on weather, ground, and lighting. (For instance, nobody would make a 1 A.M. run in the snow or under a full moon because of the light, nor would people try a run under a new moon because of the difficulty negotiating the ridge in darkness.) A drop site over the ridge was occasionally used to fetch contraband in the middle of the night—or sometimes immediately after the daily 4:00 P.M. count if the COs could be distracted by a phony disturbance in another building. That was another reason the outdated phones were so valuable: since all other correspondence into the prison was monitored, the phones were the most effective way to coordinate contraband smuggling. The going rate for fetching something was $250 to $500, depending on the contents, I found out one night after a basketball game during which my speed apparently caused a fellow inmate to think I would be an ideal "runner." I wasn't at all tempted, since I wasn't desperate for money and since anyone caught bringing in contraband was immediately sent "up the hill" to the medium-security prison packed with violent offenders, some with "elbows" (life sentences). Since there was snow on the ground for weeks after I arrived, the price of contraband had risen sharply and the "delivery fee" had skyrocketed: no one wanted to risk the treacherous route when the untrammeled snow rendered footprints easily visible.

Perhaps the defining characteristic of prison life was ingenuity. Whether it meant concocting ice cream out of vanilla pudding, coffee creamer, ice, sugar packets, milk, and bananas secretly ferried out of the chow hall, or cutting hair with toenail clippers, or cooking with spices and sauces smuggled out from the kitchen in plastic gloves, or making weights out of boulders placed in laundry bags and tied around a bar when the weight pile was closed and COs prohibited even pull-ups or push-ups, inmates figured out how to do more with less. Many of the inmates then planned to put the ingenuity they learned in prison to good use on the street* by starting barbershops (in states where ex-offenders are permitted to do so) or restaurants or personal training businesses that capitalize on the way prisoners

---

* "The street" was a catchall term referring to life on the outside, not necessarily "street life."

learn to treat their bodies as temples and sculpt them. Sadly, there was no preparation for inmates to bring their ideas to reality. No one to help them write business plans, no one to help translate their intuitive grasp of business concepts into other (legal) industries, not even an Internet connection to help them learn more or begin looking for jobs.

It's not as if U.S. prisoners ever had access to a wealth of opportunities. But since 1970, politicians guided more by notions of retribution than rehabilitation enacted ever-longer prison sentences and worked to show their constituents that prisoners were doing hard time. Whether it was the massive increase in solitary confinement, the elimination of in-prison educational opportunities and the 1994 prohibition on prisoners' receipt of Pell Grants to help pay for correspondence courses, or the advent of so-called three-strikes laws, politicians wanted to ensure that they would never lose an election by being "soft" on criminals.

There was another motive. As the carceral state metastasized, politicians sought ever-more austere conditions and even the reintroduction of chain gangs across the Sunbelt—where the nation's incarceration boom was centered—as a sort of demagogic distraction. Even as they spent increasing amounts of money to incarcerate an increasing number of people for increasingly long sentences based on an increasing variety of crimes, conservative politicians preached a doctrine of low taxes and limited public spending.[24] But all these prisons weren't built for free. And so politicians devised a series of talking points centering on austerity *within* the prison system on which voters could focus. One state legislature even implied that building prisons *was* free: Arizona lawmakers required that all new prisons be built using prison labor, buttressing their depiction of a prison system that was "cheap and mean" despite their exorbitant spending on its expansion.[25] As is often the case in politics, cheap symbolism trumped expensive reality.

In some important respects, the 2008–2009 recession accelerated the trend toward more austere prisons. The federal stimulus package backfilled strained state budgets for two years, but once that money expired, states—all but one of which, unlike the federal government, must balance their budgets—desperately searched for programs to cut. "Nonessential" prison services such as substance abuse counseling, mental health services, and vocational training were some of the first on the chopping block; the federal government, along with most states, cut its operating costs per prisoner.[26] Even those states with official policies requiring that prisons offer vocational training or other services sometimes fail to do so because frontline workers lack the inclination or necessary funding, and the opacity of prisons makes it difficult to know exactly what's happening behind prison walls. As one 2006 study concluded, "Most correctional facilities are surrounded by more than physical walls; they are walled off from external monitoring and public scrutiny to a degree inconsistent with the responsibility of public institutions."[27] Given the dearth of independent oversight—not to mention the fact that some of the nation's leading scholars doubt even the Department of Justice's own data—in an *Onion*-worthy irony, it has fallen to consumer review website Yelp to publicly review U.S. prison conditions.[28] How ironic that people banned from using the Internet (as well as those who visit them) are the only ones able to offer the world an accurate depiction of their living conditions.

The cycle of mass incarceration is daunting. One in three black men can expect to go to prison in his lifetime, one in six Latinos, and one in seventeen whites.[29] Upon release, over 650,000 of them show up each year on America's doorsteps to try to succeed in communities where they have failed before—now with the added baggage of prison records. The main reason for recidivism is financial struggle: unemployed ex-offenders are far more likely to commit a crime than are those with jobs.[30] But the idea of applying for legitimate work can seem laughable when most employers won't hire ex-offenders[31] and selling drugs pays far more than flipping burgers. And nobody forces you to check a disqualifying box when you try to get back into the drug game. One possible route around most of these obstacles is entrepreneurship.

Since most states have yet to adopt Ban the Box legislation prohibiting employers from rejecting formerly incarcerated applicants, entrepreneurial training can help reentering offenders in an increasingly tight labor market, especially those who have already started successful (albeit illicit) businesses in the past. That—along with prisoners' natural ingenuity—helps make entrepreneurship a great option. The conservative political climate that has existed since the mid-1970s inhibits the development of such programs; voters see prisons as a place for punishment, not rehabilitation. But recently, both progressives and conservative capitalists have agreed that prison entrepreneurship training is an effective approach.

Public-private partnerships to provide business training have sprouted in several men's and women's prisons, such as North Carolina's Community Success Initiative, Oklahoma's Owning Your Own Business, Oregon's Coffee Creek Prison Project, and New York's Self-Education Economic Development (SEED) and From Cell to Sell programs.[32] These programs offer a range of services, including courses on market research, website design, business plan development, and management training tailored for start-ups.[33]

The largest program currently operating is the Prison Entrepreneurship Program (PEP), which partners with the Texas Department of Corrections and hundreds of corporate executives to lead two hundred Texas prisoners annually in an intensive, forty-hour-a-week seven-month MBA-level course. Linking participants to top business and academic talent through mentorships, PEP trains prisoners to construct detailed pro forma income statements, learn EBITDA margins, and perform advanced market research. Participants develop full-length business plans and, as their final exam, present a thirty-minute business plan to a panel of CEOs and venture capitalists. In addition to a rigorous curriculum certified by Baylor University's Graduate School of Business, PEP teaches essential life skills, and the combination appears to be working: their nine-year recidivism rate is just 6 percent—one-tenth the national rate—and 100 percent of participants are employed within three months of release.

The best prison entrepreneurial education programs do more than just teach people how to craft a business plan. They explain how parole policies on traveling, signing contracts, finding housing, obtaining government permits, borrowing money, and dealing with past debts will affect their new enterprise. They provide role models: formerly incarcerated entrepreneurs who run successful businesses in diverse industries. And they offer a variety of services to ease the transition back to society—most important, housing and a support network, which PEP has accomplished by buying and managing group homes for their program's graduates.

For those prisoners lacking entrepreneurial zest, other forms of education—GED courses, literacy classes, vocational training, and even rare opportunities for postsecondary education—can also facilitate post-prison success.[34] Indeed, a RAND Corporation synthesis of findings from multiple studies of U.S. prison instructional programs found that participants in all types of educational programs were far less likely to reoffend than nonparticipants, resulting in a 13-percentage-point drop in overall recidivism—the equivalent, if extrapolated nationally, of approximately 85,000 fewer recidivists annually.[35] RAND's findings also suggest that prison education is cost-effective: while education costs average \$1,572 per person, reincarceration costs average \$9,250 less for each prisoner who received education than for those who did not. Based on a 17 percent recidivism rate for prisoners receiving education and a 30 percent rate in the control group, the additional cost of educating 1,000 offenders would be \$1.57 million, but the savings would be \$9.25 million—a 6:1 benefit.[36] As one might expect given the nature of applicants, postsecondary instruction carries the greatest postrelease benefits. The Bard College Prison Initiative, one of the nation's first in-prison college programs, offers full-time college seats in six state prisons and sports a recidivism rate of just 4 percent, while Nyack and Mercy College–run Hudson Link for Higher Education in Prison boasts a 0 percent recidivism rate for its 250 graduates.[37]

Since even minimal expenditures in this vein (that is, GED instruction, vocational education, etc.) can substantially reduce recidivism, up-front costs would be offset many times over by the savings.[38] Before these types of policy changes are possible, though, society must stop seeing prison as a warehouse for society's throwaways and start seeing it as both an expensive revolving door and a massive waste of human talent and potential. Perceptions have recently begun to change, thanks to a mix of factors as disparate as the renewed attention on over-aggressive policing that helped spark unrest in Ferguson, Missouri, and other locales and the success of the show *Orange Is the New Black* in humanizing prisoners.

Fortunately, social entrepreneurs have created programs that either won't cost public money, such as PEP, or will actually save money *and* potentially reduce recidivism, such as American Prison Data Systems (APDS). APDS provides prisons with tablet computers equipped with a full suite of educational and vocational training software. Given the dearth of technology available to prisoners, there has never been an affordable way to provide this range of material. Now, tablet computing offers a scalable delivery mechanism, while simultaneously helping prisons eliminate cost centers such as law libraries by digitizing legal books. New York alone has saved $2.3 million annually by moving this material online; this is just a fraction of the potential savings. With all incoming mail scanned onto tablets, prisons could reduce the workload of COs, who would no longer need to lug giant mailbags to housing units. Tablets could increase security by reducing incoming mail and thus cutting opportunities for the introduction of contraband. Finally, tablets with vocational training software could help prison staffers match educational opportunities with employment needs in neighboring communities.

Yet despite the fact that Manchester FCI was most prisoners' final stop before going home, the facility attempted precious little rehabilitation. Many had been incarcerated for ten to fifteen years and didn't know how to navigate the Internet, let alone search for a job on it. Instead of courses on Internet use, word processing, parenting and relationship building, sales and business development, résumé writing, job interviewing—or practical training in plumbing, electrical wiring, and HVAC work—Manchester FCI offered hydroponics, a two-week course on growing tomatoes in water. I never quite understood why that was picked, though the CO who oversaw the course always went home with a huge bag of the best tomatoes, which we assumed he sold on the side of the road. But prison did nothing to nurture these entrepreneurial instincts in a healthy way. In fact, nothing could have been further from the minds of the prison staff. This is a massive failure of a system that purports to lament sky-high recidivism rates (two-thirds of parolees are rearrested; half return to prison) and yet relies on those very rates for budget growth and, by extension, job security.

• • •

Prisoners frequently asked me for career advice. They expressed interest in home health care, automotive repair, and computer programming—and of course they wanted contacts in those fields. Though few had concrete post-prison plans, they had a near-insatiable appetite to acquire useful skills, and because the prison received a stipend from the Bureau of Prisons for each prisoner enrolled in a program, the prison was incentivized to provide programs of interest. But somewhere between conception and completion, programs disintegrated. Of course, wanting every last federal dollar available, administrators urged prisoners to enroll in programs that scarcely existed, but they evinced no discernible concern for actual outcomes.

Common sense dictates that prison administrators should team with workforce development experts to operate training programs that match participants with employment needs in their communities; hydroponics seemed like a bad joke. But it was emblematic of the failure of a system that loudly laments the same sky-high recidivism rates it quietly perpetuates. Not unlike the way private prison companies use human bodies as vehicles for profit, bureaucracies use them for job security.

Critics might argue that such coordination is asking too much of the criminal justice system. Fortunately, most major cities have reentry programs that can refer ex-offenders to jobs, coordinate with local businesses and social service agencies, and help build other creative partnerships. Prison entrepreneurship advocates should also support postrelease policies to supplement in-prison efforts: authorizing entrepreneurship as an employment option for parolees and allocating a portion of ex-offenders' supervision fees to fund start-up costs for parolees' enterprises would be two positive steps.

Yet even if prison administrators actually do want to reduce recidivism through increased education and rehabilitation efforts, that won't break the cycle of mass incarceration. That's because even in areas with official curricula, courses are often woefully inadequate or simply not offered, based on my experience and a survey of prisoners from various facilities. There is often a significant gap between written policy and the policy in practice.[39] And "street-level bureaucrats" have vast discretion in prison to do what they want because the prisoners have absolutely no political power and therefore no recourse.[40] Such discretion allows COs to become the de facto policymakers. So it is not surprising that, despite the avowed goals of most prison administrators, stated policies emphasizing rehabilitation, vocational training, and prerelease life skills preparation are essentially ignored by frontline prison workers.

An example from Manchester illuminates this. Many prisoners were anxious to learn how to operate, program, and fix computers, and dozens of prisoners had been requesting computer courses for years. So I was heartened to learn that the warden was requiring a new computer skills class for all prisoners nearing release. One day I was called to the admin building along with other prisoners in their final six months for the start of what I assumed would be a multiweek course of instruction. Two COs herded us into a computer room; one checked us off, and then we waited at the terminals for thirty minutes under his watchful eye. Shortly thereafter, the CO called roll and looked us over. "All right, it's been about forty-five minutes, so you can leave if you want." And thus ended our computer skills class. Nutrition class was similar: a CO handed out a brochure with information about the caloric content of food at McDonald's, Bojangles, and Wendy's and released us after five minutes.

The continuous release of prisoners woefully unprepared for reentry cannot be an accident. Rather, it embodies the moniker prisoners have given it: BOP, Backwards on Purpose. As the

Upton Sinclair quote suggests, prisoners are merely grist in the mill: without them, there are no food deliveries, no overpriced phone calls, no parole officers, no courts, no cops, no jobs.

When BJ cornered me one night to press me to help with his porn website—he planned to call it Whips&Heaux.com, incorporating street lingo for fancy cars ("whips") and loose women—policy solutions were the furthest thing from my mind. I realized that the excuse I might give in another life—"I'm sorry; though it's a compelling opportunity, I'm not sold on the viability of your business model"—wasn't gonna fly here. And so while I declined to invest, I agreed to help him craft a business plan.

BJ and his idea were singular, but he was also somewhat typical of the budding prison entrepreneurs I met: a compelling vision and unique niche, but little socialization or concept of behavioral norms. Perhaps he had enough of a nest egg stashed away from his days in the drug game to adequately fund start-up operations, but I doubted it; most guys said that the feds had found all their bank accounts and emptied them—or if not, that ex-wives and girlfriends had done so to support children. Even if he didn't have a felony conviction, I suspected that BJ would struggle to arrange a credit line or obtain all the necessary business permits. There were basic skills needed to operate in the outside world that many of these guys lacked. All the more reason why they deserved something more in prison than a bullshit hydroponics course and $20 for bus fare into town on their way out the door. It practically guaranteed—as some of the COs mockingly predicted to men on their final day—that they'd be back soon.

5

"THIS IS JAIL, NOT YALE"

The Demise of Country Club Prisons

"One of the things I learned quickly is you don't play basketball," said Webster Hubbell, the third-highest-ranking Justice Department official under President Clinton, referring to the eighteen months he spent in a minimum-security facility after pleading guilty to tax evasion.[1] But I'd always loved sports and naively considered myself impervious to serious injury. When I first arrived in Manchester, I counted on sports to help me get through prison—as a way to pass the time, to have fun, and, hopefully, to make friends. Little did I know I'd make almost as many enemies on the athletic field as I would friends.

People who learn of my incarceration sometimes ask if it was a "country club" prison. In fact, that once reflected my own view of prisons that housed middle-class white people. It was shaped by the vivid memory of a TV exposé I once saw about the prison that housed bankers who sparked the savings and loan meltdown—facilities complete with tennis courts and bocce courts and lush, rolling green landscapes.

Some time between the late 1980s and my incarceration, however, the federal government abandoned the concept of white-collar prisons. Tennis courts and many other amenities, to the extent that they were ever available, are no longer on offer.[2] And sentencing guidelines for so-called white-collar crimes increased in the 2000s, in part due to public outrage over corporate accounting scandals and the stock market implosion of 2000–2002. Indeed, between 1997 and 2005, the average white-collar sentence increased 24 percent, while the average sentence for drug offenses rose 2 percent.[3] (Of course, mandatory minimums for many drug offenses were already outrageously high.) Politicians, prosecutors, judges, and juries all seemed to agree that white-collar criminals, particularly those whose cases drew significant public attention, deserved long, hard time.[4] Subsequently, the Bureau of Prisons worked to establish parity between rules at minimum- and higher-security facilities.

The journalist Luke Mullins interviewed scores of minimum-security inmates, legal experts, academics, and advocates, who painted a picture starkly different from the country club prison stereotype. Based on expert and eyewitness accounts, he concluded that, indeed, longer sentences, shifting demographics, and more stringent rules had made life in minimum-security facilities similar to life in higher-security prisons. As the federal system grew ninefold between 1970 and 2007, high- and medium-security facilities strained to accommodate drug dealers serving mandatory minimum sentences; tens of thousands were sent to low- and minimum-security facilities.[5]

"This is jail, not Yale!" one Manchester CO liked to yell. Several criminal justice system employees observed that minimum-security facilities increasingly resembled their higher-security counterparts and that incarcerated white-collar criminals are no longer treated differently than drug dealers or bank robbers. Bernie Kerik, who as head of New York City's Department of Correction (before becoming the city's top cop) was responsible for overseeing the department's sixteen jails and fifteen detention centers, was later able to see the other side after pleading guilty to eight felony tax and false statement charges and reporting to a minimum-security facility in Cumberland, Maryland. "That whole Club Fed mentality, that shit that they portray in the press, is complete nonsense," he said.[6]

Of course, as I soon learned, only about 1 percent of the prisoners at Manchester's minimum-security facility seemed to be there for a white-collar crime. Nearly everyone was there on drug charges, and a few were convicted for assault with a deadly weapon. Many prisoners with drug and gun charges described incidents in which they put those guns to good use: they just hadn't been caught doing so. And based on the alacrity with which many were ready to tussle—over the tiniest of slights— most did not appear to be strangers to violence.

The other white-collar prisoners—a kind, wise, and wise-cracking stockbroker who'd siphoned off a couple of million to feed a gambling addiction, a nebbish lawyer who claimed to be the victim of a small-town political vendetta, a garrulous seed salesman who'd gotten caught up in a kickback scheme, a shady real-estate type who always seemed to be right on the verge of winning his appeal, and a straight-arrow financial whiz who took the fall for a larger accounting fraud devised by his corporate bosses— mostly kept to themselves. I sometimes ate with two of them on the weekends, when the warehouse crew separated as they spent more time in their units, relaxing and resting up for another workweek. The white-collar guys quietly lifted weights and rode the exercise bike or walked the track, mostly eschewing team sports for fear of injury or simply because they were much older than the average prisoner. But I'd signed up for all the rec leagues the prison offered and played basketball, softball, and soccer games several evenings a week, as well as weekend pickup basketball.

One Saturday a couple of months into my bid, the compound's premier players were out in force: Bama, a cocky, muscle-bound six-foot-seven slasher who had played pro ball in Europe; Weezy, a soft-spoken, silky-smooth six-foot-five swingman; and Cee-Lo, a wiry six-foot-three swingman with a range out to thirty feet. I was assigned to guard TJ, who was one of the leaders of the prison church and Christian fellowship group. TJ, six feet, two inches and sinewy, always had a warm smile and greeting for people on the yard, and on this Saturday, he greeted me warmly, pounding my fist before we checked the ball to start the game. I watched him closely the first few times; he was a confident ball handler with a slick crossover. But just like poker players, even good dribblers have tells. His fourth time down the floor, I feigned an attempt to steal it from his left hand but instead darted toward his right side and poked the ball away to a teammate, who converted a fast-break layup. On the next possession, TJ started down on the blocks, cleared his teammates to the opposite corner, and demanded the ball. I used an old trick against him, digging my heels in and pushing as hard as my short stature and small frame would allow, and then suddenly, just as his teammate prepared to make the entry pass, I slid two steps to the right. TJ, who was backing me down like a giant forklift pushing a puny pallet, was now losing his balance as he careened toward the baseline. The entry pass went into the scrum beneath the basket, where one of TJ's teammates tore it away and put up a shot. TJ had regained his equilibrium and come back for a rebound, so I found him and got my butt onto his thigh. As the shot caromed off the rim I felt hands on my back, a shove, and suddenly I was falling out of bounds face-first. TJ, meanwhile, rose high into the air and tipped the rebound softly in. Others had seen his blatant foul, but this was prison ball: to call a foul was akin to snitching. Someone who commits a foul can call it and stop the action, but the player who was fouled can only do so at risk of significant damage to his reputation and perhaps his person.

But now TJ was the object of laughter and derision for having resorted to manhandling me. "C'mon, Preacherman, you got a foot on Nash!" yelled one of my teammates; on the court they either called me "Nash" after the NBA point guard or simply "White Chocolate."

TJ remained silent and expressionless, but I'd played the game long enough—over thirty years by then—to know that it masked a quiet fury. The next time down the court, he motioned for his teammates to clear out (move to the left side of the floor) for him again, and he dribbled to the right side of the court at the arc until we were the only two players on that side of the court. He started in toward the lane, but I guessed he wouldn't drive into traffic where I'd have help, and I watched him cuff the ball as he prepared to cross back over, right for where I'd have no baseline help. I reached to poke the ball—the antithesis of everything I'd been taught growing up; *Play defense with your feet!* I could hear my high school coach yelling—but I got just enough of the ball to poke it loose toward midcourt. TJ and I raced toward it, but his momentum had started in the wrong direction and I had a clear path to the ball. I accelerated up to full speed, but just as I reached the ball, I felt another shove, this one angrier, and I found myself hurtling through the air toward the concrete wall. I bounced off it like a rag doll, banging my shoulder and knee before crumpling to the ground. I sprang to my feet, disoriented, but intent on showing that I was fine.

TJ gathered the ball and began dribbling back toward the

front court, but the howls of the other players and spectators were deafening. "Damn, nigga, you tryna kill Nash?"

TJ was the only player on the court still in motion; the others were frozen, waiting to see if I'd get up. After a few minutes I did and gamely returned to the group that had unanimously agreed that a foul had been committed and that the ball should be awarded to our team. In my entire bid it was the only time I'd ever seen unanimous agreement on a foul; on the rare occasions someone had the nerve to call one, it was usually disputed.

Our team's other guard checked the ball in and play resumed. He immediately tossed it to me and motioned for our teammates to clear out, which was the last thing I wanted: I was still dizzy and wanted to sit down but was too proud to admit it. "Do yo' thang, Nash!" he yelled.

Based on what TJ had just done to me, I knew that if I embarrassed him in front of everyone again, I could get hurt. At the same time, I had to go one-on-one at TJ, or everyone would think I was soft. I dribbled deliberately toward him, whipped the ball between my legs, behind my back, and then crossed back across my body past TJ's outreached hand as I drove to the hoop. TJ bumped me and another defender jumped out, so I dished off to my teammate, who dunked the ball. It was a good compromise; my penetration was a direct challenge to TJ, but I passed off instead of attempting a layup that, if successful, would've likely inspired enough catcalls to further enrage him.

TJ roughed me up a few more times that game, but nothing serious. What surprised me most were his two teammates who quietly, and separately, approached me on the yard the following day to ask if he had apologized to me yet. He had not, I said. Each of them then vowed to boycott TJ's sermons until he apologized. It exemplified two of the central paradoxes of the prison ethos. First, people who felt compelled to show toughness in public were often, in private, extremely empathetic. Second, prisoners who had routinely pistol-whipped people or worse on the street reacted negatively to acts of violence *if these acts were seen as dishonorable*. A good hard foul—"laying wood," in prison lingo—on the way to the hoop was one thing; that's prison ball. But a gratuitous and unprovoked act against a much smaller man was entirely another: it was seen as an act of cowardice.

I had dodged a bullet, and not for the first time. I'd already made a couple of small slipups that hadn't amounted to anything; one occurred on an afternoon when we were released from work early after an especially heavy day and I came home sore and looking forward to a shower. Just as I stepped into the one shower that consistently had warm water, a dude nicknamed Holiday—an unimaginably ripped, health-conscious, six-foot-one, 240-pound guy who routinely repped 455 pounds—appeared out of nowhere. "Unh-unh, Senator," he said, shaking his head and scowling. "Yo' clock mus' be wrong."

"Huh?" I couldn't tell if he was kidding.

"This my shower right now. Er'y day I get back from the weight pile at the same time. And er'y day I come to the same shower. Er'body know dat. So you got two choices. You can shower with me, or you can wait. But if you get in there with me, ain't no tellin' what might happen." He flashed a crooked smile. I definitely didn't want to take that risk, so I went back to my bunk and waited a half hour for him to finish his shower. I would soon establish a strong relationship with Holiday—after this incident, I often brought him stolen onions, celery, and green peppers to make sure of that—but it was a good lesson for me.

The lessons on the athletic field, however, did not seem to take; the incident with TJ constituted my third real scrape. The first was pretty basic—a minor scuffle under the basket during a 3-on-3 game had resulted in an elbow to my mouth and a pool of blood. The second, which occurred during a soccer game, was a skirmish with a volatile Mexican guy named Lulu who had been in several beefs and carried a reputation for being "loco." After this third incident with TJ, the other ex-Arena football player on the compound—a guy named Jesse who had lived just a few blocks from me in St. Louis and became a friend in prison—approached me on the yard. "Man, you betta pump the brakes," he counseled. "You know all the 044s gonna get dragged into this shit if you beefin', and then we end up back in 23-1." He meant that everyone from St. Louis—044 were the last three digits of prisoners from the Eastern District of Missouri—would feel compelled to jump in if I was getting pummeled. This wasn't something they relished; nearly all of them had come down through the system after long bids and were finally seeing the light at the end of the tunnel, especially Jesse, who was three months from the door after doing almost a decade and risked losing a year of good time if caught fighting and extending his bid by twelve months, not to mention being transferred back to a higher security level—twenty-three hours a day locked up—if caught fighting. Plus, you never knew whose slock or shank could permanently disfigure you, and nobody wanted to go home with a buck-fifty* across his face.

This was sobering for me. Thanks in part to my strategic distribution of stolen warehouse food, I had allies in different camps: my fellow 044s, the warehouse guys, and some guys from my cell block, including Holiday, the strongest and baddest dude on the compound.

However, by competing so tenaciously on the athletic field, I was not only putting myself in danger, but I was also potentially endangering others. Only then did I dial it down a notch.

---

* A cut requiring 150 stitches.

. . .

The biggest threats in prison don't come from the obvious places—the sex-crazed guy who jumps you in the shower or the muscle hired by the bookie to collect debts. The biggest threat comes from the myriad quotidian interactions that can go horribly wrong, for reasons unfathomable to the uninitiated. There was, for instance, the time an argument in the television room escalated into a fight over whether the TV should be tuned to basketball or women's track. Women's track was always popular with a certain type of long-term inmate, especially those who didn't receive any female visitors.

Rife with territorial disputes, racial and ethnic tension, an utterly undemocratic ethos, and years of accumulated bitterness, the television room is the Middle East of prison. Each cell block had two self-segregated TV rooms, one for whites and one for blacks. Mexicans split between the two. I didn't watch TV, but on the rare occasions when I walked through one of the rooms, I found the same core group of people who rarely read or developed other hobbies. Some of them spent years in front of a television, and from the prison staff's perspective, that appeared to be just fine: a zoned-out, mesmerized prisoner was their preferred type.

One quick and sure way to light the powder keg was to change the channel. As best as I could tell, the most senior prisoner in a television room at any given time controlled the channel, unless that person was a known snitch or commanded little respect on the compound for some other reason (for example, mental illness). A person's seniority at the prison was typically intertwined with the length of time he had actually been in the TV room that day, since most of the longest serving guys spent most of their day watching TV. Changing the channel without proper assent was so verboten that only once did I actually see anyone begin to attempt to do this, and people immediately stepped in before it could happen. The blacks' TV room was tuned to CNN until 4:30 P.M., at which time it shifted to Black Entertainment Television music videos when people began returning to the unit from dinner. Then around 7:00 P.M. it was tuned to the best college or pro basketball game on that night. The TV in the whites' room almost never left a NASCAR channel. Only one show had crossover appeal: *Justified,* a docudrama about crime in Kentucky, often filmed inside the penitentiary. No one knows exactly who determined the viewing schedule, but everyone is certain that anyone who disrupts it will pay the price.

A second way to start a fight was to sit in someone else's chair: seating in the TV room went strictly by seniority. I once saw a vicious fight jump off when a first-time offender fresh off the street disrespected a veteran and paid the price. Hygiene, or the perceived lack thereof, could also set off fights. I saw an argument escalate into violence when one guy who was seeking to purchase a used radio from another walked into the guy's cell and sat down on a chair after having lifted weights. In the view of the cell's occupant, the weightlifter might have contracted staph from a bench on the weight pile and spread it to the chair in the cell. I saw another fight start when one guy sneezed on another man's chips during a poker game. And I would soon learn how important hygiene—or perhaps hygiene as a proxy for control—was to my own cellie.

Yet another cause of violence was "eye fucking" or "eye hustling"—looking at someone else or their property with unnatural interest. One new prisoner with a tendency to look in other cells instead of looking straight ahead as he walked down the cell block was finally called on it by one of the old guard. "You got sum'n you want in here?" asked the old-timer. Flustered, the new dude kept walking, but the vet followed him back to his cell, glowering and awaiting an answer. The new dude apologized and was spared physically, but the old head gave him the nickname "State Trooper," and it stuck. Needless to say, that's not a nickname anyone in prison would want.

Even worse than getting caught scoping out someone else's cell is getting caught staring at someone else. As one vet put it, "Muthafuckas ain't got no business lookin' at me 'less they wanna fight or fuck, and either way I'mma beat they ass." He told me that he learned this lesson his first week in prison, when he got caught looking at one of the biggest guys on the yard for an instant too long. "Do I knows you?" asked the big fella, nicknamed Escalade. When the looker shook his head, Escalade demanded, "Then why you always got me on yo' television?"

After a few months of watching others who successfully navigated the sometimes rough waters, I began to get a feel for the place. I came up with some rules that might help incoming prisoners avoid trouble, to which I (mostly) adhered. Here are the top ten:[7]

1. As your grandma probably taught you, God gave you two ears, two eyes, and one mouth—use them in proportion.

   - When you arrive, listen, watch, and learn. You'll have a hundred questions on your first day and in one month you'll know the answer to ninety of them without having to ask and risk looking stupid.
   - Don't ever ask anybody about their crime. If they want to tell you what they did, fine. But you won't know if they're telling the truth. And if you strike a nerve, the result may not be pretty.
   - Don't talk about how you got railroaded. So did everyone else.

- Don't ask about anyone's family; it will be a sore subject with many, especially those who have not seen or heard from their children or their children's mother for years or decades.
- Don't talk about how much time you have. Someone else has more.

2. If you are a white-collar criminal, remind yourself that you're no better than anybody else.

- Do your best to blend in. Never, ever talk about how much money you used to make—even if you hear former drug dealers do it every day.
- Don't pretend you were something you're not, because they'll figure it out. Most of these guys are experienced bullshitters and can smell an amateur a mile away. However, if you were a dirty prosecutor, FBI agent, or cop, you'll have to lie to remain safe, so develop a bulletproof story and stick to it, no matter what.
- You will have a nickname. If you are an ex-politician, it will probably be your last title. If you are an accountant, they'll probably call you Andy, after the *Shawshank* character. If you're a stockbroker, they'll call you Madoff. Accept whatever nickname they give you, because the more you resist, the more likely it will stick.

3. Don't ask for trouble.

- Be polite, but not gregarious. Blend in, but don't try *too* hard to blend in. If people are talking among themselves, don't approach them. Don't eavesdrop under any circumstances. There is nothing to gain, because most of what they say will bore you and the rest may terrify you. There is much to lose, however, if you get caught. So don't do it.

- Don't stare. There is no reason to make eye contact with people unless they say your name. If you happen to bump into anyone, say "excuse me." If someone bumps into you, you should probably say excuse me anyway.
- Don't change the TV channel, especially if women's track is on or if one of the Williams sisters is playing tennis or if *Ice Loves Coco* is on. There is a stringent seniority-based regime when it comes to TV watching, and your status on the outside does not alter it in any way. So don't complain about what's on. Also, don't sit in anyone else's chair.
- Don't take anyone's clothes out of the dryer without asking. Inmates are very particular about whether their clothes are laundered appropriately and who touches them. Remember, inmates can't control much. Don't interfere with one of the few things they can control.
- Don't reach across another prisoner's tray at meal-time. And by God, don't even think about trying to eat off their tray or you could wind up with a sharp utensil embedded in your hand.

4. Stand up for yourself.

- This might seem a bit counterintuitive after the last tip. But think of it like Goldilocks and the three bears: be nice, but not too nice, lest people take advantage of you.
- Prison is like nature or Wall Street: there are predators and prey, and the predators at the top of the food

chain got there by learning how to spot prey quickly
and pounce. That's why prisoners can show kindness
but must not show weakness.

- Here are a few examples of weakness: allowing
people to cut in line at the chow hall, agreeing to buy
commissary items for people other than your bunkie,
letting someone else borrow a picture of your wife or
girlfriend. Allowing any of those things will lead to a
deluge of similar requests from other prisoners,
which you could either continue granting, inviting
more and larger requests/demands, or decline, potentially offending the person you decline given your
previous assent.

5. Be clean.

- Prisoners share a collective obsession with hygiene
and a fear of illness. This manifests itself in odd
ways: some prisoners walk around the yard with
tissues and use them to open all doors or touch any
common area, such as the valve that releases water in
the chow hall. Also, no one in prison shakes hands—
they bump fists. But, per tip 3, that doesn't mean you
should stroll down the compound fist-bumping dudes
on your first day.
- Shower every day. Brush your teeth excessively;
nothing earns opprobrium quicker than stained teeth
and bad breath.
- Never, ever sit on someone else's bunk. Occasionally
prisoners will share a meal back in the unit—several
will contribute various items and one man will cook—
and people will eat in the host's cell. But despite the
fact that there is limited seating in a cell, you should

not plop down on the host's bed or that of his bunkie. Just eat standing up.

6. Get in shape.

- You might arrive at prison in good shape, but you can always be in better shape. Not only will working out every day help pass the time, keep your endorphins pumping, and reduce anxiety, but all else being equal, the bigger you are, the less likely you are to be preyed upon.
- Play sports, but if your taste runs to contact sports like basketball, you may want to think twice, and if you decide to play, be very careful. Some people who have it out for you may exploit the opportunity to try to hurt you on the athletic field and not get in trouble for it. Most prisoners stop playing contact sports a year before their release, to avoid injury or fights that could cost them their good time.

7. Don't complain about how bad your prison job is, and don't brag about how good it is.

- Many people in prison work normal forty-hour weeks, so they spend most of their waking hours at work. So there is great competition for the best jobs, such as working in the library or at the rec center helping organize rec ball. But if you don't get a "good" job, don't complain about it. As with anywhere else, no one likes complainers. But in prison, people really don't like them, because it's a given that everyone is miserable.
- If you do get a good job, don't brag about it. Because pretty soon, the COs will find some contraband at

your job site that mysteriously appeared just after
your shift. And you'll be out of a job, possibly in the
SHU, while someone whose envy you sparked may
well replace you.

8. Use your knowledge, skills, and position to help
   other inmates and build alliances.

   • This doesn't mean that a former accountant should
     set up a questionable tax dodge for a drug kingpin, or
     that an ex–public relations pro should manage the
     campaign for the dude vying to be the next head of
     the prison's Aryan Brotherhood sect. But everyone
     comes into prison with a unique perspective and a
     different skill set, which can help a vulnerable pris-
     oner build a network that provides protection in case
     of strife.
   • Some examples of quiet ways to do this: a former
     attorney could use his legal background to help a pris-
     oner bringing an appeal pro se (representing himself);
     a former teacher could tutor a guy working toward his
     GED; a former salesman could help an aspiring
     entrepreneur figure out potential sales channels as he
     crafts a business plan.

9a. Don't break prison rules. The prison underworld
    can be a brutal and unforgiving place.

   • Don't gamble. If you lose, you'll be in debt, a very
     compromising position in a dangerous place. If you
     win, someone will be very angry and may figure out a
     way to get his money back—in a way that might leave
     you unrecognizable.

- Don't "hold" anything someone asks you to hold, even if it looks innocuous; it's probably got contraband inside of it.
- If you need a hustle to survive (such as stealing and selling food from the kitchen or running a tattoo joint), try not to encroach on someone else's hustle. Competition can be fierce.

9b. Don't snitch on anyone who breaks prison rules, under any circumstances. This may seem to conflict with 9a, but it doesn't. And it's the most important tip, so if you neglect every other one, follow this one.

- The only people in prison who have it harder than child molesters are snitches. You need to learn how to see things (weapons, drugs, hooch, pornography, etc.) without seeing them; that is, learn to look away before anyone has seen you see the contraband, because if someone sees you see it and you are not trusted, you could be blamed if COs uncover it.
- Stay away from snitches, and in general, watch the company you keep: in prison, you are your car (that is, the people you "ride" with). Because of their size and the stature gained by helping the rest of the prison access otherwise unavailable products, hanging with the warehouse crew benefited me a great deal.
- If you committed other crimes for which you were not prosecuted or are plotting any, don't discuss them. As I know all too well, you never know who's listening— and there are a lot of guys in prison desperate for a time cut, which they might be able to get by offering new information about an unsolved crime.

- Don't be seen talking to the COs. You cannot be "friends" with them. Sure, there may be gangs and racial or ethnic division among prisoners. But there are really only two teams: prisoners and the prison. Never forget this rule.

10. Don't eat sweets that are offered to you.

- Prison rape is real. But many prison relationships lie somewhere on a complex continuum between rape and consensual sex; some prisoners agree to sex with one predator in explicit or implicit exchange for protection from other predators.
- When a sexual predator is interested in another prisoner, he may hand him something sweet, have a candy bar delivered to him, or put one in his cell. If this happens to you, assuming you are not interested, don't eat it—figure out where it came from and send it back.

A first-time prisoner would significantly increase his odds of staying safe by following these tips. I learned most of this the hard way.

6

"YOU BEST NOT GO TO SLEEP TONIGHT, CELLIE"

Exploring the Prison Psyche

By my fourth month at Manchester FCI, I floated between three different groups: the guys from my unit I'd met on my first day (Red, Dred, BJ, and others), the warehouse crew, and a couple of white-collar guys (both named John) I sometimes ate with. My social structure—as is often true in civilian life—revolved around my neighbors, my colleagues, and a couple of my hobbies. Indeed, throughout society, one's social structure is largely determined by where one lives. If you live on Park Avenue, you are surrounded by people with stratospheric net worths. If, on the other hand, you live in Appalachia, you are surrounded by poverty.

Real estate and social structure in a prison operate in almost exactly the same way.

The upstairs unit where I lived, which was mostly black, younger, and noisy at all hours, was referred to as "the projects" or "the ghetto penthouse." The first-floor unit, conversely, was older, whiter, and much quieter—not just at night, but all day. It was widely referred to as "the suburbs."

But the divisions began out in the prison yard. Small groups of prisoners who lift weights together—who ride together in the same "car"—have their set times and places on a prison weight pile, and any interruptions to these routines are unwelcome at best, antagonistic at worst. As with all recreational spaces in prison, nearly all groups are composed exclusively of one race. Sometimes I lifted with a former stockbroker and accountant; other times I lifted with black warehouse colleagues, which initially drew a mix of curious glances and hostile sneers. One white bystander asked, "You know you laying right in nigger sweat when you work out with them?" But after that, it was not remarked upon. Either segregation wasn't as stringently enforced on the weight pile as it was in the chow hall or old-guard whites assumed that after six months I knew the score, and if I wanted to risk a problem by working out with blacks, they weren't going to protect me.

The weight pile at Manchester, as at other prisons, was revered above any other prison activity. As scholar Alex Tepperman and countless prison films have documented, weightlifting—referred to as "gettin' right" or "gettin' money"—shapes the broader social structure, culture, and economics of a prison yard.[1] Bodybuilding is so fundamental to prison life that the only acceptable currency other than stamps is mackerel—the high-protein, low-quality bags of fish sold at the commissary that pack a big protein punch into a dollar bag, precisely what prison bodybuilders crave. Weightlifting also dictated many prisoners' schedules for cooking, eating, and showering, and you didn't want to mess with their routine, as I had learned the day I inadvertently interrupted Holiday's shower regimen.

Bodybuilding informed nearly every single activity in the daily life of many prisoners, from sleep to diet to, yes, masturbation: one Manchester bodybuilder used to brag that he hadn't masturbated in nearly a decade so as to conserve protein. Prisoners associate sleep with building muscle mass, a link confirmed by research.[2] Manchester's most serious bodybuilders were also some of our longest sleepers, some sleeping almost any time they weren't eating. Waking them up was an offense subject to a beating, but I saw that happen only once, probably because anyone who can sleep through prison noise could also sleep on the runway during a 747 takeoff.

Soon after arriving on the compound, I dedicated myself to a daily workout regimen. I needed to be able to protect myself in a sometimes hostile environment and gain strength to unload warehouse shipments without injuring myself. Even if I was exhausted from my warehouse job, I'd work out pretty religiously, four days on (chest and shoulders, back and arms, legs, and core), one day off. When I was confined to our cell during lockdowns, I'd do five hundred push-ups, five hundred sit-ups, and one hundred body lifts suspended off the ground between my bed frame and the wall. During my routine, I initially got tongue-in-cheek comments due to my stature, but soon I began putting on muscle; in about six months I went from 117 to 142 pounds. Others began to take notice, which made me more confident on the basketball court—too confident, in retrospect.

I soon learned that getting into a "car" is more like joining a gang than a gym: your car is your first line of protection if something "jumps off," that is, if you are attacked. Often the leader of an old-guard car checked your "papers"—your legal file—for evidence of pedophilia or snitching before accepting you. Because of clippings about my case passed around by a St. Louisan who received the hometown newspaper, people knew the nature of my crime and that I didn't get a cooperation agreement from prosecutors, so two of the warehouse guys invited me to train with them early in my bid to help me get in good enough shape to handle the heavier warehouse loads. The real upside for me was that it was almost like having a small team of certified personal trainers, all of whom probably had spent a lot more time pumping iron than your average twenty-three-year-old trainer at the local gym.

The serious bodybuilders—along with the prisoners nearing release who wanted to impress women upon their homecoming—sparked a vibrant black market that we in the warehouse fueled, along with the kitchen crew who siphoned off their share as well. Any protein source automatically went for a premium, especially since the prison did all it could to fill stomachs cheaply by serving tons of starch. Of course, such a diet was anathema to the typical bodybuilder, who sought to avoid the empty calories of simple carbohydrates and thus seldom graced the chow hall except on the rare occasions that actual whole chicken parts were served—Memorial Day and the Fourth of July. Chicken legs, chicken and hamburger patties, peanut butter, and eggs were some of the warehouse products that were in highest demand. Fish—mostly low-quality canned tuna and mackerel—was also in demand, but that came through the commissary, not the warehouse. Creatine was the most expensive; it was smuggled in at visits or through COs. That was the vehicle of choice for many men who were "short" (nearing release). Often guys in their final months doubled up on protein by smearing gobs of peanut butter onto mackerel.

Prison weightlifting is very competitive. Everyone watches to see what other people are putting up and monitors others' bodies to see how big they are getting. People step up their training to superhuman levels during their final six to twelve months in anticipation of release, working out twice a day, rain or shine. We always took perverse pleasure from lifting in snowstorms. As crazy as it might sound, one of my fondest prison memories is of lifting in 15-degree weather, clad only in prison flannels, work gloves, and a stocking hat, with the snow and wind whipping against my face. If you can do that, what can't you do?

People dropped weights and sustained injuries, but that didn't deter anyone: you just had to "get money," particularly if you were a short-timer and needed to get right, fast. And especially if you saw your racial rival—for me, a five-foot-five, 140-pound black guy named Shorty who probably had about 2 percent body fat and could dunk a football, though he couldn't get his small hands around a basketball—lifting more than you were.

Respect was earned largely by how much someone bench-pressed. When someone who used to consistently rep 455 pounds struggled to put up 405 even once, people on the yard would be abuzz: they just didn't fear the guy in the way they had. The biggest rivals on the compound were Holiday and Superman, a bulky, doughy white guy who somehow kept up with Holiday and occasionally even outdid him. Of course, they never lifted together; they just eyed each other warily. Each swaggered when he outperformed the other and quietly seethed when he was outdone.

Some states removed all weights from their state prisons in the 1990s and 2000s.[3] And even prisons with decent weight piles suffer from periods of denied access, such as during extended lockdowns; at one point Manchester went nearly a month without weights. But prisoners don't let that stop them. During lockdowns I saw (and often emulated) prison ingenuity at its finest: men doing dips pushing off their bunk and the side of their desk, curls using huge buckets of water, bench presses using giant rocks tied to long sticks, and pull-ups off the top of a cinder-block cell or the side of a shower stall since, for understandable reasons, there's nothing to hang from inside cells.

. . .

Most inmates at Manchester FCI were nonviolent offenders
(though as Ville often reminded me, that didn't mean they hadn't
shot people—just that they didn't get caught). Most were crack
or meth dealers at their last, lowest-security-level stop on a multifacility national tour. And since most people were close to the
door—you couldn't be at Manchester unless you had less than
ten years to go—most inmates avoided beefs, lest they be shipped
to the hole.

Still, this was prison. And many prisoners viewed violence
as a necessary, even desirable tactic for addressing even the
smallest conflict, for getting revenge, and for showing that
one was not to be fucked with. "So whatchu gon' do 'bout ya
boy?" Red repeatedly asked, referring to Steve Brown. "I knows
you ain't gon' let him get away with that shit. You let him off,
same shit gon' happen again once you hit the street." He spoke
as if I were a drug kingpin needing to cultivate a rep that would
ensure none of my future co-conspirators ever crossed me again.
But this was the logic of prison. The ability to emit a credible
threat of violence was precisely what ensured that one would
rarely have to actually engage in violence. The most feared guys
never touched a soul, because they didn't need to—usually because they were said to have badly mangled somebody who'd
crossed them. It was the least feared—and the least connected—
guys who always seemed to be beefing over petty matters that
escalated when neither side could retreat without losing face.
Those with the least stature scrapped tenaciously so as not to
lose what little rep they had.

Not everyone was animated by vengeance, though. When a
similar conversation occurred in a different setting and a fellow
inmate offered to have Steve "bumped off" (I assumed he was
kidding), KY told me his own story of betrayal: his brother-in-
law had told the feds the location of KY's stash. "Damn," I exclaimed. "What you do to him?"

"Wasn't shit I could do, I'se already in custody," he replied. "Thought about the motherfucker for my first three years straight. 'Bout killed me. But then one day I let it go. Jus' like that. Cuz you can't do time like that. Your boy with the wire, man, you can't even *think* about the motherfucker. It'll make you crazy."

"I hear you. 'Preciate that, KY."

"Think about it," he said. "You gon' have one fucked-up year. But that motherfucker got a life sentence. He just don't know it yet." It was the best advice I got in prison. From that day on, my bitterness toward Steve dissipated, with just a few fits and starts.

Still, violence usually simmered just beneath the surface, threatening to emerge the moment someone cut in line, or fouled someone a little too hard on a layup, or teased someone until the object of derision cracked, or simply looked at the wrong guy in the wrong way on the wrong day. "Why you always eye-fuckin' me?" I once heard a guy ask somebody who glanced at him for a beat too long on the way back from dinner, and the alleged voyeur was bloodied within seconds.

Most often, though, violence was rooted in debt: prisoners who didn't pay their bills faced collections in a far more methodical, certain, and effective manner than do people on the street. In this way, violence was critical to the compound's smooth functioning—the enforcement mechanism for every transaction in a world that relied on liquidity and market trade no more or less than the free world. Much as the federal government had to inject trillions into the financial system when U.S. credit dried up after the 2008 subprime mortgage meltdown, prison bigs step in to restore order when debtors prove unable to pay up, sometimes by providing liquidity (stamps) and then if necessary by violently reminding other economic actors that in order for the system to operate effectively, debts must be paid, one way or another.

When things "jumped off," guys might attack each other with fists or a variety of prison-made weapons: slocks, tin can tops smuggled out from the warehouse or kitchen and sold back on the compound, homemade shanks (sometimes called "guns") shaped from aluminum soda cans, or pieces scraped off buildings. "Give him a buck-fifty!" onlookers would shout, or "Give him a buck-ninety."* Once I saw one of my warehouse colleagues badly beaten and bloodied over a few small packets of purloined peanut butter that were diverted into the guy's coat pocket instead of being divvied up equally among the conspirators. Of course, when asked by our supervisor, I hadn't seen anything at all—I'd been "in the bathroom" during the fight. Even Amigo, the petty thief who'd taken the beating from KY, wouldn't say what had happened. "I slipped," he told Miss Horton.

"Yeah, you slipped onto somebody's fists," she scoffed. She probably figured KY had done it since he hadn't removed his gloves despite the warm weather, and as she constantly told us, she'd have loved to have gotten rid of the lazy, thieving Delgado. But perhaps she also figured that she couldn't get rid of one without losing the other, and she likely valued KY's diligence and management of the crew too much to say or do anything more about it. In any event, she gave neither KY nor Delgado a shot.

Other violence, of course, was premeditated—sometimes planned weeks or even months in advance. Often people crafted or bought weapons with a specific plot in mind and then sold or disposed of the weapon immediately so as not to get caught with it—COs frequently swept cells in search of weapons, and anyone

---

* As defined earlier, a buck-fifty was a cut requiring 150 stitches. A buck-ninety meant dousing a sleeping rival with scalding water, the number symbolizing 190 degrees.

caught with one faced a year in the SHU and a return to a high- or medium-security facility—probably the one up the hill.

It was critically important, of course, not to show weakness after a hard foul or a shove on the compound. When I was first elected, a fellow Missouri senator who would soon become attorney general told me there was one key to success in the state senate: being feared. To do that, he advised me, "Find someone a lot bigger than you, and punch 'em in the mouth." As it turned out, this was good advice for prison as well. I learned this early on when someone gave me a gratuitous elbow on the basketball court and I went right back at him, harder, on the next possession. Just as in politics, if you get rolled once, everyone will try you.

I was involved in a few scraps on the basketball court: one earned me a fat lip; the other a bloody nose. I didn't get into any full-blown fights, though I nearly came to blows with my cellie. One Friday, a few months into my bid, we got into an argument— the same one we'd had every week for a month. The difference between this argument and the others was that this time he threatened to kill me.

He talked often about "pushing steel" during brawls when he was housed at a high-security institution, but I didn't think he'd stab me—he was too close to the door after twenty-five years, and wouldn't want to take the risk. Of course, I might have been wrong. In prison, anything can happen.

I'd arrived back in my cube on Friday after a bruising week at the warehouse. Red worked as a unit orderly, mopping for five minutes a day. When I left for work at 6:45 A.M. he was asleep. When I returned for lunch, he was asleep. And when I came home at 3:15 P.M., he was usually asleep. That Friday was no different. Exhausted after a big milk delivery, I removed my shoes and climbed up into my top bunk to read. A half hour later, the intercom announced the 4:00 P.M. standing count, at which federal correctional officers around the nation count every single federal prisoner—to a one.

Rooms are examined during count and must be in perfect order. As I crouched on my knees to tuck in the top corners of my sheet, the prison-issue tube sock on my right foot hung a few inches over the bedside. "Get yo' muthafuckin' stank-ass foot outta my face!" yelled Red.

He was obsessed with hygiene, so much so that he screamed whenever one of my hairs fell onto his bunk and demanded that I shower after coming home from the warehouse or the weight pile.

"It's not in your face," I replied, since it was a few feet away.

"Yeah, it is, and I'm gonna slap the shit outta you and yo' mothafuckin' foot when you get down."

As I descended from the top bunk, I replied, "Sorry my feet don't smell like roses. If you worked at the warehouse or did anything besides sleep all day, neither would yours."

"Yeah, I'mma do sum'n 'sides that, sho'nuff. You ain't gon' be talkin' slick when I bust up that muthafuckin' grill and you ain't so pretty at yo' next visit."

Inmates crowded in the corridor and started whooping. Red and I were inches away from each other, the distance closing. Someone said to calm down. He tugged at his black do-rag and announced to no one in particular, "Yeah, I'll push some muthafuckin' steel, sho'nuff. I'll *go* back behind the fence—I give a fuck. But if I'mma go, I'mma kill me a Caucasian!"

Pushing steel meant using his shank of razor blades. But instead of lunging for me, he just glared. "You best not go to sleep tonight, cellie," he warned before storming off.

For thirty seconds, the unit was as quiet as a morgue. Then a well-respected veteran from the neighboring cell approached. A week earlier he'd heard Red castigate me upon finding a "European hair" on his bed, after which Red threatened to "cut a cracker." There had been other incidents, and the veteran wanted to avert disaster. "Yo, Senator, you need to get the fuck outta there," he said with concern. "That motherfucka is crazy. Next time, he gon' crack."

The next day I requested a rarely granted cell transfer. I approached Mrs. Lamorie—a fat woman with skinny legs and freshly crimped hair—who was in charge of the housing unit. She was married to Mr. Lamorie, a CO who did not disguise his dislike for me, spitting out my name as if each syllable were a shard of glass. So I figured it was uphill.

I caught Mrs. Lamorie while I was out at the weight pile and asked if she had a moment.

"What happened to your lip?" she responded.

I told her I caught an elbow in a basketball game.

"Hmm. So what do you want?"

I asked to be transferred to a new cell.

She pointed at my lip. "Your cellie did that to you."

I explained that it happened playing basketball in the gym.

"So he did it in the gym?"

I needed a new angle. I knew the warden didn't want to see a media story about a high-profile prisoner getting hurt—in fact, I got the sense that no prison employee ever wanted to deal with a media inquiry about anything. "No, Mrs. Lamorie, he didn't have anything to do with it. But yeah, there's been some tension, so I'd like to get out of there before anything happens."

She considered this for a moment and then nodded. "Okay. Find a white guy you won't have a problem with. But you better keep your mouth shut. If a single inmate comes to me looking for a transfer anytime in the next week, you're going back in with him and whatever happens, happens."

I returned to my cell, where Red was sitting sullenly on his bed, hand on his skullcap, sucking his teeth. I pulled out a laundry bag and began shoveling clothes and other items into it.

"Aight, so it gon' be like that," he said with disdain.

"Guess so."

Upon reaching my destination across the corridor, which mostly housed whites in prison on meth charges, I plopped down my laundry bag and was greeted like a long-lost prodigal son by a group of white men who gathered around me. "Sen-uh-tuh, Ah don't know how you survahved ovuh there long as you did," said Cornbread, the pack leader. I'd remained cordial with him since we first met, right after my racial faux pas in the chow hall. I'd made a point of maintaining a safe distance, though. "I couldn't live in the middle-uh all them nigguhs like that."

Another guy named Banks echoed the sentiment. "Don't worry," he assured me, "we keepin' this corner pure. Welcome to the Gated Community." It occurred to me that if I sought their protection, they might try to initiate me, but I didn't have much time to think about it. I needed to retrieve more stuff.

I returned to my old cell to get some pictures of Teresa and my family that I'd pinned to a makeshift cardboard "frame," and my cellie was standing there with another black guy I barely knew, both of their arms folded, forming a barrier that kept me from reaching the pictures. "How was the Klan rally?" sneered Red, still sucking his teeth.

"Huh?"

"The Klan rally they havin' to celebrate you comin' home? Y'all gonna go lynch some niggers now, huh?" He cackled without smiling.

I wanted to look back to see if Cornbread or any of his lieutenants were monitoring the situation, but I knew it would signal weakness. So I quickly brushed in between Red and the other dude and grabbed my pictures. Red closed in on me. "This ain't yo' room no more, so you best keep yo' muthafuckin' paws off my board."

No one from the warehouse crew who might have had my

back lived on my floor. As I saw it, I had several choices: back away and leave without my pictures; call for reinforcements from my new white "allies"; propose a deal whereby I would give him something in exchange for the pictures; or try to plow through him, gambling that he'd let me go without a fight. Choosing option 1 would invite predatory behavior for the rest of my bid, endangering me. Option 2 would be a serious escalation, and I would likely be severely harmed in the twenty seconds it would take for aid to arrive—if it arrived. Option 3 would be weak though not fatally so. Option 4 was strong but risky with both guys right there, especially since I knew Red carried a shank. I did a quick mental calculation and chose a hybrid of options 3 and 4.

"Guess I gotta take Coco with me," I said, pulling a magazine from the desk drawer and starting toward them.

Red, who'd been locked up for most of the past thirty years, enjoyed looking at pictures of near-naked* women and wasn't shy about it. He'd often announce that he was off to "see my baby Coco" before heading into a bathroom stall with a magazine featuring the impossibly curvaceous (39-23-40) bleach blonde who would later burst onto reality television as rapper Ice-T's wife. He'd return fifteen minutes later, announcing, "Now I needs a muthafuckin' cigarette!" When I told two of my friends on the outside about this, they offered to send in a new magazine featuring the latest pictorial of Coco that I could let my cellie borrow, which he did frequently while we'd been getting along. But now Red was faced with the threat of losing access to Coco.

"You leave my baby here," he said forcefully.

---

* The prison allowed magazines as long as women's vaginas, anuses, and areolae were not fully exposed. Most magazines circulated pushed those boundaries, although some hard-core pornography exceeded them.

I made a show of grudgingly tossing the magazine back onto the desk and then squeezed in between the two men on my way back to my new home on the other side of the cell block.

That was my last substantive interaction with Red. My new bunkie, Danny, a quiet but pleasant guy from Tennessee, was not looking for any drama.

My heart was still pounding as I began making up my new bed when Cornbread approached. "Welcome home, brother," he nodded with satisfaction.

I noted the A-B etching across his chest. "Anheuser-Busch, huh? You from St. Louis?"

He flashed a sinister smile. "This the Aryan Brotherhood, man! You funny, though."

On the street, I'd have taken issue with this. Now, knowing there was no vicious gang of crooked Jewish accountants to protect their brethren, I kept my mouth shut and pretended to have been kidding.

One of the hardest things about prison is learning to numb yourself. Old-timers say not to get too high or too low—emotion is vulnerability, and vulnerability is dangerous. Since my initial anger upon finding out Steve was wired, I'd willed myself into numbness. But a few things I saw in prison broke me down.

In prison, you learn quickly not to ask people about their family, because the stories are often difficult to hear, and surely even more difficult to tell. For many, the reminder of the forced separation from family—and their culpability in that—flooded them with guilt and angst. While I was waiting to use a phone, it was hard to avoid hearing their anguished phone conversations with ex-girlfriends who controlled access to their children, with rebellious teenagers who—lacking a male authority figure at home—were in some cases following in their fathers' footsteps, and with dying parents far away who know they'll never see their sons again.

The differing lengths of the commissary lines before Mother's Day and Father's Day explained a lot about my fellow prisoners and the households in which they'd been raised: Mother's Day cards were sold out two weeks in advance, while Father's Day cards mostly sat unsold. The week before Father's Day was like any other week, but the week before Mother's Day it was all anyone could talk about. I'd never heard other prisoners so frequently use a nonexpletive following "mother."

Other prisoners were very curious about Teresa and other family members whose pictures I posted, but taking my cue from some of the older guys I'd observed, I revealed little. My warehouse colleague and friend Big E was one of many who seemed noticeably reticent to discuss family.

Because of mandatory minimum drug sentences, most cocaine dealers got an automatic ten years to start; many had a gun for protection, which added another five years. Other sentencing enhancements added more time. Many prisoners, such as Big E, had been in prison for as long as they had been free. He'd gotten busted at age nineteen and was sentenced to seventeen years. He showed me his case file and explained that his public defender had advised him to accept a plea deal, even though he had been caught with powder but was prosecuted under the harsher crack cocaine statute. Under some sort of "relevant conduct" theory, they charged him with possessing the amount of crack that the powder he actually possessed could have generated. Big E had also received a two-year sentencing enhancement for being caught in a so-called school zone and claimed that he wasn't nearly as close to the school as his prosecutor had claimed. He asked me to check on this for him as the basis for a possible appeal, and sure enough, he was right: I asked a friend of mine on the outside to map the location of the school against the intersection where the indictment said that he had been apprehended, and the distance was well outside the threshold to establish proximity.

But the public defender was unfamiliar with the details of Big E's case, he recalled, and spent most of the hearing attempting to please the judge and prosecutor. The public defender urged him to agree to the first deal offered, and he did: seventeen years for a first-time nonviolent offender.

Big E was one of our warehouse supervisor's favorites. He had huge hands and an unmatched work ethic, and he never complained about the work. I'd vouch for him for any similar job on the outside.

One day an ACC basketball game came on television. Normally, there was jousting in the TV room on Saturdays; everyone had his hometown team, and there were frequent conflicts about which games we would watch and when a game was no longer close enough to remain in the rotation.

But this day no one changed the channel, not even during commercials. When one newbie made some crack about missing the women's track meet and rose to change the channel, one of the old heads glared at him and ordered, "S'down, short-timer." Whereas usually such an order would cause whooping all around in anticipation of a fight, the room was silent. Wordlessly the new guy obeyed, a barely audible grumble his only attempt to save face.

Big E's son was a freshman guard playing in his first conference game. And Big E, the best shooter on the compound, had never seen his son play. He sniffed once, which may or may not have been an attempt to conceal an approaching tear. No one said another word about it, and the game continued.

Moments like this reinforced my belief that the justice system should adopt electronically monitored home confinement or work release for nonviolent first-time offenders. Given the 2.7 million U.S. children with an incarcerated parent, such a policy change could help break the cycle of poverty, crime, and family breakdown that devastates poor communities. Parental incarceration impairs a child's behavior, academic performance, financial situation, and emotional and physical health,[4] causing severe anxiety, developmental regression, acute stress, and reactive behaviors[5] that make them five times more likely to end up incarcerated themselves.[6]

While these effects depend on the existing parent-child relationship and the degree to which parents supported their children before confinement, the conventional wisdom of minority male offenders as absentee parents is false: half of all incarcerated fathers lived with their children, a quarter served as primary caregivers, and over half provided primary financial support.[7] Consequently, these children become more likely to receive public assistance and experience multiple school changes and divorce, and are four times as likely to end up in the child welfare system.[8] A new program of electronically monitored home confinement for selected offenders could reduce those adverse impacts and help break intergenerational poverty cycles—not to mention saving a projected $16.9 billion annually "without any appreciable deterioration in public safety," according to research.

Around this time, halfway through my bid, the GED exam came up, and several prisoners asked me to tutor them. Most were functionally illiterate. Using books that people had sent to me, borrowed newspaper sports pages, and a few old magazines from the prison library, I spent many nights and weekends for about two months working with four men, helping them read, answer reading comprehension questions, and do basic algebra and geometry. After they passed the exam, I continued working with two of them, sharing articles and books and trying to help them think about politics, public policy, and their place in the community to which they would return.

I lived and worked and sweated and played and laughed with these guys every day, and during the day, they ribbed me, clearly relishing the fact that they had the upper hand in their interactions with a former lawmaker. But at night, as we sat going over material, they deferred to me, cut the prison bluster, and thanked me sincerely when I left. I had mostly enjoyed teaching at Washington University, but nearly all the kids came from affluent families; it had been a long time since I'd engaged in sustained work with people who really needed the help. These moments were some of the highlights of my bid.

The guys, in turn, were teaching me how to survive—and many of them had my back in ways small and large. It was a pretty good deal for me, I realized.

More difficult were the occasional moments when the depth of my fall hit home. For example, I'd joined the church choir as a drummer and played a set as part of an annual prison event to thank outside volunteers. Exactly two years earlier as a senator, I realized, I'd visited a prison to watch Shakespeare; now I was the performer. Sometimes the juxtaposition overwhelmed me.

For the most part, though, I tried not to feel anything in prison. In that way, prison resembled politics: emotions are your worst enemy. Sad that your son hasn't written in months? Keep it to yourself; your cellie may not have heard from his son in years. Excited about your girlfriend's upcoming visit? Don't get too excited: she might inadvertently wear prohibited clothes (khakis, for instance) and have to spend almost three hours of your precious five hours together driving to the nearest town to buy appropriate clothes; or she could have to cancel because "work has just been so exhausting and I got sick, I'm sorry," giving you weeks to stew about whether it was actually work or some guy she met; or there could be fog, delaying all visits for hours since prisoners can't leave their cell blocks in the hazy conditions so frequent in a desolate Kentucky hollow for fear they'll try to escape. You may even have to call your visitor the evening before and tell her that she can't come after all because no one ever approved the visitor form she sent in three weeks ago. Each of these things happened to me.

Yet I saw far worse happen to fellow prisoners who'd been locked up much longer and did much more to prepare for visits. Most guys would get "creased out" for visits—they'd pay five stickies or a cigarette to a guy who worked in the laundry room to iron their greens in order to look extra sharp for their visit, given what a special occasion it was. I saw one guy get creased out and wait three hours for a call down to the visiting room that would never come; he never again heard from the woman he was expecting, who declined to accept his calls or reply to his letters afterward. He was never quite the same; he quit playing sports and working out and often ate alone, or essentially alone with others at the same table.

I quickly learned that before you breathlessly mention your upcoming visit from a lady friend, remember that some inmates haven't had a visit for decades, if ever, and might not share your excitement. And so picking a fight with you at chow time— something I watched a sullen long-termer nicknamed Chi-Town do after another guy bragged about how much he would get laid when he got out the following month—will get you both sent to the SHU for three to six months, denied contact with the outside world, and possibly moved to a more secure facility, which was no skin off his back, just a change of scenery. Seeing something similar happen to a guy I became friendly with taught me not to mention upcoming visits to anyone but a close friend or two. Some people, like a St. Louisan named Sykes, had been locked up almost twenty years and hadn't had a visit in fifteen. So when they tried to tell you things you already knew, such as when Sykes would try to tell me what restaurant was at a certain intersection near my house in St. Louis despite it having been torn down over a decade earlier, I just nodded.

Visits themselves were fraught with emotion. It was hard being away from my family, but even harder to face them when they visited me in prison. My dad was a golf coach, then a sportswriter, then an advertising copywriter; my mom spent two decades working with kids who had special needs. Had you asked them a year earlier, they'd have told you they were more likely to go to the North Pole than Manchester FCI. As much as I wanted to see them, I didn't really want them to visit. First of all was the obvious: I didn't want them to have to see me locked up like an animal, degraded by guards, under constant surveillance and stress. Given their ages—seventy and sixty-six—I also didn't really want them driving fourteen hours in two days. I found it terrifying to be called down to the administration building; I had nightmares about being called down and told of my parents' death in a car accident on the way to see me, leaving me racked with guilt before waking in a cold sweat. Of course, having watched several other prisoners be denied permission to attend their parents' funerals, I was acutely aware that one or both could conceivably die during my incarceration without my being able to tell them good-bye. The thought was almost too much to bear.

When I entered the visiting room, I could see how much it rattled them to see me in my greens. My dad appraised me. "You look good," he said. "Jesus, what have you gained, twenty pounds?"

"Yep," I said.

"I don't care about that!" interjected my mom, half smiling, half wincing. "Just tell me you're doing okay?"

"I'm fine, Mom. Don't worry." Only the most selfish prisoner would do anything other than put on a good face during visits. You never discussed the dark side of prison life. Any mention of that could wait until you were safely home.

"Where did you get all these muscles?" asked my dad.

"I work in the warehouse. We move a lot of food."

"What?" exclaimed my mom. "You can't do that! Why don't you explain to them that you have no business doing that? Can't they have you teach or something?"

"Well, that's where they assigned me," I said.

"Can't you get moved? Can't you explain to them that you've been a professor?"

I shook my head. "Mom, it's not that simple."

"Why not?"

"Mom, the captain here saw this letter I got . . ." I didn't want to go into the details.

My mom turned ashen and then broke down in tears. "Jeffrey, when will you learn not to be so reckless? Not to always push the envelope and disobey? Will you ever learn?"

It hurt that she conflated this with what got me there in the first place, but it definitely wasn't the time to say so. "Look, Mom, I didn't actually *do* anything *wrong*. . . ." It wasn't worth trying to explain, and I didn't really want her to understand just how powerless I was, just how arbitrary prison discipline could be.

My father and I sat helpless while she cried.

As sad as that was for me, one thing I frequently saw was even sadder: watching young children cling to their fathers as visiting hours ended, as mothers and grandmothers and big sisters peeled them off. In one such case, the CO stepped in and physically separated an inmate from his sobbing son. Hugs were allowed to last for only one second, so the kid was violating prison rules. For many COs, that could not be tolerated.

There were many other areas in which prisoners were well served by keeping their emotions in check. Dozens of prisoners had appeals pending, usually based on ineffective counsel; several told me stories of public defenders who fell asleep in court or barely knew their names, let alone the basic facts of the case. These prisoners could be up or down depending on the results of an appeal, but the veterans knew not to ever get too high or low: nearly every decision was subject to another appeal, in front of another judge or panel, which likely meant another year before they'd really know anything.

Prisoners also quickly learn not to show fear. In politics, you couldn't back down from a fight because it tarred you as somebody who could be rolled. Prison is the same, but with graver consequences. Both inmates and COs prey on weakness, fear, or pain; both groups are mostly bored and unhappy, so once they see a festering wound, many will arrive gleefully with salt.

But no emotion is more dangerous than anger. Once someone knows how to set you off, he controls you. There's no hiding in prison, no way to avoid someone who wants to "try" you. The benefit of a low-security prison is that inmates have free movement much of the day. The downside is that would-be predators have full access to you—and unlimited opportunities to try to manipulate you. Anyone who thinks politicians are cunning ought to spend a week in prison.

And yet, at some of the most unexpected times, decades of pent-up emotion spilled out in entirely unexpected, sometimes even sweet ways. One night, as a special privilege for having the cleanest unit, several dozen of us were able to screen *The Blind Side,* a film based on the Michael Lewis story of a giant, nearly homeless black boy adopted by a white family and groomed to be an NFL star. In one scene, the protagonist's adoptive mom tells his birth mom of her family's plans to adopt him. The birth mom, ashamed of her drug addiction and soiled clothes, declines to see her teenage son to wish him good-bye. In the next scene, Michael's new family asks if he would like to become a part of their family, and he replies that he thought he already was. At that point I looked around me to see a roomful of hardened criminals wiping their eyes.

Even as I steeled myself to feel nothing, I found myself unusually attuned to the feelings of others—fellow inmates or friends and family on the outside I'd been too self-absorbed to consider before. I also developed a Pavlovian response to certain regularities of prison life. I remember seeing visitors watch me tense up when I heard keys jangling (the sign of an approaching CO) or rise abruptly when a CO entered and motioned for a standing count during visiting hours. My visitors didn't notice these signals, but noticing them was now a reflex—so much so that I could focus on other people's responses. I'd become a trained animal that feared punishment if it didn't immediately return to its crate after hearing its master call.

This was after eight months. I couldn't imagine how people with eighteen years felt . . . or if they felt anything at all. Many of them simply slept their time away; at one point my cellie Red was sleeping approximately sixteen hours a day. As ex-prisoner Daniel Genis wrote, "Prisoners are often like cats, able to sleep enormous amounts of time because they prefer their dreams to reality." What seemed clear was that the adaptive behaviors of inmates needing to cope rendered the healthy expression of human emotion upon release nearly impossible. And that adaptive behavior, increasingly, was bodybuilding.

So while it may seem a no-brainer to eliminate an activity that makes prisoners bigger and stronger, I'd think twice when a legislator proposes eliminating weights from state prisons. The benefits of prison weightlifting go far beyond body sculpting.[9] Genis argued that weightlifting helps prisoners who have struggled in life "see a better version of themselves" by giving them "a concrete achievement in a place meant to degrade and diminish." My experience backs this up. As Genis writes:

> Most men are in prison not because they're strong, but because they were weak. . . . For the guys that could be termed "losers," bodybuilding is a path towards perhaps their only success in life. After all, most prisoners have not succeeded in education or employment. They haven't built families or bought homes. Many have never been on an airplane. Their life is entirely without any memory to be proud of. . . . To say that prison weightlifting is good for self-esteem isn't enough. It also builds willpower and dedication, and gives men a sense of accomplishment. For many, it's the first time they've felt any sense of achievement.[10]

I'd never been dubbed a "loser." I was high school co-valedictorian and three-sport captain, a National Merit Scholar. I'd cofounded a charter school, earned a Ph.D., nearly gone to Congress, and gotten elected to the state senate by thirty-two. Even the race I'd lost was like a win, thanks in part to the documentary film about it. Yet I'd thrown it all away, and for nothing, which appalled most of my fellow prisoners. "Fuck is wrong with you? You got locked up and you ain't even get no money?" These words I heard nearly every day, whenever a newly intrigued prisoner approached. They expressed utter disbelief at my stupidity, compounded by the fact that I had two months in office after finding out about my friend's wire and *still* didn't find a way to steal public money once I knew I was going to prison anyway. On one level they respected me for having once had a little juice and for not being a snitch; on another level, these men, many locked up half their lives and nearly illiterate, thought I was a complete fool. Somebody dumb enough to get caught with his hand in the cookie jar without even getting any cookies.

In short, a loser.

7

"YOU DON'T WANNA GET A CELLIE WITH BOOBS"

Sex and Intimacy in the Cell Block

Rape: it's the one aspect of prison life that every friend or relative you see on the way in is worried about, and the one thing about which everyone you meet upon release is curious. Going in, I tried not to think about it. But when I arrived, there was no escaping it—or, more accurately, the specter of it.

A few weeks after my arrival at Manchester, about two dozen of us were ordered into a barren room in the administration building. After a half hour or so, a CO wheeled in a television set and shoved a videocassette into the VCR. The video featured a nondescript white guy, who might have been an accountant or a civics teacher, warning viewers not to eat any candy bars placed on the pillow in their cell. He had eaten the Snickers bar on his pillow, unwittingly signaling his predatory bunkie that he was ready and willing. He then described the horror of life as a recurring rape victim for the rest of his bid.

All the guys in the visiting room laughed. So did I, though

I was quickly embarrassed at having done so. I knew this man's story was not unique; hundreds of prisoners are raped every day across the country, and once victimized, a prisoner is often repeatedly subjected to gang rapes or must trade submission to one or more men in exchange for protection from the rest. Since I came into prison at 117 pounds and knew that I would have a tough time protecting myself in a jam, I made a mental note not to accept any sweets, no matter what.

During my maiden walk up the compound, the cacophony of shouts in my direction—and the men who came up to sneer and leer and inspect us like so many pieces of meat—had been disorienting. I only vaguely noticed the hulking, forty-something white guy with wavy brown hair who hollered at one of the guys walking in next to me. This was not an uncommon scene; most inmates who came in had done time somewhere else. But this massive mustachioed man known as Big C was unique: he'd been locked up so long, and at so many different prisons, that he seemed to know almost everyone who came in. If Manchester FCI were a morning talk show, Big C was Regis Philbin: the goofy, garrulous host of the weekly event at which new prisoners debuted on the compound.

My trouble with Big C had begun early in my stay, the very week that my work colleagues had given me the unfortunate nickname Booty-face after a particularly clean shave. KY had joked that Big C was going to love my smooth face. In fact, that very day, as the seven of us arrived back on the compound following a long day of work, chicken patties Saran-wrapped around our chests and green peppers stuffed in our jackets, Big C approached me for the first time with a pat on the shoulder that was one part friendly, one part menacing. I remembered KY's goading and tensed up.

"So yew werkin' fer Miss Horton," he said archly.

"Yup," I said.

"She's a tough bitch, that one," he said. "She'll werk the shit outta you."

"Sure will." My first day had been miserable, and unlike my crewmates who had mocked me for grunting when I caught the eighty-pound boxes hurled at me that day, here was someone who understood. "You used to work out there, too?"

"Hell, yes, I did," he said. "Done werked there twice. Ah know Miss Horton better than any uh these dudes. You jes' remember, she don't give two shits about you. Well, you tell her I said hello. Name's Smith, jes' like yers, but everbody 'round here calls me Big C."

I looked around to see who had witnessed our conversation and didn't see anyone.

Sure enough, though, KY started razzing me about it at work the next day. "Yo, Miss Horton," he crowed, "Big C pushed up on the Senator last night!" Everybody laughed.

"That true, Smith?" she asked.

"No, ma'am," I said, although I knew there was a certain amount of self-delusion involved. "He just introduced himself and asked me to tell you hi."

"So now youse doin' his errands," she barked.

I bristled. "No, ma'am. I wasn't even gonna say anything if you hadn't asked."

"You ever hearda that song 'Prison Bitch,' Smith?"

The warehouse crew roared. "No, ma'am," I said.

"Well, maybe you shoulda." Miss Horton never even broke a smile. "Y'all can laugh all you want, but you know I ain't kiddin'."

That afternoon, after Miss Horton drove us back to the compound, a throbbing noise drew our attention. We looked up and Big C was pounding the windows of his cell yelling, "Senator, Senator!"—just as he would nearly every day at 3:15 P.M. for the next several weeks, to the delight of the rest of the warehouse crew. KY would holler to anyone listening, "Big C on the prowl!! Big C gon' get at the Senator!!"

I just shook my head and kept walking. At that point, still in my first few weeks, the warehouse crew didn't know quite what to make of me. If I had been built like them, that might have been grounds for caution. Since I was not, they mocked me with abandon. I didn't know how seriously I should take Big C as a threat.

The next month, a couple of the warehouse guys saw me playing pickup ball and asked me to join their prison-league basketball team, which I did; playing in a hotly contested basketball game was the only time I forgot where I was. My ability helped me build friendships with the warehouse guys, our teammates, and even some opponents. During one of our first games, Big C cheered me on with ominous enthusiasm, his booming voice audible above that of the gamblers, bookies, sycophants, and haters. Two nights later at our next game, Big C was back. And then after every game, right there for a fist bump when I came off the court. "Man, Senator, you really schooled 'em out there! Ah cain't hardly believe the way you handle that ball!" The double entendre only made the episode more disconcerting.

I bumped fists with him as well as with several other spectators. I didn't want to snub him and risk angering him, given his size, but I was determined not to give him any extra attention, either positive or negative, that might reveal any hint of interest. But he was undeterred. He continued to pound on his window nearly every day when I got home from the warehouse, wink at me, and generally act in a way that amused others. At first I could not ascertain if others sympathized with me, simply enjoyed my unease, or took some kind of perverse sexual pleasure in seeing me squirm.

As winter turned to spring and softball season began, Big C's pursuit was now into its third month. Softball games were played on alternating nights with basketball; during softball games, Big C was up in the bleachers cheering for me, while on basketball nights he was in the gym. My father had been a devout attendee of all my soccer, baseball, and basketball games growing up, but Big C was giving him a run for his money, rarely, if ever, missing one of my contests. And Big C was typically the loudest voice in the bleachers when I made a diving stop at shortstop, and the most vehement guy in the gym hollering at the refs when they ignored hard fouls against me.

After one particularly boisterous performance, KY told me that Big C's boyfriend had recently gone home, and he was apparently "lonely" and looking for a new one, which I completely understood and empathized with as a human being but could not allow myself to understand and empathize with as a vulnerable prisoner.

The next day at lunchtime—well, 10:00 A.M., but lunchtime in prison—I was eating chili con carne at the chow hall with the warehouse crew when Big C dropped by the table. "Man, Senator, Ah ain't never seen nuthin' like you done to that dude last night!" he exclaimed. KY sat there grinning at me, already thinking of jokes for later. Big E just looked down at his food and kept eating. Ville, though, stared straight at Big C, who continued to rave about my performance. "You done made that dude fall down trying to guard you! You the quickest white boy Ah ever seen! Man, you was sum'n else!" He held his fist out to bump mine, and then he smacked his lips.

I sat stone-faced. I'd tried keeping a friendly distance, but after a month of Big C pounding the window when I walked by his cell, attending my games and cheering for me, this was too much. If he wanted to say "Good game last night," then okay, but this was ridiculous; he was basically hitting on me in front of three other dudes. I knew I needed to do something to stop this from going any further, but I didn't know what. I briefly considered rising to punch him in the face, which wouldn't have ended well, and then I looked across the table at Ville, my mammoth warehouse coworker, who was now looking straight ahead and untying his braids slowly, methodically, so that his hair protruded outward wildly in every direction.

Ville slowly looked up at Big C and said icily, "Naw, man, Senator ain't on that type of time. You betta take that faggot shit somewhere else."

Big C curled his upper lip, sucked his teeth for an instant, and skulked off.

I nodded at Ville casually and neither of us ever mentioned it again. A part of me wanted to thank him profusely, but had I done that, I'd have been exactly what Big C wanted to think I was: somebody who needed protection.

Big C would never bother me again after that. Of course, few are as fortunate as I was to have a strongman like Ville around, having my back. I didn't think about what might have been.

Victims of prison rape are usually the smallest, the nonviolent, the "fresh fish" (first-timers), and those charged with less serious crimes. Middle-class prisoners, those with college degrees, those without gang affiliations, and those not part of the racial or ethnic group dominating an institution are also likely to be targets.[1]

For those keeping score at home, I was eight for eight.

Although I looked the part, I had experience in other situations (politics, sports, etc.) where passing certain kinds of tests got me in trouble in the short term but helped shield me over the long run. More important, the bonds I'd established by proving myself in the warehouse afforded me the protection I needed at critical junctures.

Prisons have been called "training grounds for rapists," and according to one estimate based on two decades of surveys, nearly 300,000 rapes occur annually in U.S. prisons, compared to

135,000 reported rapes of U.S. women.[2] One researcher studying Philadelphia prisons estimated that 2,000 rapes occurred
during the two years studied.[3] Another study found that
14 percent of California inmates (and 41 percent of homosexu-
als) reported having been raped.[4]

The most recent Justice Department data concluded that
from 2003 to 2012, nearly 2 million inmates were sexually as-
saulted, costing society as much as $51.9 billion annually, includ-
ing the costs of victims' compensation and increased recidivism.[5]
Advocates hoped that passage of the 2003 Prison Rape Elimination Act (PREA), which sought to prevent, uncover, and address
sexual assault, would help, but six states comprising 20 percent
of the population have (with little consequence) refused to comply
with it, hindering its effectiveness.[6] Accordingly, in 2011—nearly
a decade after its passage—a prisoner's likelihood of being raped
was roughly thirty times higher than that of a given woman on
the outside; one top government statistician confirmed that nearly
two hundred thousand prisoners were raped in 2011 alone, suggesting a depressingly steady trendline since PREA's passage.[7]

And yet the states that disregard PREA do so with impunity. Why? Perhaps rape has become so embedded into prison
life—and pop culture's depiction of prison culture—that it has
become a critical component of prison's deterrent effect. "[Many
believe] rape is . . . what makes learning your lesson in prison
scary," complained Elizabeth Stoker Bruenig, "and scary prisons are what keep bad people in line."[8] The implication is that
criminals should expect to be raped, which helps explain the non-
chalance with which state-sanctioned PREA noncompliance is
greeted.

Since reporting assaults will only bring more trouble from
fellow prisoners and COs alike, most victims who agree to sex
in exchange for protection from gang rape remain quiet, rendering official prison data unreliable.[9] Exacerbating this is a

dearth of postrape psychological treatment during incarceration or reentry, which increases the likelihood that victims will
suffer from post-traumatic stress disorder. Research has found
that this hinders victims' efforts to successfully reenter society
and increases their odds of recidivism—especially sexual assault.[10]
Tragically, prison rape often causes compensatory aggression
as untreated victims commit rapes upon release to reclaim
their manhood in the same way they imagine it was lost.[11,12]
This vicious cycle by which (frequently) nonviolent offenders
become violent is the opposite of the duty that "correctional
institutions" are meant to perform.[13]

Even the earliest researchers studying sexual behavior among
prisoners concluded that many experience some form of sex. But
of course, for the vast majority of prisoners, sex takes a different
form than it had for them on the outside. Basic laws of supply
and demand operate in prison just as they do on the outside:
when a good or service is scarce, it becomes more expensive to
purchase and consume. But given pervasive material depriva-
tion, sex can replace other unavailable goods and become a key
commodity driving a prison's underground economy—and thus,
the source of violence.[14]

At Manchester, prisoners frequently alluded to sex, but usually through dark or caustic humor. Sometimes when KY and I
would walk down the compound together, he'd get funny looks
from veteran black prisoners for hanging out with this little
white guy hardly anybody knew. A few times he grabbed me and
joked "Two books!" to the oncoming dude, suggesting that he
"owned" me but that he'd "rent" me to the other dude for two
books of stamps—about $12 in prison terms. For appearance's
sake, I would have to faux-wrestle him when he would do that,
to show that I wouldn't take it, but then he would manhandle
me—he was one of the strongest guys on the compound and

undoubtedly had the best combination of strength and agility. Even when it was clearly a joke, and even when I knew I was sorely outmatched, that was not the kind of comment I could laugh off in prison.

I often wondered what Big C's introduction to prison had been like, wondered what he might've needed to do for protection. I wondered if he was actually gay or if it was merely "situational," a function of circumstance, architecture, and environment?[15] "Gay for the stay," some called it. And I wondered how his tactics might adjust to real-world courting. How would he pursue a desired mate if he ever got out? Would he pound windows to attract him or her? Stalk him or her at rec league softball games? Was he too warped by decades of prison to ever woo someone in a socially acceptable fashion? Like many inmates who appeared to have lost any sense of proper social interaction, he would find that his prison approach would not go over well on the outside.

Sex was never far from the mind of a typical prisoner, no matter how hard one tried to banish it. Any time several hundred men are confined in a small area without the benefit of female interaction—other than a pair of (arguably) female prison administrators—certain niceties get lost. Some evinced an insatiable desire for sex, talking about it constantly—sex they wanted to have with female prison staff, females in visiting delegations on tours, the rare deliverywoman. Some of my work colleagues at the prison warehouse even fantasized about one squat female CO who had the demeanor of a drill sergeant and the sensuality of an amoeba. "Lemme catch homegirl in the club once I'm sprung, bihhh," said Ville as he pumped his hips. "I'd run four miles of dick up in that."

Others tried to get men suspected of being gay to wear "makeup"—that is, grape or strawberry Kool-Aid mixed with lotion—so that they would look more feminine and leave slightly less to the imagination. And one of the quickest ways to get into a fight was by switching the channel during a women's softball game or track meet, events that were watched with as much whooping and hollering as homemade porn at a frat house.

For other men, like my former cellie Red, pornography generally sufficed. Outside muscle-building substances, these magazines were perhaps the most prized possessions on the compound. But even Red took the occasional break from Coco to consider the female staff.

During our time as bunkies, Red told stories of so-called gunslingers he had met during his time. There was one woman CO who occasionally patrolled, and one day while she was patrolling the chow hall, he contemplated whether it would be worth it to "gun her down."

"You crazy?" I asked. "You're almost to the door!" He'd been locked up off and on for twenty years, but had only a year left. "What she do to you anyway?"

He spoke to me slowly, as if I were a child. "Prance around in front of me wit' dat fat ass, is what she done did. Fuck they gon' do, throw me in the hole?"

"Cellie, they'll give you life!" I exclaimed.

He scrunched up his face. "How they gon' gimme life fo' gettin' off on some bitch?"

Only then did he realize that I didn't understand his slang. He explained that "gunslingers" were men who ran strings from their toes up their leg to lubed-up toilet paper tubes fitted around their penises. To "gun her down" would've been to wire himself and go to the chow hall at mealtime, position himself at a table near her post, and toe-tap away until he . . . well, I won't extend the gun metaphor any further.

• • •

One day a few months into my bid, while Red and I were getting along fine, I was on my way down to the visiting room to see Teresa and Red approached me with a business proposition. "Ten stamps if you can get me a lil' Teresa on here," he said, thrusting a tissue into my hand and inhaling theatrically. "Mmmm-mmmm, I bet she do smell like fresh strawberries!"

He was astonished when I declined his offer. "Cellie, you ain't even got to DO shit. Easiest ten stamps you ever make. And I bet she love that shit, knowin' I be gettin' off on her."

No, cellie, actually, I don't think she *would* love knowing that. But thanks for thinking of her.

I would not have been surprised had others accepted his offer. First, some inmates were financially desperate. One was nicknamed Five-Stamper; word was, there was nothing he wouldn't do for five stamps. Second, visiting room shenanigans were not uncommon. Given our security level, we didn't have to visit "through the glass" but could actually sit together in a setup similar to an airport waiting area. Visiting room rules were fairly simple: no exchange of any material under any circumstance, no kissing, one hug on the way in, one hug on the way out, and no touching in between. But some prisoners exploited the fairly loose arrangement. For instance, one newbie got sent up the road to a higher-security facility for manually pleasuring his girlfriend in the visiting room one day as I sat nearby.

I should not suggest that I was somehow above these carnal urges. One day when Teresa came to visit me, we struggled to contain our affection and violated the rules repeatedly. A few hours into the visit our kiss was rudely interrupted by a booming voice.

"Inmate Smeeth! Git! Over! Here!" thundered one of the COs on duty. I looked up, chagrined. "You know how many kisses I done just counted?" he demanded, and exchanged sneers with his partner.

"Nope."

"Twenty-seven. Yup, twenty-seven kisses."

I quickly replaced my chagrin with prison insouciance. "How many we allowed? Fifty?"

"Yew got a reeee-al slick mouth, Smeeth. How much time you got?"

"About six more months."

"I oughta put yew in the SHU for six months so we can bring yer little missy back here and 'vestigate just where yew put them twenty-seven kisses on her." His black eyes bored through me and his top lip curled upward.

I figured that saying either "No, man, don't do that," or "See if I give a fuck," two of the most frequent responses to that threat, would only increase the likelihood that they would put me there. So I chose a middle ground. "Do what you gotta do, I guess," I said.

The CO sized me up. "Yew used to have a lil' clout, a lil' juice, on the street, back when you was guvnah, mayuh, whatever you was."

"I guess so."

"That's why all them pretty young things come to see ya, huh? Well, maybe you oughta tell 'em you ain't no guvnah no more, yew jus' a convict now."

"They know that," I said. "They still come." I winked. Irreverent, risky, probably stupid of me.

Suddenly the CO cackled, and his partner quickly joined in. Then, just as abruptly, they both stopped and fixed their glares on me. "Well, your visit's over today. Go tell her good-bye, and if you try for number twenty-eight, the next one won't happen for six months, and it's gonna be through the glass." That meant I'd go to the SHU for six months, and then to a more secure prison where physically separated prisoners and visitors could speak only by phone.

Needless to say, I did not go for number twenty-eight. But in just sixty seconds, I had dramatically enhanced my rep on the compound. By the time I got back up to the unit, word had already spread. "The Senator a straight peee-omp!" hollered a young black guy they called Cee-Lo. "Man, the Senator had his muthafuckin' tongue down his old lady THROAT!!!" exclaimed an unfamiliar guy with braids. Then Cornbread chimed in. "This the third week runnin' the Senator done hooked up with a different one! This shit don't make no sense." A Mexican named Chino added, "You don't even know, bro. Then the Senator done got up in the CO face and tell him to fuck hisself!"

It was still going strong that night. Other inmates—two of the most feared and highly regarded guys on the compound, "Black" and "DC"—called me over to their huddle. "Yo, Senator, you goin' hard, huh?" said Black. "Look like you tryna put a baby in her right there in the damn visiting room!"

In truth, while it was a fact that I'd had a few different women visitors, all but Teresa were of the purely platonic variety. But there was no use trying to correct the record. From then on, they constantly warned me about Teresa surprising me and visiting when another woman was there. "Lemme find out yo' old lady bitch-slapped some ho' up in the visiting room one day!" exclaimed DC to much laughter. "This dude like Shaft!"

This was typical of what people called inmate-dot-com: the compound was like a big game of Telephone in which legends grew faster than you could contain them even if you wanted to. And based on the respect I was gaining, I definitely didn't want to.

Prison produced a longing not just for sex but for intimacy. Only rarely did inmates let their guard down and admit this, and such moments required careful handling. One day a few weeks into my bid, I was approached by Dred, a Jamaican guy with dreadlocks he had nurtured since he was first locked up fourteen years earlier at age seventeen for possessing, with intent to distribute, enough cocaine and ganja to intoxicate a small state. "Yo, Senator, who them be writin' you all them letters?"

In addition to being the compound's chess champ, Dred was probably the best cook—he was well-connected to kitchen workers and obtained jerk spice, paprika, and anything else he needed to concoct an authentic Jamaican meal by either letting them eat the meal or offering chess lessons or calligraphic letter writing in return. Meals were a big deal, as they are in most medium- and low-security prisons in which inmates have time outside their cells to collaborate, and access to a microwave or "hot pot" that warms but does not boil water. Dred and other prison chefs created a variety of exotic treats, most using ramen noodles or rice purchased from the canteen as a base and adding meat, vegetables, and sauces smuggled from the warehouse or kitchen to round out the meal. Cooking helped inmates pass the time, helped give them a sense of freedom (from prison meals) and mild rebellion (given the pillaged ingredients), and offered a semblance of community.

Dred had a hybrid barter-sale business model: four of us in the cell block would contribute ingredients to a huge "nacho" or other meal he'd make, and then he'd cook for us in exchange for ingredients and sell the rest for stamps. I was often included at least as much for my access to warehouse vegetables as for my companionship.

Most of his (and our) waking hours, Dred sang reggae in a mellifluous accent, which became the soundtrack to my weekends. He almost never removed his headphones, not while cooking, sleeping, playing chess, or working out, so you could never be sure if he heard you when you addressed him. But this time, about two months into my bid, he'd shed his headphones, so I could tell he was interested.

"Lotsa people," I replied cryptically. "I write anyone back

who writes me, except for crazy people." I liked Dred, and I would grow to trust him as much as I trusted anyone on the compound, but he was about six-foot-three, 230 pounds, and I'd already heard stories about a dude he'd beaten to a pulp, so I thought I'd tread carefully.

"Senator, lemme get a pen pal, yo?" asked Dred.

"Yeah, okay, I could probably do that."

"It's been, like, ten years since I done talked to a girl, yo?" he said gingerly. "So I jus', you know, get kinda lonely."

"I hear ya. I got someone in mind."

Dred's face lit up like a Christmas tree. "Really, mon? Who she is? What she look like? Tell me about her, Senator!"

"Well, she's a redhead," I began, and then my Red burst in, fresh from the weight pile.

"Who a redhead?" my cellie demanded.

Dred grinned sheepishly.

"Dred's pen pal," I said.

"You got him a redhead pen pal?!" exclaimed my Red. "Shit, lemme get one!"

"You like redheads, too?"

"I don't give a fuck if she a redhead, a blond-head, or a brown-head. I need pussy so bad I'd take a muthafuckin' bald-head long as she got a hole for this muthafucka!" he exclaimed, gesturing at his crotch.

"Quit dippin' in the Kool-Aid, brah,"* said Dred. "Yo, Senator, what her name is again?"

"Kailey." Kailey had been my most trusted aide, a lovely young redhead who had, as a college freshman, e-mailed my office at 2:00 A.M. one night during my first state senate session and told me she'd seen the documentary about my first campaign and dreamed of interning for me, and that it could be the first

---

* Prison slang for entering a conversation without invitation.

step toward her goal of being the first woman president. "Dear Future President Burger," I had replied that same night, beginning a lasting friendship. We were so close that Kailey agreed to serve as a pen pal for a prisoner if it would help me navigate prison, though she drew the line at sending lewd photos.

"Oh Sen-a-tor," sang Dred happily. "I'mma make Kailey fall in love wit' me." Then he walked outside with a spring in his step. "I can't WAIT to get up out this muthafucka and CUDDLE a bitch!" he announced to no one in particular.

An hour later, Red approached my bunk and whispered, "You can get me a pen pal?"

"Sure, I'll try."

"A different one from Dred? So I can have my own?" For once he was almost kind. He sounded like a little boy, far from his usual wisecracking dealer-pimp posture.

A couple of hours later I returned from the weight pile and Dred stuck his head into my cell conspiratorially, then solemnly handed me an unsealed letter with his return address printed calligraphically. "Yo, Senator, you could look at sum'n?"

"Sure," I said, and started reading.

"Hello Kailey, Before I begin, I would like to apologize to you for how we're meeting under these circumstances. However, I am not sorry for writing you. After hearing about you, I simply could not help myself. I feel it would have been a crime to allow such an incredible person escape me. Especially without giving things a try for an everlasting friendship."

"That's beautiful," I said. "You're a really good writer." But I didn't even have Kailey's address yet, and I looked at him to tell him and he quickly turned away. "What's wrong, Dred?"

"What if she no like it?" he whispered, quivering. I noticed a tear running down his cheek. "I wanna find a partner, you know, mon, to share my life. . . ." His voice trailed off. More tears.

This was a tricky situation. He had revealed too much. This

made him vulnerable and so it was possible he'd strike out at me. Nonetheless, I wanted to comfort him—put my arm around him—but this was prison. You didn't embrace; you bumped fists. And so instead, I reassured him that Kailey would like the letter. He then proceeded to tell me about his dreams of owning a restaurant and having a family to take care of, and then about his ex-girlfriend in Hawaii and the fourteen-year-old daughter he'd never met. He had a picture, though, and he wanted to show me.

"Yo, Senator, you think I ever see her? If she's doin' good I no wanna bother her, but if she in trouble, I wanna help her, you know, mon?"

Now I was afraid I might cry, too. I just smiled and told Dred that he'd be a great dad one day. And then we played chess. He beat me two out of three.

I never mentioned the incident to Dred again, and he never opened up to me again, or to anyone else as far as I know. It helped me understand yet another reason inmates walk out of prison so woefully unprepared for the trials of life on the outside: they spend years, decades even, bottling everything up inside, afraid of showing any vulnerability. The first lesson of prison, of course, is to show no weakness, to never give anyone clues that might let them exploit you. But the price of this is that when they walk out the door, at the very moment of their lives requiring maximum coping skills, they have few, if any. Does that mean every inmate should have free psychotherapy for the duration of his bid? No. But institutions must develop ways to foster deep bonds among men that will help them express emotion, support one another, build resilience, and, ultimately, learn how to fit into a community again.

If felons were cars, Porkchop was as standard issue as a Ford Taurus. Like several others (Popcorn, Peanut, etc.), he was nicknamed after his favorite food. He was six-foot-two and husky, with close-cropped dark hair, a goatee, and more tattoos than teeth. Porkchop spent every waking hour smoking, working on the weight pile, or watching TV. He had been in and out of state and federal prison for nearly twenty years, his offenses ranging from selling meth to kiting checks to stealing cars. A habitual offender, the law called him. To us he was just an ordinary thug, always trying to get over for a cigarette, a beef jerky, or a pack of mackerel.

The minute JT hit the compound, Porkchop had his eye on him. JT wasn't flamboyant—not one of the dudes who wears makeup (grape Kool-Aid on the eyes, cherry on the lips, Tang on the cheeks). He wasn't the type we got warned about by the gruff veteran staffer during orientation: "You might wanna move now if you got a single and go move in with somebody you know," he'd warned. "You don't wanna get a cellie with boobs."

No, JT was a typical meth dealer—nondescript, mostly kept to himself other than the occasional poker game. But Porkchop took a shine to him, pursuing him quietly but relentlessly. First he brought JT into his car. Then he taught him how to make a good nacho. Finally, he started ironing JT's greens before visiting hours.

And then one day, as I walked down to the bathroom late one night, I saw it. They were in bed together, snuggling and talking quietly. I saw a newbie snicker, and then a veteran ice-grilled him. "Ain't none o' yo' muthafuckin' bidness," said the look, and the newbie scurried back to his cell. After that, no one said a word about it. It would remain that way every night for the next three months until I left.

8

"THIS AIN'T T-BALL, LITTLE SENATOR, WE AIN'T GIVIN' YOU NO TEE!"

Prison Culture, Explained

On the street, there are morning people and there are night owls. But in prison, no one wants to talk in the morning. It's hard to get a solid night's sleep, since every night a CO comes in at midnight, 3:00 A.M., and 5:00 A.M., letting his keys jangle loudly, sometimes amusing himself with his burping and farting, shining a flashlight into our eyes before bouncing it off all the walls like a strobe light, just because he can.

The alarms for the kitchen workers start to go off around 4:15 A.M., and just after 6:00 A.M., a familiar voice booms out over the loudspeaker: "CHOW HALL IS OPEN FOR BREAKFAST." At Manchester FCI, that's a good night: between the surprise "fog counts"—for which we were hauled from bed a half hour earlier than usual and counted to ensure that none of us had taken advantage of the cover of fog enveloping the hollow and escaped—the deliberate racket made by patrolling COs, and the various nighttime noises of so many men trapped in one room together, it was basically impossible to get more than two consecutive hours of rest a night. No, prison was no place for a light sleeper like me.

Most nights I went to sleep a bit after midnight and woke up at 1:00 and 3:00; my mind would then race until after the 5:00 A.M. count as I'd anticipate all the alarms honking; then I'd fall back into a fitful sleep until the 6:00 A.M. call over the loudspeaker for breakfast. I tried not to think about the prosecutor's condescension, or Steve Brown sleeping peacefully with his wife while Teresa slept alone (I hoped), or how I'd make a living when I got out.

Other nights I was awakened when someone was told to pack out at three or four in the morning; they were being transferred with no notice, no chance to say good-bye to people they'd lived alongside for years. It seemed so arbitrarily cruel, given the bonds that formed between people who shared this experience. And there was a certain powerlessness in going to bed every night and knowing there was a chance you could be roused in the wee hours and bussed out for diesel therapy. Some nights my mind was besieged by all those things, mixing with the nocturnal soundtrack of grunts, farts, snores, and occasional ejaculatory moans from the showers, rendering sleep impossible.

After a difficult night on the street, you can hit snooze and catch a few extra minutes of sleep. But at Manchester FCI, a bearded prison staffer named Mr. Smith ensured there would be none of that. He seemed to take special pleasure in flipping on all the lights and barreling down the corridors at 6:00 A.M., screaming, "EVERYBODY UP AN' OUTTA YER BEDS! THIS AIN'T YER HOUSE AND I AIN'T YER BABY-MAMA! UP AND AT 'EM, YOU CONVICTS! THIS IS JAIL,

NOT YALE! SO GET THE HELL UP AN' MAKE YER DAMN BEDS!"

I could've used the extra few minutes of sleep because I was always tired and I didn't need to be at work for another hour. But I didn't have the option of sleeping an extra half hour and grabbing breakfast on the run. Tossing and turning every morning between the 5:00 A.M. count and the 6:00 A.M. screaming, dreading the inevitable, I was reminded of just how few choices I had anymore. Even the basic choices that should exist or could exist usually don't, for a pretty simple reason: it would inconvenience the COs.

Prisoners cope with the stresses of incarceration in a variety of ways.

"Bid" is both a noun and a verb in prison; it also describes how people do their time; some "bid off" weightlifting; some, off their hustle, sports, books, television, or just playing the dozens, known simply as "biddin'." The one thing nearly everyone shared as a coping mechanism was a reliance on ritual. The old heads taught you that having a daily routine made time pass faster and somehow eased the tension of prison life. I could never quite figure out why that was the case, but the veterans were right: my daily ritual of work, workout, standing count, dinner, basketball or softball, shower, journaling, and bedtime reading helped bring some measure of predictability to an environment in which you otherwise had very little control over anything. The quest for control manifested itself in odd ways, such as the aforementioned obsession with personal and room cleanliness. Some guys, for example, requested a floor buffer every single day so they could buff the floor of their cell in the morning. Many prisoners had their OCD tendencies, and they didn't necessarily jell with the equally rigid routines of other prisoners. All of them seemed,

though, to be rooted in the same desire to reclaim some semblance of autonomy. As my cellie Red explained to me in my
first week, "Prison ain't Burger King. You cain't have it *your*
way."

For most, weightlifting was a way of life; others supple-
mented the weight pile with other forms of recreation. Basketball and softball were both big events; even those who didn't
play would often attend to cheer on their homies or cellies,
or razz enemies or friends, or place wagers on various com-
ponents of the games. During my very first softball game, a
stocky dude named Roscoe, who was notorious for his incessant
and mean-spirited heckling of players, started up on me as soon
as I stepped into the batter's box. "This ain't T-ball, little Senator, we ain't givin' you no tee now!" Everyone in the stands
howled.

Every minute or two, a pair of onlookers would call out a
bet with each other, usually after an argument about the relative talents of two players—whether or not a guy would make a
hit or make an error in a given inning or hit it in a certain
direction. Batters would often bet heckling spectators, adding
an extra dimension of pressure to an at-bat. The bets frequently
led to major disputes, and occasionally to actual fights, about
whether a runner was safe or out or whether a play was a hit or
an error. The incessant gambling also led to a lot of on-field show-
manship, such as one shortstop who would mock runners by
fielding the ball flawlessly and then rolling it speedily to first
for the putout instead of throwing it.

Some prisoners focused almost entirely on their hustle. That
was especially true for those with complex hustles that required
constant, surreptitious attention, such as the smuggling of contraband or the mixing of hooch. The hooch boys—a group of Ken-
tucky- or Tennessee-bred rednecks, including guys nicknamed

Roadkill, Tadpole, Catfish, and Cockring—often huddled up in one cell at odd times checking on the progress of their concoction. As far as I could tell, they'd tie some stolen garbage bags together and pour Kool-Aid mix, water, moldy bread, and overripe tomatoes and apples obtained through swaps with kitchen or warehouse workers. They would hide the bag for a week and let it ferment in a separate bag under a layer of trash inside a trash can, with a straw poking through a hole to release the carbon dioxide. Then on Friday night they'd be in there clowning around, playing cards, and singing Kid Rock songs at the top of their lungs until the COs were spotted on the way up to the unit. Once a CO came in during a makeshift hooch party in a cell that was the rednecks' base. "SMELLS LIKE A GODDAMN JACK DANIEL'S DISTILLERY UP HERE!" he screamed. "YEW BETTER EITHER GIMME SOME OR DUMP THAT SHIT DOWN THE TOILET 'FORE I GET THE WARDEN UP HERE!" Since he didn't seem an ideal drinking buddy, Cockring and the boys guzzled what they could and flushed what they couldn't sell down the toilet after he left.

Other prisoners who weren't preoccupied by sports, hustling, or other unsavory enterprises gravitated toward reading, drawing, Bible study, or music. Since the only way to play a musical instrument was to join the makeshift prison church's gospel choir, and since they needed a drummer, I joined and even learned a little scripture. Not bad for an agnostic Jew. Quite a few prisoners attended church services; the message of redemption was a resonant one. Of course, it didn't resonate with everyone. "I gave myself to God and he did a background check and sent me back," said Jesse, one of my homies.

Still others spent their leisure time focused on their legal cases or studying for the GED or preparing résumés or writing business plans. I spent a lot of time with fellow prisoners helping them with all of the above and giving other guys pop quizzes on things they'd read to improve their reading comprehension; many of them could read a whole passage and, after they finished, have no idea what it had been about. Guys would come by my cell every day to borrow books; my ex-girlfriend's mother sent me at least two books every month I was there, which made my cell like a second prison library: by the end of my bid, I had nearly as many books as the library did. There were also several news junkies who religiously read what we referred to as *USA Yesterday,* a sly reference to the two-day delay on all mail into the prison.

Once I was helping Cee-Lo study for the algebra portion of the GED. I was having a tough time explaining algebra via alphanumeric expressions. Almost all of the people I tutored seemed to struggle with abstractions, such as the fact that x and y actually didn't mean the letters themselves but were stand-ins for numbers.

Another guy came up and kidded Cee-Lo. "Nigga, quit wastin' time, you ain't never use no algebra no way." But I was determined to reach him, so I tried a different tack. "Think of it like this," I began. "One dude from the warehouse is trying to sell you four chicken patties for ten stickies. Other dude's offering you twenty patties for two books.* You only really need four right now to eat, but you also spot a potential business opportunity in the twenty, which you could likely resell. But first you have to figure out if the mass purchase is a good enough deal to allow you to make a decent profit off the excess patties, given the time and effort it might take to market them—as well as the inherent risk in storing them, if only for a couple hours. You ever been in that situation?"

Cee-Lo was mesmerized. "I *steady* in that situation," he replied, as if he'd had an epiphany.

---

* Two books = forty stamps.

"Then you do algebra every day," I said.

"Day-umm." He beamed at the other guy. "I be a mutha-fuckin' mathematician!"

One CO who was known among prisoners as "Teach" was re-sponsible for overseeing GED courses, but according to one of the inmate-instructors—an occasional workout partner of mine—Teach made one appearance in each course, for five minutes during the first class. During the next few months of the class, his management style could politely be called laissez-faire; he re-quested daily attendance sheets and then, at the end, collected the final exams. Given his foul disposition, this approach may not have been a bad thing for prisoners; the prisoners who did the teaching generally brought enthusiasm and smarts to the task. I got a taste of Teach during the final month of my bid, after I was transferred from the warehouse to the education de-partment. During my first few weeks at the warehouse, before I'd gained strength and the hundred-pound bags were still crush-ing my back, and before I'd developed a rapport with the rest of the crew, I'd made written requests to teach courses on civics, personal finance and budgeting, résumé writing and job in-terviewing, and African American history. Each request was ignored, though I would later find that the prison counselor, who handled work assignments, had checked with Miss Horton before deciding to scuttle the requests. Periodically, she'd scoff, "Smith, yer here with me for a year and a day, like it or not. That's right, son, ain't a thing you can do about it."

Then one day in the warehouse, about a month before my release date, Miss Horton told us to retrieve some equipment from its storage area above an industrial freezer, about thirteen feet high. As the smallest of the group, I was the designated climber, so KY lifted me up, put one of my work boots in each hand, and extended his arms above his head until I grasped the top of the freezer. I was preparing to use my grip to hoist my-self to the top of the freezer. Suddenly I heard some commotion beneath me and then I felt myself tumbling to the ground, landing on my back with a huge thud.

The warehouse crew doubled back toward me to see what happened. They'd been distracted; our regular Hostess delivery-man was out for the day and a black woman in formfitting khaki shorts and a snug polo shirt was substituting for him. This had attracted the attention of the whole crew and distracted KY, who prematurely let go of my foot, causing me to land on my back. Everyone gathered around as I writhed in pain. "Yo, Miss Horton," yelled Ville. "You better come out here."

She surveyed me and immediately called the admin build-ing to send a van for me so that I could see a doctor. "You gonna die, Smith?"

"No, ma'am."

"Well, just don't move 'til they get here."

A few minutes later a van arrived with a stretcher. Miss Horton helpfully informed the guys who ferried me off, "KY told him to go up there, not me." It was a consistent theme of the lawsuit-wary prison staff's comments in similar situations: they weren't involved; they weren't to blame. I have no idea how badly I was hurt because no doctor was available that day and a nurse simply gave me a bottle of maximum-strength ibuprofen, but nearly five years later, I have severe back pain every morning.

By coincidence, Peter Kinder, Missouri's lieutenant gover-nor, was slated to visit me the following day. He came and was allowed to see me outside of normal visiting hours. (This was also characteristic of Manchester FCI prison administrators: when Teresa visited, she was sometimes delayed from entering for as long as three hours, but when someone they perceived to have influence wanted to visit, they could bend the rules to allow it.) Peter had become a friend during my time in the state senate;

he was the rare conservative Republican who spent much of his intellectual and political energy on the plight of St. Louis's urban core and, in particular, its struggling schoolchildren. He and I often sent articles back and forth, sometimes agreeing about their theses and other times arguing, but always good-naturedly. During our visit, we caught up and talked politics and policy, not prison, but the visit had an unexpected salubrious effect: within an hour of my return back to the compound, a prison administrator informed me that I was being moved from the warehouse to the education department and directed me to report immediately. I was gratified: although I had only a month left in my bid, I'd finally get the opportunity to put my teaching background to use and hopefully have a broader impact on the prisoners than my one-on-one tutoring could accomplish. Perhaps I could even teach one of the civics or black history courses I had designed months earlier and persuade some of the men I had tutored to enroll.

I went back to the warehouse to tell Miss Horton that I'd been transferred and to say good-bye. I found her seated in her usual chair in her office, surrounded by all the small items that she kept close because they were so easily stolen, like the things kept behind glass at a shitty convenience store. I approached her, curiously forgetting her iciness after my fall, suddenly struck by a deep tenderness I hadn't felt in ages. "I want to thank you for taking such good care of me over here, Miss Horton. I really appreciate it."

She grunted without looking up from her desk as she jotted some numbers on a sheet.

"I mean, not just the food and the snacks. I appreciated our conversations about, you know, the system and stuff. I learned a lot over here. It was nice to be able to talk to someone who'd worked in the system for a long time, knew the ins and outs, and could help me see the big picture." I grinned. "And the work wasn't as bad as I thought it was going to be. It was actually probably good for me to do more than push pencils, like Cowboy said."

Miss Horton did not look up. "You ain't gettin' any bananas outta me, Smith," she said. She would never give me the satisfaction of a Hallmark moment.

I told the warehouse crew that it was my last day and they just shook their heads. "Miz Horton gon' be there to git yo' lil' ass outta bed if you ain't out there fo' the bus, so you go on thinkin' whatever you want," said Ville. Nobody really believed I was leaving; the only way anyone ever escaped the warehouse was by getting caught stealing.

I resisted the temptation to try to make off with a big haul on my final day and took the van back to the compound with the rest of the warehouse crew. With a spring in my step, I hustled past a group of men milling around toward the classroom. "Fuck you in a hurry for?" asked a guy on my basketball team, laughing. "You think you goin' to give a speech? You in prison now, Senator!" I smiled and kept moving quickly. One of the hardest things to get used to in prison was how slowly everyone moved and how long all the lines were to do just about anything. Lines were difficult for me at first, physiologically and psychologically. First of all, I was so addicted to my BlackBerry during my time in politics that even during the first months of my bid, I constantly felt phantom vibrations in the pocket where I'd kept my phone while standing in a line with nothing to occupy me. Second and more troubling for me was the comparison to my past life as a senator, in which people waited in line in my office to see me. Lines were a constant reminder of my status.

One of my trademarks as a politician had been speed: I'd raced from meeting to meeting, often more than a dozen per day, drove like a maniac, and jogged between doors when canvassing voters—behavior that most of my staff and interns emulated. My philosophy was that every campaign had a different amount of money, endorsements, and volunteers; the only equal quantity was time. Since every minute was valuable, we would use ours more effectively than our opponents. For instance, I estimated that I needed to raise $450,000 to win my congressional race, so I aimed to raise $10,000 a week for forty-five weeks, which meant $2,000 per weekday, which meant $500 per hour of call time and extra hours on the phone any day I did not meet the daily goal. I had my life scheduled by the minute, which only intensified after I got elected and became chair of the Missouri Senate Democratic Campaign Committee. Prison felt like Bizarro World for me: all anyone had was time, and the goal was to get your activities to expand to fill the day, not the other way around.

But now my time would finally be put to good use, I thought to myself as I entered the education department and tentatively approached Teach. "Sir, I'm Jeff Smith, reporting for work—I just got transferred here from the warehouse."

He greeted me with a forbidding glare. "Sit down," he ordered.

I waited and watched him shuffle papers for about fifteen minutes, and then he peered at me over his glasses. "What's your education background, Smith?"

"I have a Ph.D."

"In what, horseshit?" He chuckled for a few seconds at that.

"Political science."

"Oh, I don't really care what. You know what they say, Piled Higher and Deeper. In horseshit, get it?"

"Yep, I get it." That I was not visibly amused seemed to annoy him.

"So Smith, or should I say *Dr.* Smith, you ever taught before?"

"Yes, I've taught at a few universities. Most recently at Washington University."

"Never hearda it. How many years you teach?"

"For about a decade, as an adjunct or visiting professor."

"Good to know, Smith. Good to know." He handed me a broom and smirked. "We'll start you off sweepin' the classrooms and see how you do."

Though I tutored over a dozen men, I was unable to teach in a formal setting.

In the hotly contested prison rec league, my team reached the semifinals, which were scheduled two nights before my departure. My head told me not to play—why risk injury? Most guys stopped playing sports in the final year of their sentence to make sure they left in one piece and on time. KY and Ville told me that under no circumstances should I play. But I was the point guard—the floor general—and it was the semis, and I wasn't going to take my team all the way there and then sit out my last game. Maybe my mom, who had accused me of inveterate recklessness, had a point after all.

I opened up with the hot hand—a jumper from the elbow, a steal and layup, a crossover penetration move and dish to Popcorn (my center) for the dunk. We were up twelve points at half and came out of halftime prepared to run some clock. Going into the fourth quarter it was a three-point game.

The fourth quarter seesawed back and forth until the three-minute mark. The other team's point guard, a gazelle-like six-foot-two bald guy everyone called Jordan but who was overhyped, was bringing it up the floor. I feigned a reach on his left side to entice him to switch hands, then lunged to his right side when the ball arrived in my hand as smoothly as if I'd taken the last dribble myself. My momentum gave me a few steps on him toward the hoop, but he was lightning fast and making up ground; the crowd's screams swelled as we neared the hoop. I rose for the finger-roll, and as I released the ball I felt my body hurtle through midair before hitting the wall with a thud.

"An' one!" yelled someone, and then the crowd gasped, waiting to see if I'd get up. Jordan had shoved me hard just as I leapt. Being in prison, I probably should've anticipated it, but in the middle of a game, you don't remember you're in prison—that's why you play in the first place.

My teammates rushed to help me up. Popcorn picked me up and nuzzled me, and the crowd noise again swelled. "Lock that nigga up fo' assault!" yelled someone, to which somebody replied, "Naw, man—lock the Senator up fo' larceny!" in reference to the steal, which brought down the house.

On the way back to the free-throw line, the other team's power forward, AK, a muscled-up guy and former Arena football wide receiver, got in my face. I tried to walk right through him, except that he had nine inches and 100 pounds on me, so instead I bounced sideways off him and then had to circle back to the free-throw line. The crowd laughed at that, too.

I missed the free throw, but we were still up six with two minutes to play. I brought the ball up against a full-court press and yelled, "Four corners!" so that my teammates would spread the floor. With no shot clock, all I had to do was dribble around and protect the ball.

I crossed half-court and the floor was wide open. Jordan was hounding me, so I faked a drive with both the ball and my right hip, then whipped the ball under my right leg over to my left hand. Though I'd scarcely moved from half-court, Jordan lurched back near the free-throw line to defend my anticipated penetration, got tangled up trying to recover, and was sprawled out on the floor. The crowd whooped.

In the suburbs, spectators cheer politely when you hit a jump shot but don't appreciate the finesse and psychological impact of a move like this. In the ghetto, a jump shot rarely moved the crowd, but fancy ball-handling and footwork could produce ooohs and ahhhs.

Though I should have, I did not anticipate what happened next.

Jordan rose and approached me with the strangest look on his face. His eyes gleamed and his mouth was twisted into a crooked smile. The last thing I remember seeing was his forearm as it jerked up toward my chin.

We won the game, but I didn't finish it. I don't know how long I was unconscious. KY and Ville walked me up to my unit slowly, arm in arm, lecturing me. "Smith, how many times I tell you not to play tonight?" asked KY. "Once people found out you was leaving, you was already gonna get fucked up. Then you go and do that fancy-ass shit? Don't you know these dudes with a dime* to go gonna do somebody at the door—'specially your little ass? You lift a few weights and think you tough!" He laughed and shook his head.

I lay down in my bunk that night and thought about what had just happened. One day and a wake-up† from the door, my future bride waiting for me, having ridden with me all year long, and I was risking it all in a basketball game. Not even to win the game, but to look good.

The way I had antagonized people on the court shocked me, now that I reflected on it, and I couldn't believe how selfish I'd been by playing throughout my bid. I should've either found the right noncontact sport to help me stay in shape or I should've disciplined myself not to showboat. All I'd thought about was flaunting my slick moves. I'd never even considered how it would feel for somebody with eight more years to see a guy leave after eight piddly-ass months, and then have that guy—a little white politician, for chrissake!—embarrass him in front of the whole prison as the runt waltzes out the door.

---

* Ten years.

† Two days from going home.

Unable to sleep that night because of the pain, I had many hours to consider it, to think about the anger that simmers inside of veterans as they watch short-timers come and go. Especially short-timers with just a year and a day. And a graduate degree, family and community support, financial savings, a strong professional network, and decent prospects on the outside. Short-timers who got visits most weekends, always seemed to have money for a phone call, got new books sent in almost every week. Short-timers who spent their year playing basketball, writing a book, taking notes on their conversations, *studying* them. Almost like they were on a fucking *sabbatical*. A *vacation*.

I got up around 5:00 A.M. with the kitchen workers, head throbbing, and gingerly climbed down from my bunk to clean up before breakfast. People approached, asking me if I was okay and if I was going to try to get back at Jordan. "I'm out," I told people. "If somebody wants to get at 'im when I leave, fine, but I'm walking out that door and goin' to a motel with my old lady!" There weren't many times that turning the other cheek in prison was even marginally acceptable, but this was one of them—and since my licentious visit was legend, the motel line was credible.

As it turned out, on my final day I ended up in line with Jordan on the way to lunch. He approached me with a mile-wide, gap-toothed smile. "They say you leaving, Senator! You mean you ain't gonna be here for winter league?"

Ha-ha, I thought. "Naw, man, I'm down to a wake-up now."

"Sheeee-it," he replied, sounding like *The Wire*'s Senator Clay Davis. "If I'da known you was leaving, I'da *really* laid some wood."

9

"YOU'LL BE BACK, SHITBIRD"

Breaking the Cycle of Mass Incarceration

"You'll be back, shitbird."

If I heard it once, I heard it a dozen times. It's what COs told inmates nearing their release date, especially inmates who had "slick mouths" or otherwise created problems. Once I learned the date at which I would be released to a St. Louis halfway house (where I was slated to stay for two and a half months), I became increasingly conscious of the way COs treated outgoing prisoners.

Research indicates that abusive correctional officers impair attempts to reduce recidivism, but the COs were either unaware of that or did not mind—most likely, both. "Jackasses like you are how I know I'll always have a job," one CO frequently told wayward inmates. It was his way of reminding us that not only did he expect us to return, but his livelihood *depended* on it. The attitude sickened but did not surprise me. After all, COs spend their lives in prison just like prisoners do. They have the power, and they often wield it gratuitously. One particularly egregious example was the CO who would occasionally drive the warehouse crew back to the compound after work and after loading us into the back of the van where we stood during the ride, make needlessly sharp turns and slam on the brakes before sadistically cackling to himself as we careened into the sides of the truck and each other. I felt like this would have been far less troubling had he been showing off for another CO. That he was entertaining only himself suggested a disturbing purity of pleasure from our pain. It would be folly to think that COs could somehow remain psychologically unscathed after spending years or even decades in a dehumanizing environment.

The broader Manchester milieu helps explain the cycle driving the prison system. In surrounding Clay County, Kentucky— the nation's most miserable county, according to the *New York Times*—there are not exactly a lot of great professional options. The *Times* writes that it "might as well be a different country": half the people are obese, median household income is barely above the poverty line, and the disability rate is nearly ten times the national average.[1] Addiction to methamphetamine and oxycodone is rampant; a dozen onetime public officials were convicted on federal charges for participating in a massive scheme whereby elected officials, sheriffs, and others condoned drug dealing in exchange for a share of the profits, which were then used to buy votes.[2]

Clay County was once the heart of coal country, but these days, that industry employs just fifty-four people; its unemployment rate is more than double the national average.[3] During my sentence, job opportunities for local residents were scarce—I didn't view all the COs as power-hungry tyrants who applied for the position to fulfill some sick fantasy. Many, if not most, probably started out as decent people looking for a steady job with benefits, a rarity in an economic wasteland. When COs flashed fleeting moments of humanity—allowing me to linger an extra moment in a visiting room hug, or looking the other way after catching me with an illicit orange—I tried to imagine what they might have been like as carpenters or plumbers on my beer league softball team.

But the saddest thing about COs and their obnoxious bluster is that their malicious taunts often proved correct: most inmates probably *were* coming back. Some seemed resigned to it; a few even seemed fine with it. Long-term veteran Roscoe, the single loudest and most insufferable guy on the compound, refused to leave his cell for his final ten days of incarceration, terrified at the prospect of life on the outside. Cee-Lo, nearing the end of a long bid, shoved a CO for no apparent reason and got sent back to the medium-security prison with his "good time" revoked, meaning another two years instead of two weeks. At first I didn't get it. *Why would he do something so dumb right when he was going home?* I wondered. *No self-control. Probably wouldn't have made it on the outside anyway.*

I didn't really figure it out until the end of my bid, when a new prisoner showed up on the compound who had apparently been at Manchester before. The old heads greeted him like a long lost brother or a prodigal son. But one turned to me and said knowingly, "I seen dudes like that. Can't hack it, end up homeless, throw a brick at a post office window."

"Why the post office?" I asked.

"Fed time easier than state time. Less chance of gettin' mixed up with murderers and chomos* here."

It struck me that the guy who started the fight just as he neared the door actually had extraordinary discipline—enough to know that, without support, he wasn't ready to make it on the outside. Knowing he wouldn't be able to keep his emotions in

---

* Child molester.

check on the street, he sacrificed his shot at freedom—the thing each of us prisoners wanted most, at least ostensibly—for his own good.

Controlling one's emotions is often an impossible task for a prisoner out on parole, and a significant factor in recidivism. After suppressing their emotions for years to avoid showing weakness, many ex-inmates struggle to manage emotions and stay calm amid conflict—an essential workplace skill. Another is fear of the unknown: inmates are often terrified upon release— of finding a job, an apartment; of reuniting with old friends still in the dope game. They didn't exactly like prison, but after a decade or more, they were used to it. It was *home*. They had a routine. If you steered clear of trouble, it wasn't too bad. That's what it meant to be institutionalized.

Institutionalized. This is the biggest insult you can hurl at a fellow prisoner, other than calling his mama a ho. Being institutionalized is lifting weights outdoors in the driving snow without thinking twice because you can't miss a day. It's smearing peanut butter on mackerel after your workout for an extra boost. It's the ability to recite from memory the weekly menu, the COs' shift schedules, and the disciplinary handbook. It's squirreling away cafeteria sauces in the fingers of stolen plastic gloves all week to prepare a weekend feast.

But above all, being institutionalized suggests that you are almost *comfortable*. And while prisoners have respect for those who know how to do their time, they have deep contempt and pity for those who learn how to do it too well and become practically content.

In small but persistent and accumulating ways, I found that I was developing habits characteristic of those considered institutionalized. Without realizing I had done so, I memorized the last three digits of every federal court jurisdiction that fed into Manchester FCI. I hoarded small bits of food to store for lockdowns or special midnight snacks. And my body reflexively tensed up as soon as I heard the clanking of Tuck's steel-toed combat boots, because who knew if my cell would get tossed and a stray piece of smuggled bread would become my ticket to the SHU.

On my final day at Manchester FCI, I awoke during the 3:00 A.M. count and couldn't get back to sleep. The minutes felt like hours. I thought about what my first cellie had said, shortly after we met: that he'd done more time in this joint on the toilet than I had time. He was right. Compared to almost everyone with whom I served, my stay was ephemeral, a blip. Notwithstanding a few of the habits I'd developed, I wasn't there nearly long enough to become institutionalized. I was ready to start a new life. The only tinge of remorse I felt about leaving was that I couldn't bring some of the guys with me. I went out to meet the warehouse crew before they left for work.

"I'm out, y'all—I'll be in touch, though."

"Yeah, right," said Ville.

"I will!" I protested. But the guys seemed oddly subdued.

"You gonna act like this year done never happened." KY laughed, but I could tell he meant it.

"Naw. I really won't. I saw some shit I'm never gonna forget."

"You gonna try to forget it, though," chimed in Big E.

"That's just not true. I'm not gonna forget you guys—uh, the warehouse, ya know?" I wanted to personalize it, I really did, but all of a sudden, it felt like they had shut off.

"You write about me in ya book, yo, Senator," said Ville as he walked toward the bus. "I should be the hero of that motherfucker. But you gon' give yoself all the good lines. Just remember I'mma read that shit when I get out, so you betta keep it one hunnid, yo? And tell Teresa I'll be up to see her in a few years." Of course they laughed at that.

We all bumped fists, and with that, they were gone. It was hardly the good-bye I'd secretly hoped for, in which we all share soul shakes, and I thank them for having my back, and they tell me I wasn't anything like they thought I was gonna be, and so on. They had silently cued me not to get nostalgic. They couldn't afford to. Unlike me, they still had years to go.

I headed back to the chow hall for breakfast and ran into C—a friend with whom I occasionally worked out and played basketball, not Big C, who had courted me—who collared me and looked me in the eye. "Don't you forget 'bout us in here," he said.

"I won't," I pledged.

"You my nigga, ain't nothin' bigga."

I smiled and we bumped fists, letting the fists linger for a few seconds—about the deepest show of intimacy you'll see among prisoners who are not romantically linked.

I walked back up to my cell, packed up a bag of things, and then walked around the compound giving away a few dozen books I'd saved for people. Then I gave away my Walkman, some peanut butter I'd stashed, and other incidentals that have little value on the street but are cherished in prison. It was considered poor form to walk out with anything but the clothes on your back or things of sentimental value, and that is as it should be.

I walked down to the admin building, excited to get out, elated to see Teresa, and yet with a tinge of nostalgia. I vowed to stay in touch, and I planned to, but I realized that I'd probably never see any of these guys again. For a brief moment, I was overwhelmed with sadness and gratitude and love, really—and deep remorse for not having told them any of that earlier in the morning. And yet I instantly realized that if I had said it to them, they'd have laughed and said, "Go on with that political bullshit, Senator. Now git the fuck outta here to yo' old lady."

After what seemed like an eternity of paperwork and waiting, I was released late that morning. At my mother's suggestion, Teresa greeted me with a coffee cake from my favorite childhood bakery in St. Louis. Before getting on the highway we stopped at the Best Western at the end of Catfish Hollow Road for a few blissful minutes that made me feel seventeen again, and then at Walgreens for a pint of milk to go with the coffee cake. I jumped out of the car and hustled toward the store, and much to my surprise I saw Chester, the Flav-O-Rich driver who delivered to the prison. He was befuddled. At first he couldn't place me.

"Chester, it's me, from the warehouse!"

His eyes widened. "Senator, how did ya . . . wait a minute, did ya—"

"No, no, don't worry, I got out this morning!"

Relief spread across his face. "Well, sonofagun! C'mon up in the truck and get anything ya want!"

I'd spent seven months unloading milk from that truck under the watchful eye of Miss Horton, who was constantly trying to catch one of us pocketing a chocolate milk, an orange juice, or a Twinkie. Now Chester was giving me free rein over all his snacks. It was almost too much to bear. I was paralyzed.

"I ain't got all day!" said Chester good-naturedly.

I hesitated, grabbed an orange juice, then replaced it and grabbed a chocolate milk instead.

"Hell, take both of 'em, I don't care!" He grinned.

I couldn't decide which one to drink first, but there wasn't time to dawdle. I had eight hours to be at the halfway house, so I bid Chester a warm good-bye and we were on our way.

On August 9, 1977, a New Mexico district court judge named Jack Love was reading the comic strips and noticed that Spider-Man was facing a new impediment in his daily battle with the forces of evil. The Kingpin, a menacing villain who had captured Spider-Man, held the superhero at gunpoint and attached a bracelet to his wrist. "This electronic radar device will allow me to zero in on your location whenever I wish!" warned the Kingpin. "Even your awesome power cannot remove it! Nothing can— except my hidden laser key!"[4]

Judge Love reversed the Kingpin's idea. Instead of monitoring superheroes, he thought, an electronic bracelet could monitor offenders, reducing prison overcrowding and cutting costs while giving nonviolent offenders a chance to serve their sentences in a more humane way. The judge approached several electronics manufacturers to no avail. But a friend of his—a midlevel Honeywell salesman named Michael Goss—was intrigued. Goss futilely spent years trying to persuade his bosses of the idea's potential, and in 1982, he quit Honeywell and dumped his savings into a start-up firm that soon developed an anklet that emitted a radio signal, instantly relaying it to a computer system, which then alerted security personnel if the user tampered with the device or strayed outside its 150-foot range.[5] Judge Love ordered selected nonviolent offenders to be outfitted with devices, and a California joint legislative committee soon found that home incarceration would give courts "an intermediate disposition between state probation and . . . jail, as well as a better control mechanism following jail given as a condition of probation."[6] Though Goss ran out of funding before the idea spread, a larger firm purchased his and expanded worldwide as more states and countries adopted the devices.[7]

I saw many examples of waste in my warehouse job. But they all paled in comparison to the systemic fiscal and human waste that could've been avoided in many cases via electronic monitoring. Half of the prisoners with whom I spent any amount of time at Manchester appeared to be no proactive threat to anyone (though few would turn the other cheek if provoked). The average annual cost of prison is approximately the price of tuition at a private university: $31,286.[8] This is only the portion that is counted in state corrections budgets; it does not include attendant health care or social service expenses.[9] In my former home of Missouri, for instance, budget figures understate the cost of a prisoner by nearly 26 percent.[10]

It makes even less sense to lock people up in a facility without a barbed-wire fence surrounding it. If our system trusts prisoners enough to afford them the opportunity, however dangerous, to scale a ridge and run for it, then why not electronically monitor prisoners confined to work and home, at least once a nonviolent offender has served, say, the first half of his sentence without incident?

That those of us in the warehouse were trusted to handle all incoming materials indicates that we were capable of responsibly performing a similar job on the outside for $17 an hour instead of the average $17 a month prisoners received. We could have been sentenced to electronic monitoring rather than time in prison: instead of draining taxpayers, we would have *been* taxpayers, paying monthly fees to offset the cost of electronic monitoring, helping extend Medicare's solvency, and supporting other critical programs. Moreover, research suggests that electronic monitoring substantially reduces recidivism, leading to additional agency savings at each stage of criminal case processing (arrest, court, probation, jail, prison).

Half of all incarcerated Americans are nonviolent offenders who would not require taxpayer-funded housing, clothes, food, or constant human supervision if electronically monitored. If half of those nonviolent offenders could qualify for home confinement based on the above criteria, taxpayers could save $16 billion annually—and the reduction in human misery and familial damage would be incalculable.

Mandatory minimum sentences mean that one of every nine nonviolent offenders—or about 160,000 people—are serving life sentences, a third of them without the possibility of parole.

Mandatory minimum sentences are widely acknowledged to be the equivalent of using a bulldozer to remove an anthill. But they obviously serve a purpose in ensuring longer and more certain stays. Prisons house hundreds of thousands of mentally ill people, and they function as a de facto substitute for mass unemployment. Removed from the workforce, prisoners aren't counted in our unemployment rate, but they do provide employment for the prison-industrial complex. They aren't counted as part of the electorate and have no voice to participate or protest, yet criminal justice policies they have no voice in shaping literally determine their freedom or lack thereof.

Given that, eliminating mandatory minimums would require that government formulate a real plan to deal with mass unemployment and that it prepare to hear and incorporate the voices of incarceration into the policymaking process. It would require the construction of fewer prisons, the employment of fewer guards, and fewer purchases from the vendors who supply everything from food to uniforms to appliances. Given the powerful lobbies at work—from massive private prison operators like Corrections Corporation of America and food vendors like Sysco Corporation to correctional officers' unions and stubborn prosecutors—there are potent forces working to prevent commonsense and cost-saving reforms. These overlong sentences create a vicious cycle: the longer people are locked up, the harder it is to adjust to the outside—and the more likely probationers are to reoffend.

It's well-known that some prisoners develop an antiauthoritarian strain—or augment an existing one—that serves them poorly upon reentry. What is less well understood is that the survival mechanisms they develop are unlikely to serve them well, either. Anyone who has spent a weekend at a bachelor party understands how testosterone drives the behavior of men separated from women. Imagine what it does over decades—when many of the impulses that can be satiated at a bachelor party must be suppressed. It's not just about blowing off steam or excess testosterone, though. After coping with incarceration by teaching themselves to feel nothing, how can prisoners learn to appropriately express emotion upon reentry?

The challenges of reentry are both large and small, but even the seemingly small ones can be intense. The number of choices in a supermarket can be overwhelming, as can the myriad of decisions required every day—which clothes to wear, which bus to take, what to say and how to act in unfamiliar social situations. After a decade of obeying orders, the sudden deluge of choices can overwhelm people. One set of choices many ex-offenders are not allowed to make, however, is a choice among political candidates. Many policymakers are only beginning to see the irony of a system that asks probationers to be law-abiding citizens while simultaneously denying them that most essential element of citizenship: the right to vote.

More broadly, many ex-offenders experience symptoms of post-traumatic stress disorder not unlike war veterans: despite leaving prison physically, it takes some ex-offenders years to leave mentally. For those who can't cope on the outside, returning to prison seems comforting and familiar—just one more factor helping explain our sky-high recidivism rate.

I wasn't entirely free yet. I still faced two and a half months at a halfway house. To paraphrase an old expression, prison was a lot like politics, minus the riffraff. I would soon find out where the real riffraff was: in the halfway house to which I was assigned.

Dismas House was the polar opposite of prison. A three-story federal-style turn-of-the-century building just off a main thoroughfare, it sat in the heart of my old state senate district.

A fence enclosed the yard, although not the front of the building. The first and most immediate difference was the location and its demographics. Manchester FCI was tucked deep in a mountain hollow in Kentucky's overwhelmingly white southeast edge, on top of a former coal mine; Dismas House sat in St. Louis City's nearly all-black Twenty-second Ward, where neither mountains nor forests penetrated the concrete jungle.

A second difference was that prison culture was almost entirely interior: most people weren't getting out any time soon, so most prisoners were inwardly focused. They focused on their hustles, their workouts, their sundry prison conflicts and dramas. Since the fifty or sixty men in the halfway house were at least somewhat free, they were focused on all that the world had to offer, with special attention to the long-forbidden fruits of wine (Boone's Farm and Mad Dog were favorites), weed (always blunts, never bongs), and women (in this realm, people seemed to be less particular).

Third, whereas prison rules were often enforced to a tee, halfway house rule violations were often ignored. The rules were pretty simple: once you had a job you could go to it, but then you had to be home within an hour of your shift ending. Your parole or probation officer could roll up on you at work or anywhere else, at his whim. Once you spent a few weeks working without incident, you could start receiving a limited number of three-hour evening passes, and if that went smoothly, you were in line a few weeks later for a six-hour weekend day pass. Assuming that you were always where you said you'd be and always picked up land lines when Dismas House or your PO called the place you promised to be, you could apply for a full weekend pass, and after doing that successfully, you were ready for full home confinement, which meant only that you had to get to Dismas House for twice-weekly drug tests and pick up the phone in the middle of the night when they called.

The relatively lax enforcement of rules resulted from the staff's orientation, which was completely different from that of the prison guards. COs were agents of the warden, almost always unequivocally on Team Prison, but halfway house staff were far more ambiguous, some seemingly aligned more closely with residents than management. One employee in particular looked the other way when residents scaled the fence to get drunk, high, and laid, and again when they hopped back over in time for evening counts. Some boasted about already having returned to their old lifestyle. The counts occasionally interrupted raucous dice games from which emanated the strong scent of marijuana; one staffer just shook his head, sighed, and moved on to the next room.

A fourth difference was the nature of crimes committed by men in the two facilities. Although nearly everyone I spoke with at Manchester FCI had done time in higher-security facilities, most were convicted of nonviolent crimes. They talked about the need to carry guns and some described gunfights, but that wasn't why they were locked up. Conversely, most of the guys in the halfway house appeared to have done time for armed criminal action, manslaughter, or even murder. One day I asked a dude in the weight room how much longer he planned to work out with the sixty-pound dumbbells, and he just stared at me. So I asked again, and he stared some more. I said, "All right then," and walked away. A third guy who was there waited about ten minutes until the dude with the dumbbells left, and then told me that the guy was a murderer and that I should probably be more careful, especially when he had dumbbells in his hand.

A final difference was personal. I had the sense that prison officials knew my story and were not enamored of it. During the first week, the captain intercepted my correspondence and called me down to scold me. Soon afterward, I was placed in the prison's most physically taxing job, though I had teaching experience that might have helped others. Conversely, when I arrived in the halfway house, I was treated well by the staff. In an eerie parallel, the halfway house director told me almost the exact same thing that the counselor had told me during my prison intake: "I saw what happened with your political career—what a waste that you're even here." But unlike the prison counselor, a midlevel cog in a massive system, the director was in a position to do something about it. When I told him that I was in the process of lining up a job to which I'd be going nine-to-five each day, he shook his head. "What do you have here, almost three months?" he asked, scanning my forms. "We oughta be able to get you outta here in three weeks so you're not taking up space somebody else really needs. Let me try to get you out of the barracks in the next forty-eight hours." The barracks was the basement: a ramshackle setup of bunk beds inhabited by the newest of arrivals, most of whom lacked jobs and the house privileges that accompanied them, such as night or weekend day passes—no one without a job was allowed out of the building for leisure. True to his word, I was upstairs with a single bunkie in forty-eight hours and out in three weeks, moved to home confinement for the end of my sentence.

And yet, as different as the two locales were, they were bound by a common poverty and desperation. Manchester was the capital of Clay County, the second-poorest majority-white county in the country, plagued by prescription drug abuse and violence, with a 2010 median household income of $16,271, leaving 40 percent of its residents in poverty. Similarly, the Twenty-second Ward was often cited as the city's most dangerous because of the inordinate number of murders that occurred there during the past decade. The areas both bred a deep sense of despair, even nihilism, about their future.

The men in the two facilities also shared a common survivalist instinct. Men at Manchester demonstrated amazing ingenuity and emotional strength, in some cases going over a decade with-out a single contact on the outside. Men in Dismas House also knew how to do exactly what was necessary to get by. One eve-ning about a week after I arrived, I earned my first evening pass. Gleefully heading toward the exit, I saw a cornrowed resident I recognized from the barracks; he put his arm around me and led me arm in arm out to his car. "This yo' first pass, Senator?" he asked.

"Yup," I said, grinning broadly.

"Yo' old lady ride witchu?"

"Yup. Came down to see me every month."

"Day-um! Thazza good woman. Look now, Senator, you be good to yo' old lady, yo?"

"You know I will, startin' in about thirty minutes!" We both laughed. I was only one week in and found this to be an unusually friendly gesture in a place where embraces seemed as rare as they were in prison. We reached his car and he released my arm, abruptly bid me good-bye ("All right"), and ducked inside.

The next day another halfway house resident who said he and his cousins used to play in my charity basketball tourna-ments approached me and urged me to stay away from the guy with the cornrows. Apparently, the cornrow guy was a snitch marked for revenge, and our friendly interlude had simply been his way of getting me to serve as a shield. Several murders oc-curred near the halfway house during my time there, and ac-cording to Dismas residents, that made perfect sense: this would be the first chance anyone in the area who believed he got snitched out by a resident—or had some other beef with one—would have to get revenge.

Just like everybody else leaving prison, I needed a job. Yes, I had some savings. Yes, my parents had money they could've loaned me in a pinch. But the quickest route back into the real world was a job. Not necessarily a career, but a job. So I contacted an old friend who wrote a daily political tip sheet covering Missouri politics and asked if he needed any help for a few months. He said sure, he couldn't pay much, but he totally understood and would be glad to have the help. He'd covered me from the beginning of my political career and saw where I might be able to add value: he had me quietly research potential subscribers for his newsletter and also do some writing for him. He was right: it didn't pay much, by the standards of journalism. But after making $5.25 per month unloading food trucks, I felt like Donald Trump when I opened my first paycheck.

I soon realized why my friend had less than a hundred newsletter subscribers: he hated to sell. Whereas he enjoyed talking to sources and could immerse himself in writing for hours, a single phone call to pitch a prospective subscriber exhausted him. But having known him for years, I knew what could motivate him: beer. And so one morning before work I stopped by a convenience store and picked up a six-pack of Bud Light bottles. Each time he closed a deal, I would hand him a beer, which he would swig like a parched man stranded on a desert isle.

After a very successful morning in which he nabbed three new subscribers, we left for a late lunch, after which we planned to head home. I packed the remaining brews into my backpack, and we walked up the street for barbecue wings at our favorite joint, Three Monkeys. About five minutes into our walk, a car pulled up behind us and then swerved to the side of the road, startling us. Out jumped Raoul Williams, my probation officer.

As probation officers go, Raoul was as good as I could've hoped for. Nearing retirement and having achieved a senior position, he didn't need to prove anything to anyone, and he wasn't trying to catch anyone in a violation and send them back to prison. He was clear in his expectations of me—that I must adhere to the rules of the halfway house, most notably that I notify the front desk every time I changed locations. As long as I did so, he was fair and reasonable.

But on this day, I had forgotten to notify him that I was leaving for lunch. And that wasn't my only mistake.

Over a year earlier, I'd been into the U.S. Department of Justice office to meet with a pretrial-services officer, who would write the presentencing report given to the judge slated to determine my fate. During that meeting, the investigator asked hundreds of questions, one of which had involved alcohol consumption. "How many times a week do you drink?" he asked.

"A few," I replied.

"When you drink, approximately how many drinks would you say you typically have?" he asked.

"A few."

"And would you say you've been drinking less than usual, more than usual, or the same lately?"

"Well, I'm about to go to prison," I replied. "So I'd say probably a little more than usual."

The investigator, a heavyset, baby-faced young man, did not acknowledge the attempt at humor, but the judge did, belatedly: she added a condition to my two-year probation that forbade me from drinking alcohol.

I was suddenly reminded of that prohibition as Raoul Williams rapidly approached us. "Mr. Smith," he greeted me with the tone of a scolding nun, "you appear to have gone missing."

"Oh God, I forgot to call and let the front desk know I was headed for my lunch break," I said apologetically.

"You need to call every time you change locations."

"Yes, I know. I'm sorry. This is my boss, he can confirm that we—"

"Yes, that's fine," Raoul interrupted. Then he squinted at me. "What's in the bag?"

Oh, shit. "Stuff for work." That was technically true.

The comment floated in the air. My heart pounded, and my stomach tightened as I forced a relaxed smile onto my face. I could see my mom shaking her head at me, handcuffed back in front of the same judge, who was also shaking her head as I tried to explain to her that I wasn't, in fact, drinking the beers but had just been using them to incentivize my boss and was carrying them back home with me and that any Breathalyzer would've confirmed as much and that, yes, I understood that it sounded implausible, but I was just trying to be a good employer and help sell subscrip—

"Okay," said Raoul, "have a nice lunch. And let me know before you leave next time."

Bullet dodged.

It was a bullet not unlike the ones that felled so many of the guys I'd done time with, many of whom were back on probation violations after one dirty piss test or one night when they slept through a 2:00 A.M. phone call trying to confirm their whereabouts or one failure to show for a meeting with a PO when the bus was late. I dodged the bullet in part because Raoul never saw me as someone who would violate. At most of our weekly appointments, he'd ask me about various politicians or the upcoming election or some public policy in which he was interested. This was, I am sure, nothing like the probation experience of most of my Manchester colleagues.

Finding employment was far more difficult for most of the other residents. Many spent the day literally pounding the pavement, going from fast-food joint to body shop to laundromat, looking for work. To say that it was inefficient is to state the obvious, but again, some of them had no idea how to look for work online. It was sad to watch a man lose a little bit more of his dignity each day he came back to Dismas House without a job, as was the case for a few of the guys I met.

Finding employment for ex-offenders has huge benefits—for them, for their families, and for communities—but none is more important than reducing recidivism. High recidivism rates have far-reaching impacts. Except in cases of parole violations (failing to apprise halfway house monitors of one's whereabouts, not showing up for meetings with parole officers, missing a drug test, etc.), recidivism means first and foremost that new crimes are being committed, which jeopardizes public safety and creates new victims, at significant financial and psychological cost to individuals and society at large.

Second, high recidivism rates damage the lives of individual offenders: whereas onetime offenders are occasionally granted a true second chance by employers and society, repeat offenders are usually written off, even by family and friends.

Third, recidivism damages the families of offenders. Children bear the brunt of this, often experiencing severe psychological trauma, material hardship, and prolonged family instability as a result of parental incarceration. These effects often cause reactive behaviors that lead the children of incarcerated parents to their own bouts with the criminal justice system.[11]

Fourth, recidivism increases the already burgeoning costs of prison, including land and construction costs, personnel, training, health care, facility upkeep, energy, and food. Even a slight reduction in recidivism rates would generate massive cost savings in many of these areas, and allow for the closing of some facilities.

Fifth, recidivism has a broader impact on society. When approximately two-thirds of all prisoners reoffend, society dismisses offenders as irreparably flawed and will be even more reluctant to make modest investments in rehabilitation that might ultimately break the mass incarceration cycle.

Recidivism reduction would have significant positive human and fiscal impacts in each of those areas. And yet, as we've seen, the prison system is practically designed to encourage the terrible outcomes we get. But until prison reform advocates are able to overcome the layers of political, psychological, and procedural resistance—much of it shaped by the political and financial goals of self-interested actors—prisoners won't learn any new practical skills on the inside that will help them get back on their feet upon release. They'll just learn new hustles.

Instead of ten weeks, I had to spend only three in the halfway house, thanks to my journalist pal and a helpful Dismas House director. Moving back in with Teresa went exactly as I'd spent the year hoping it would. Soon we were planning our wedding—but suddenly there was a hitch. Teresa's father—a preacher in Amarillo—was slated to perform the ceremony, and we had to call him to inform him of a slight change of plans: we had to move the wedding up a few months. Here I was, a Jewish agnostic, unemployed, an ex-felon—four strikes against me. And now I had impregnated his daughter. Would he still be willing to perform the ceremony?

"Reckon you all got things a little out of order," he said gruffly, pausing dramatically for an extra beat. "But every baby's a blessing." We heaved a collective sigh of relief and adjusted all of our plans in order to have a much smaller wedding.

As we prepared for the big day, I applied to consult for the Missouri Workforce Housing Association, an umbrella group of organizations that support the development and maintenance of affordable housing for struggling families. It was a small, lightly funded group that wanted help recruiting new members, raising money, and managing government affairs. It seemed like a great chance to work on an issue that had inspired me to run for office in the first place. The interview was my first in a decade. Without a car postrelease, I arrived in a sweat-soaked suit after riding my bike over. "Why should we take a chance on you?" pushed a board member near the end of the interview. "Why should *we* be the ones to take a hit for hiring you? Wouldn't it be smarter for us to let someone else do it first and then bring you on later?"

Maybe I was still arrogant from my senate days. Maybe I was more candid after my lie led to trouble. Maybe I was displaying the surliness of somebody fresh out of prison. Or maybe I just had nothing left to lose. "You know, for what you're paying, you'd be getting a heck of a deal," I replied. "If you have another candidate who gets grassroots organizing, fund-raising, Missouri politics, and the legislative process as well as I do, can call senators or the house speaker to see what's going on—and would work for this price and isn't fresh out of prison, you should hire him."

Then I politely thanked them for their time and left. Here I was, a guy who had a Ph.D., years of relevant political experience, deep contacts among the policymakers who would be determining affordable housing policy in the years to come, and three hundred references, in essence—the letters written on my behalf by many of the state's leading figures. And I was struggling to get a part-time consulting gig that paid an entry-level salary. As I rode home that day, I thought about all the obstacles to employment the guys from Manchester would face without the benefits of my education, my professional experience, my many and prominent contacts, my fluency—my whiteness. It would not be easy for them. Hell, it wasn't easy for me.

I found out later that some of the organization's board members were appalled by my "take me or leave me" attitude in response to the final question. But they hired me to consult for them, and I remain with them in a role that has deepened over the past four years.

Around the same time, I also decided I'd try to return to teaching. I visited a website for political scientists and saw an opening for a professorship in urban policy at the New School in New York City, and decided to apply. That was another interesting interview; when I profusely thanked the search committee chair for overlooking my criminal record, he replied drily that my background "definitely helped me stand out from the other applicants." I again benefited from advantages available to very few ex-offenders, including reference letters from other academics. I received an offer, and now I teach graduate courses on the legislative process, campaign management, policy analysis, urban political economy, and incarceration, as well as a wide-ranging course called "Power, Strategy, and Social Change."

Literally sixty seconds after I walked into my first New School class and began introducing myself, Teresa's water broke. It was a bit bizarre to tell them that I was a former state senator who had spent the previous year in prison and regrettably had to leave before getting to know them because my wife and I were about to have a baby. Indeed, I overheard one of them reference the MTV series in which celebrities fall prey to elaborate practical jokes as I walked out. "Yo, I think we just got Punk'd," he said, to much laughter. Teresa and I now have an energetic and defiant three-year-old, Charlie, as well as a delightful eighteen-month-old, Sydney.

The last piece of my reemergence is the one that could ultimately have the most impact. I speak about prison reform to various state legislatures and at universities and advise several organizations working to reform our criminal justice system to provide more education and opportunities to current and just-released offenders. They include American Prison Data Systems, which seeks to put a tablet in the hands of every incarcerated American, and the Prison Entrepreneurship Program, a seven-month university-certified program that, among other things, leverages top executive talent to help prisoners craft full-scale business plans. I work with other organizations as part of the New School's innovative client projects, in which I connect graduate students with various public and nonprofit sector agencies seeking to improve various aspects of New York City's criminal justice system. Some of the organizations we've advised focus on convincing policymakers of the need for in-prison educational opportunities, a role for which I feel well suited after seeing the system from many different angles. And perhaps, in some karmic way, all of this helps me partially repay the guys who befriended and protected me in Kentucky.

Perhaps because I spent over a year suppressing so many of my emotions, my post-prison experience has given rise to a much wider range of emotions than did the actual serving of the sentence. Certain sounds or smells flood me with memories and feelings relating to my prosecution and incarceration. Several times, I would hear an unexpected knock at the front door, and my heart would pound as I crept to the window only to see the UPS guy, not an FBI agent. While sitting alone in my office at work late at night, I would hear a set of keys jangle and feel all my muscles lock up before realizing that it was just a janitor, not Tuck coming to toss my cell. And on a hot night, lacking a bar, I might do pull-ups off the balcony of my house, a lockdown-style improvisation, only to see a passerby, alarmed by this strange behavior in a town where normal people joined gyms, steer her child to the other side of the street as if she could smell the convict in me. These were fleeting moments, but not a day passed in which my mind was completely free of them. And again, many of the people I did time with, in the memorable words of my first bunkie, did more prison time on the toilet than I did time. And their scars no doubt took far longer to fade.

Many experiences felt surreal, as the specter of prison floated above so many conversations and situations. One such experience occurred shortly after I arrived in New York, when a New School colleague invited me to a party. It was a bright, accomplished group, intimidatingly so, and with their thoughtfully trimmed beards and Susan Sontag glasses, they seemed to me the embodiment of the Brooklyn hipster-intellectual fashions then in vogue. They were young college professors, *New York Times* reporters, social entrepreneurs, and other assorted do-gooders. The only person I knew was the host, who kindly introduced me around as a New School prof teaching in their public policy graduate program (yawn) who once ran for Congress (yawn) and served in the Missouri Senate (slightly more polite yawn).

Midwesternness emanated from me like stink from a skunk, or at least that's how it felt when I used the word "wife" instead of partner, the self-consciously gender-neutral term they used when referring to spouses or longtime companions. But when the host told them where I'd spent 2010, they perked up; the curiosity was insatiable.

Was it white-collar? (Maybe 5 percent.) *Was it violent?* (Occasionally.) *Did you get in fights?* (A couple.) *Did you get hurt?* (Yes, but not too badly.) *What were the people like?* (More interesting and less pretentious than you.) One stammered, *Did you get . . . uh . . . was there a lot of . . . uh . . . sex?*

At that point I hadn't thought about Porkchop and JT for over a year, since leaving prison. But at that Brooklyn party, I found myself feeling defensive on their part. Those incomparably enlightened and erudite hipsters, themselves mostly unattached and plotting their next conquests ("So, she's not looking for anything too serious, right?" the host asked me when I mentioned a dating prospect to him), were visibly fascinated with the sexualized brutality of prison rape. I found myself wondering if any of them would ever experience the type of intimacy—and the indulgence of it, community sentiment be damned—that JT and Porkchop shared. I doubted it. In some ways, everything after prison seemed so much shallower.

"There was some," I replied. "And some love, too."

Then there was a different kind of emotion—pure gratitude. There was one day in particular that stands out in my mind, a February day when I was headed downtown from Penn Station to the New School on my bike to substitute-teach for a colleague. As I sped down Seventh Avenue, ice pellets whipped against my face, thanks to an Arctic mix of icy temperatures and gale-force winds. I suddenly felt annoyed. *Why did I ride my fucking bike today? If I was gonna ride, why didn't I just lock it up at Penn Station? Why did I even agree to sub for some guy I barely know? Why didn't I just call in sick?*

And then suddenly it hit me, hit me harder than sleet or wind, harder than a double-decker tourist bus: I was free. Wind? Ice pellets? Who gave a fuck?! I was on my way to teach brilliant and engaged grad students, in an incredibly vibrant city, and when I finished, I would be free to go home and snuggle up with my wife and kid. I flashed back to my year of backbreaking work in the prison warehouse, and the prison beefs I got in, and the human misery I saw, and the looks on the faces of Teresa and my parents and brother when they visited. What I wouldn't have given on any of those days to ride out of that prison into a frigid sleet thrashing my face, free to ride anywhere I liked! At that instant on Seventh Avenue, I knew that I would never again take any of it for granted.

That gratitude stayed with me. Even years later, when I attended a conference at the dawn of 2015 but found that my luggage was four days late, a friend marveled that I didn't balk at having to wear the same clothes for three days. "Look," I replied, "when you wore the same clothes for three hundred days, three doesn't seem so bad." I felt such gratitude that I was amused, not annoyed, when I heard that after seeing me discussing politics on MSNBC, prosecutor Hal Goldsmith was telling people that he "made" me.

Prison made me a better teacher, advocate, friend, father, and husband than I'd have otherwise been. It helped me understand why Steve made the choices he made, and why I made the choices I did. It helped me see what is truly important; nothing gives you perspective like the sweetness of your baby's breath at dawn. Politics equipped me with the savvy I needed to get through prison intact. But prison gave me the perspective I needed to successfully reenter society.

Post-prison—especially after the Ferguson mess embroiled St. Louis, and the region cried out for leaders who could build bridges across racial lines—some suggested that I run for office again. But now I knew what the game was like. When I went away, I had nine thousand numbers on my cellphone. After resigning and pleading guilty, I never heard from eight thousand of those people. This helped reinforce my appreciation for the people who reached out to offer support, and especially for those who continued writing me in prison. I wanted to spend the rest of my days focused on my true friends.

I found irony—and sometimes tragedy—in the stories of disgraced pols who rush for immediate reinvention in the same ego-nurturing and soul-crushing arena that initially got them in trouble. It's as if the Weiners and Sanfords of the world have determined that the artificial politico personas they have so painstakingly created are the only versions of themselves that they can still recognize. True redemption requires you to hit the pause button, to sublimate ambition and reflect on what truly matters. And it requires you to reevaluate your mistakes.

About ten feet from the bottom of the cliff that served as one

of Manchester's natural barriers was a boundary line. In reminding us of that line during orientation, a stern prison administrator alluded obliquely to the COs on alert in nearby guard
towers, whom we often heard doing target practice in preparation, we assumed, for a riot or the possible sighting of an inmate
attempting to make a run for it.

One thing was certain, and seems even more so today, given
the spate of police-involved shootings occurring in the far more
transparent outside world: if you wandered near the line and
a sniper imagines you to have crossed it—or gets a little trigger-
happy or is just having a bad day—it could be all over for you.
And when they report your death, no forensic investigator will
conclude that you were actually—barely—on the right side of the
line. You'll just go down as another escapee intercepted by a
lawman's bullet. So you learn quickly not to go *anywhere near*
the line.

In the haze of a campaign, when you are sleep-deprived,
frayed, and under intense pressure from donors, staff, volunteers, voters, and yourself, it can be easy to lose sight of the
larger picture. And in business, near the closing of a huge sale,
merger, or acquisition; or in sports, in the heat of battle; or in
your personal life, it can be tempting to seek an extra edge, shade
a truth, cut a corner. Making that mistake cost me my political
career, my reputation (temporarily, I hope), and a precious year
of my life.

I decided that in my new life—long before I would ever reach
that climactic moment of decision—I would try not to go anywhere near the line.

Like the majority of ex-offenders, I would be back inside a prison
in less than three years.

But unlike most of the others, I was returning as the commencement speaker for the Prison Entrepreneurship Program's

spring 2013 graduating class at Cleveland Correctional Center in Texas.

The four finalists who presented their business plans as venture capital pitches to over a hundred executives prior to the commencement ceremony were more polished than just about any graduate student I have ever seen make a public presentation. Each was substantive, analytic, and persuasive—and each made contacts that day that could help them turn their ideas into reality. Perhaps even more important than the practical skills participants gained was the camaraderie they developed: a special brotherhood was clear when the winner was announced and was immediately and genuinely congratulated by the other three finalists and dozens of other inmates. It was exhilarating to see a group of men inside a prison—a place thought to embody the oppositional culture that characterizes so many troubled youths, a place where gangs exemplify racial hatred and division—supporting each other so positively and without regard to color or ethnicity.

After my speech, I spent several hours meeting inmates and their families, hearing stories, answering questions, giving advice on reentry. As I left for the airport, one inmate pulled me aside. "You got a good heart, brother. I know you were makin' moves, doin' good things—like that bill to help dads. But you know what, you gonna have more impact now than you coulda ever had before. Trust me."

I took that as my charge: my activism would be a small way to repay the inmates who'd befriended and protected me—and the millions of others like them. Politics had helped give me the savvy to get through prison intact. Prison gave me the perspective to understand how we must transform the politics and policies of our criminal justice system—and the impetus to help make it happen.

EPILOGUE

Much of this book has examined the problems of mass incarceration through the lens of my experience. Several ideas offered within would reduce the size and oppressive nature of the carceral state. Encouragingly, some similar proposals finally appear to be gaining traction in various states, thanks in part to the tremendous work of many longtime advocates, as well as the policy leadership of the Pew Foundation's Public Safety Performance Project (PSPP). The PSPP diagnoses the factors driving prison growth and helps develop evidence-based policies to reduce prison costs and recidivism rates while enhancing public safety.

There is also new momentum at the national level. An array of grassroots and elite-driven groups from across the ideological spectrum have sprouted up in recent years to challenge mass incarceration. Organizations ranging from JustLeadershipUSA, which trains formerly incarcerated people who lead state-level efforts to "humanize" prisoners and build a broad-based reform movement, to the Texas Public Policy Foundation, a leading libertarian policy institute advocating for shorter sentences, have gained grassroots strength and national media exposure. These groups have joined the well-funded, transpartisan Coalition for Public Safety, which is working to bring the successful reform efforts from the Sunbelt states, where they have recently gained traction, to the new Republican-controlled Congress. After his reelection and without the prospect of another one, President Barack Obama has rather belatedly evinced interest in criminal justice reform. Attorney General Eric Holder recently directed prosecutors to seek lesser sentences for certain non-violent offenders, and bipartisan legislation has been filed by Senators Rand Paul, Cory Booker, and Pat Leahy to reduce mandatory minimum sentences for nonviolent drug offenders, expunge certain offenses from records after a period of time, ban employment discrimination against ex-offenders, and restore voting rights and access to various federal benefits for ex-offenders. Paul has taken the lead in scrambling traditional party politics on mass incarceration. "Three out of four people in prison right now for nonviolent crimes are black or brown," he told the Urban League in July 2014. "Our prisons are bursting with young men of color, and our communities are full of broken families. I won't sit idly by and watch our criminal justice system continue to consume, confine, and define our young men."[1] One might argue, of course, that it is far easier for a white Republican seeking the presidency to raise these issues than it was for a black Democrat. The Obama experience, of course, must be understood in context. He was the first Democratic president since Bill Clinton—who sought a right-of-center posture on crime so badly that he flew back to Arkansas from New Hampshire just before its 1992 presidential primary in order to execute a mentally handicapped black man who had insisted on saving the pecan pie from his final meal for later.

Given the disproportionate impact on blacks, Democrats' most reliable voting block, black Democrats were until recently the most prominent voices on the issue.[2] But Republicans have lately taken the lead, which can be explained in part by a cursory analysis of the two parties' respective electoral coalitions. There are three main wings to the modern Republican Party—Wall Street, Main Street, and Easy Street—and all have compelling reasons to support criminal justice reform. Fiscal conservatives are concerned about balancing budgets and belatedly realizing how much the United States spends to incarcerate people; religious conservatives influenced by Charles Colson's Prison Fellowship see offenders' opportunity for redemption, and many support more humane treatment of them; and libertarian conservatives chafe at intrusive surveillance and draconian drug laws that can put people in prison for life after a third drug offense.

While Democrats decry the prison-industrial complex and its vast human toll, prominent Democrats like Senators Dianne Feinstein and Chuck Schumer actually helped build it. Feinstein and Schumer cut their political teeth in the early 1980s when the Democratic Party was doing pretzels to avoid being tagged as soft on crime and struggled to shed the cartoonishly libertine 1960s image that presidential candidates Walter Mondale and Michael Dukakis seemed only to reinforce. This effort had the Democrats "outbidding" Republicans on the number of crimes subject to mandatory minimums and on sentencing lengths for these crimes—and doing so on crimes disproportionately committed by African Americans.[3] Their cynicism is striking, particularly given the policy impact on their party's staunchest constituency—African Americans. Following the 378–16 House passage of the 1986 Anti-Drug Abuse Act, which expanded mandatory minimums, one House Democrat observed that anti-drug legislation is "out of control . . . but of course I'm for it."[4]

Though some Democrats admitted that their efforts were rooted in electoral calculations, certain cases seem to suggest terrible miscalculations. For instance, liberals such as the late senator Edward Kennedy initially conceived of the U.S. Sentencing Commission as an agency that could reduce sentences and racial inequities; instead, its incorporation of mandatory minimums into a larger sentencing grid ended up increased other sentences proportionally.[5] Other liberals backed funding to professionalize police forces in order to reduce brutality but ended up institutionalizing an urban police state that swept more citizens into the system.[6] More offenders meant more prisons, empowering correctional officers' unions who would later help pass noxious "Three Strikes" laws in California and two dozen other states.

While significant constituencies of the Republican Party move toward criminal justice reform, the Democratic Party's major wings remain split on the issue. In some states, the party is constrained by the staunch support it receives from correctional officers' unions, who are skeptical of any major reform that would threaten their jobs en masse. Even some young progressive stars like California attorney general Kamala Harris are not pristine.[7] Harris said she was surprised to learn that lawyers from her office had argued against the release of eligible nonviolent prisoners so the state could retain them as forest firefighters. Indeed, few congressional Democrats have been as outspoken or eloquent as Rand Paul in advocating reform, despite his relative lateness to the cause. Though reform may be years away, Paul's advocacy may be opening up enough political space to make it feasible.

The recent, relative depoliticization of criminal justice issues is a positive development, given that historically, heated partisan competition fostered carceral state development. Look, for instance, at the region where incarceration boomed more than any other since 1970. Criminal justice issues rarely rose to prominence during the first half of the twentieth century when conservative Democrats dominated Sunbelt states from North Carolina to Arizona. More broadly, ideological conflict was suppressed since battles were fought entirely within the Democratic Party, often around personality and symbolic issues.[8] But starting in the 1950s, these states began to develop two-party competition with newly visible ideological schisms: Republicans first gained ground in silk-stocking Sunbelt suburbs during the 1950s and in rural areas starting in 1964, while more liberal urban Democrats successfully challenged old-line conservative Democrats.[9] Conservatives had new electoral incentives to emphasize wedge issues such as crime, and amid widespread urban unrest in the mid- to late 1960s, they did not hesitate to do so. Indeed, Nixon's 1968 "law and order" strategy and less subtle 1972 Southern strategy were designed with Sunbelt voters in mind. That was the beginning of a half-century-long trend toward party polarization, which facilitated the "hyperpoliticization of penal policy."[10]

But now every major faction of the modern Republican Party has stopped pushing "tough on crime" policies—and some Republicans are even taking the lead in condemning them, as Rand Paul did in the wake of the heavily militarized police response to unrest in Ferguson, Missouri. By 2015, Republicans rarely bludgeoned Democrats over crime issues, so Democrats had little need to match or outbid them in an attempt to neutralize the issue.

Rather, transpartisan coalitions have formed to try to overhaul our penal system and substantially reduce incarceration. Left-leaning groups such as the ACLU, the Brennan Center for

Justice, the Sentencing Project, and the Center for American Progress have joined with conservative luminaries such as Grover Norquist, Newt Gingrich, Rick Perry, and the Koch brothers to champion major reforms. Many of these groups have a stated goal of cutting the prison population in half by 2030 and have formed a well-funded, transpartisan Coalition for Public Safety to pursue that goal.[11] Observers have expressed a new optimism about the reforms that could emerge from this strange-bedfellows coalition at a time of divided government in Washington. "I've been working in this field since 1990, and this is certainly the most hopeful time I've seen in that twenty-five-year period," said ACLU National Prison Project director David Fathi. "There is an openness to fundamentally rethinking our approach to crime and deviant behavior in a way that I've never seen before."[12] Vikrant Reddy, top policy analyst at Texas-based Right on Crime, struck a similar note. "There's a bill to reform federal mandatory minimums that is co-authored by both Rand Paul and Patrick Leahy," he said. "You just can't conceive of people with more different world views in Washington, D.C."[13]

And so giddy advocates and progressive commentators (myself included) have heralded the arrival of a criminal justice reform "moment." They point to encouraging state-level reforms in more than a dozen (mostly Republican-governed) states; federal directives instructing prosecutors to seek lighter sentences; and recently filed bipartisan legislation that would reduce mandatory minimums, add expungement opportunities, ban employment discrimination against ex-offenders, and restore voting rights. And they cite exhaustive new research debunking the theory that incarceration deters future crime; in fact, an exhaustive 2015 study showed that despite massive growth in the prison population, incarceration has had essentially zero impact on crime rates. Crime rose during the 1970s and 1980s as prison populations increased; it plummeted in the 1990s and

2000s as incarceration continued to surge, making the non-correlation between the number of people imprisoned and the incidence of crime fairly evident.[14]

But advocates may be wise to take a cue from prisoners and manage expectations. Disappointment is a constant in prison, but many prisoners seemed particularly stung when their high hopes for reform after President Obama's election were dashed upon learning that the crack-powder disparity reduction legislation he signed would not be retroactive. "One black man in the White House," went a familiar refrain, "one million niggas in the Big House."

Reformers' ambitious goal to cut the prison population in half is admirable and may even be possible; a similar strategy to halve the (much smaller) number of incarcerated juveniles proved effective. Indeed, advocates may be able to persuade policymakers to enact alternative sentences (i.e., home confinement) for certain crimes or divert more people to mental health or substance abuse programs. But since more than half of the 1.3 million people in state prisons are convicted of violent crimes, halving the number of incarcerated people would likely mean touching the "third rail" of penal reform by paroling or cutting sentences for some violent offenders, not just the so-called non, non, nons—nonviolent, nonserious, and non–sex offender criminals.[15] Assuming a relatively steady stream of offenders, some would need to be released early to cut the prison population in half, even if all nonviolent offenders were released early or detoured from prison. Of course, removing low-level offenders from prison would likely lower the violent population, too, since often-brutal prison conditions can have a "criminogenic" effect, turning neophytes into repeat offenders.[16]

Reformers should also remember that even if Democrats rebuff their party's correctional employee unions to pass disruptive reforms, prison staff may impede policy implementation.

As scholars Jeffrey Pressman and Aaron Wildavsky as well as Michael Lipsky argue, high-level policy change may not lead to effective implementation if frontline actors (wardens, prison program staff, and COs) disagree with or feel threatened by the thrust of the new policy. Based on my experience, persuading prison staff that inmates are worth any type of investment may be the most difficult obstacle to surmount. It is at least possible that the views of prison administrators would adjust to comport with the rapidly evolving views of political elites, but successful implementation of major prison reform requires such changes to filter all the way down to "street-level bureaucrats"— the COs who must be relied on to help implement any program.

Indeed, there's no clearer proof of Upton Sinclair's theory that man won't accept change that directly threatens his financial interests. He will continue to see things the way he wants to see them. We may call him willful or selfish or exactly what's wrong with the system, and certainly his attitude is each of these. But it's just another form of self-preservation, and that's what makes it so hard to change.

You may be wondering what became of KY, Big E, Ville, Big C, Dred, and the other characters described herein. During my first year out, I sent Christmas presents (money) to several of them, and then Father's Day presents (books about different career options, mostly) the following spring, and more money for some of their birthdays—even though no one in prison celebrated birthdays, which served mostly as a sad reminder of their lives ticking away. But when we moved to Hoboken, New Jersey, for my New School job, Teresa, Charlie, and I were crammed into a five-hundred-square-foot apartment, and we had to store all of our books and papers. One day after our belongings arrived from St. Louis and we had hauled them down into basement lockers, Hurricane Irene hit. I lost several hundred books to the floodwaters, but more important, much of what I wrote in prison sustained water damage. The piece of cardboard on which I had written the addresses and prison numbers of people before leaving was almost completely unreadable.

I stopped writing the guys in FCI Manchester. I stopped wiring money and sending gifts.

I could've figured out their information. It wouldn't have been that difficult. But I had a new job in a new city, a new apartment, a new wife, a new baby, and soon, another baby on the way and a new house. I stayed in touch with some guys who had already gotten out—that was easy. We could be Facebook friends, we could e-mail or text each other. But I didn't make time to stay in touch with the guys on the inside, which was a lot harder—most couldn't afford to use the prison's primitive but expensive* e-mail system, requiring old-fashioned snail mail. And who has time for that in this era of Google chats and Twitter messages and Snapchats, where instant communication equals instant gratification?

I'm ashamed of this, and I'm trying to remedy it. I hope that there is a second edition of this book and that in it, I am able to report success.

But this is instructive. It's indicative of what happens to long-term prisoners as people fade out of their lives during their bid. I was gone for less than an entire year, and many people faded out of mine. Riding with someone for a decade or longer requires tremendous dedication. It's a dedication few people have, which helps explain why so many men lose touch with friends and relatives during long bids, which research suggests helps explain the sky-high recidivism rate at the root of

---

* The prison's e-mail system allowed one to compose, reply, or delete on a black screen. It cost prisoners $6/hr, which was prohibitively expensive for most of them.

American mass incarceration. As I commit myself to reconnecting with the warehouse crew, I hope that everyone reading this strives to reconnect with anyone they know who is behind bars or recently did time. And for those readers who don't know anyone currently or recently incarcerated, I hope you will volunteer to help people who are, either inside or outside of prison. Even my mom, so impatient with her son's mistakes, is doing so and has employed and helped turn around one ex-offender's life over the past four years. She recently signed up for a second mentee. So while broad policy reform remains critical, until we achieve it, my mom offers an unlikely example of a grassroots strategy to ameliorate our nation's carceral crisis: one person at a time, just like her son's first political campaign.

ACKNOWLEDGMENTS

This book was possible because so many of my fellow prisoners shared their hopes, dreams, fears, and aspirations with me. I want to thank all of them for doing so.

A special thanks to KY and Big E from the warehouse, who taught me the proper way to stack boxes—it's counterintuitive— and looked out for me more generally. You guys saved me from myself more than once.

Thanks also to Gill for the laughs, to Lewis for storing my scribbled notes far away from the COs' hunches, and to Danny for helping design lockdown workouts.

My parents have put up with more than any two parents should have to endure from one child. Enough said.

I won't soon forget telling my brother I was going to prison, outside an Oberweis Dairy store. After asking if I thought he could get away with harming certain involved individuals, he lent me the money to help cover my legal bills.

Speaking of my legal bills! Thanks to Richard Greenberg and Kevin O'Malley, whose wisdom guided me through the process and helped me achieve a slightly below-the-guidelines sentence.

More thanks to:

Everyone who reached out and offered to write letters to the judge on my behalf, and especially those who did so at risk to their own political careers. I'm lookin' at you, Steve Tilley, Don Calloway, Chris Koster, Jason Crowell, Brian Wahby, Eric Schmitt, Susan Montee, and many, many more.

Scott Rupp, I list you separately, for offering to pay my mortgage while I was away, despite having five kids of your own to support.

My stalwart ex-aide, now attorney/children's advocate Kailey Burger, who received the earliest versions of this, freshly transferred from napkins to paper, and transcribed my scribbling.

Jen Haro, who along with Kailey helped me keep in touch with the outside world during 2010 and who along with Jack Coatar helped me mollify Red via Coco.

Connor Raso, for helping me with way too many things to mention over the past fifteen years and for your unsurpassed loyalty.

Dave Buckner, my lifelong friend and teammate to the end, for keeping me up when I was down and knocking me down the minute I got too high.

Adrienne and Lis Smith, for the steady stream of political and historical biographies, which helped sustain me through many difficult nights in prison.

Dave Drebes, for the reentry help, the Jack Daniel's, and the wings.

Chris Hite, for the total lack of pity with which he reached out to me upon my return about a job opportunity in affordable housing. ("Frankly, I'm calling because I know you'll do a great job, and we'll be able to pay you a tenth of what we'd have had to pay you had you resigned under different circumstances.")

Kathy Sorkin, for helping convince MOWHA to hire me, despite my sweaty interview.

Gary Miller, Paul Frymer, Bill Lowry, Brady Baybeck, Jay Barth, and David Kimball for shepherding me through my dissertation and offering professional guidance upon my reentry, and lasting friendship since.

Jonathan Miller, who reached out and asked me to write a blog post for *The Recovering Politician,* and thereby became the first editor of what would become this book, as well as a lifelong friend.

Andrew White, who chaired the search committee that hired me and has committed his life to improving the lives of New York City's invisible children.

All my colleagues at Milano, but especially Dean Michelle Depass, Alec Gershberg, Alex Schwartz, and Lisa Servon for their patience with my peripatetic nature and conference calls interrupted by screaming toddlers.

Julia Foulkes, for inspiring me to merge my two lives, coteach a course on incarceration, and situate my experience within the broader phenomenon of mass incarceration.

Krystal Ball, my first friend in New York City—two Midwesterners and ex-politicos trying to survive in new careers in the big city. Thank you and your family for making life here a little better for all of us.

Jeremy Gregg, former chief development officer for the Prison Entrepreneurship Program, and Adam Smith, formerly of American Prison Data Systems, for reaching out and introducing me to two amazing organizations.

Adam Eaglin, my agent at Cheney Literary, and Elyse Cheney, for taking a chance on me, and to Adam in particular for his precocious understanding of the inscrutable literary world.

Yaniv Soha, for believing that this book deserved an audience.

Tim Bartlett, my editor, on whose desk this book fell once Yahiv moved to a different publisher, and who turned out to have an uncanny sense of me, the book, and the audience; and Tim's assistant, Claire Lampen, whose book description nailed it on the first try, and who had to deal with the angst and befuddlement of a first-time print author.

And of course, to you, Teresa, for riding with me when nearly everyone figured you'd leave and for giving me the greatest and most maddening gifts in the world, Charlie and Sydney.

NOTES

Introduction

1. Jill Filipovic, "America's Private Prison System Is a National Disgrace," *Guardian,* June 13, 2013.

1. "The Missile's Already Left the Silo"

1. Sam Dillon, "Study Finds High Rate of Imprisonment Among Dropouts," *New York Times,* October 8, 2009.

2. Dave Drebes, "Smith's 1.6% Loss in 3rd District Inspires 'What-ifs,'" *St. Louis Business Journal,* August 8, 2004.

3. Jeff Smith, *Ferguson in Black and White* (Amazon Publishing, 2014).

2. "Have Some Respect, Mr. 90210!"

1. United States Sentencing Commission, *Report to Congress: Mandatory Minimum Penalties in the Federal Criminal Justice System,* October 2011.

2. Fatema Gunja, *Race and the War on Drugs,* American Civil Liberties Union, May 2003; www.aclu.org/files/Files/ACF4F34.pdf.

3. David Arenberg, "A Reflection on Anti-Semitism on the Yard," Southern Poverty Law Center Intelligence Report, Winter 2009, Issue 136,

http://www.splcenter.org/get-informed/intelligence-report/browse-all-issues
/2009/winter/a-jew-in-prison.

4. Leo Carroll, "Race, Ethnicity, and the Social Order of the Prison," in *The Pains of Imprisonment,* eds. R. Johnson and H. Toch (Beverly Hills, CA: Sage, 1982); also see Alice Goffman, *On the Run: Fugitive Life in an American City* (Chicago: University of Chicago Press, 2014).

5. United States Sentencing Commission, *Report to Congress: Mandatory Minimum Penalties in the Federal Criminal Justice System,* October 2011.

6. Arenberg, "A Reflection on Anti-Semitism."

7. Kevin N. Wright, "Race and Economic Marginality in Explaining Prison Adjustment," *Journal of Research in Crime and Delinquency* 26, no. 67 (1989); see also Jennifer L. Skeema, John F. Edens, Glenn M. Sanford, Lori H. Colwell, "Psychopathic Personality and Racial/Ethnic Differences Reconsidered: A Reply to Lynn (2002)," *Personality and Individual Differences* 35 (2003): 1439–1462.

8. R. Johnson, *Culture and Crisis in Confinement* (Lexington, MA: Heath, 1972).

9. Frederic Block, *Disrobed: An Inside Look at the Life and Work of a Federal Trial Judge* (New York: Thomson Reuters Westlaw, 2012).

10. Edward Huntington Williams, "Negro Cocaine 'Fiends' Are a New Southern Menace: Murder and Insanity Increasing Among Lower Class Blacks Because They Have Taken to 'Sniffing' Since Deprived of Whisky by Prohibition," *New York Times,* February 8, 1914.

11. Block, *Disrobed.*

12. Maya Szalavitz, "Blacks, Bias and Marijuana: Did Drug Stigma Contribute to Trayvon Martin's Death?" *Time,* March 27, 2012; Rashad Robinson, "Unite the Two New Yorks: End Discriminatory Marijuana Arrests," *Huffington Post,* June 18, 2012; Mick Dumke and Ben Joravsky, "Mind the Grass Gap: Nearly Nine of Ten Chicagoans Convicted with Pot Are Black Men," *Chicago Reader,* September 6, 2011; Lucia Graves, "Gross Racial Disparities in California Pot Arrests," *Huffington Post,* May 25, 2011.

13. Maya Szalavitz, "Study: Whites More Likely to Abuse Drugs Than Blacks," *Time,* November 7, 2011; see also tables at Substance Abuse and Mental Health Data Archive, 2011, http://www.icpsr.umich.edu /quicktables/quickconfig.do?34481-0001_all.

14. Human Rights Watch, *Decades of Disparity: Drug Arrests and Race in the United States,* Table 2: U.S. Rates of Adult Drug Arrests, 1980–2007, 7; http://www.hrw.org/sites/default/files/reports/us0309web_1.pdf.

15. United States Sentencing Commission, *Report on the Continuing Impact of United States v. Booker on Federal Sentencing*, 2012, 8; http://www.ussc.gov/news/congressional-testimony-and-reports/booker-reports/report-continuing-impact-united-states-v-booker-federal-sentencing.

16. J. B. Jacobs, "Race Relations and the Prison Subculture," in eds. N. Morris and M. Tonry, *Crime and Justice: An Annual Review of Research*, vol. 1 (Chicago: University of Chicago Press, 1979), 1–28.

17. Ibid.

18. Laurel P. Richmond and Corey W. Johnson, "'It's a Race War': Race and Leisure Experiences in California State Prison," *Journal of Leisure Research* 41, no. 4 (2009): 565–580.

3. "The Senator Be Embezzling . . . He a Regular Convict Now!"

1. Hedwig Lee and Christopher Wildeman, "Things Fall Apart: Health Consequences of Mass Imprisonment for African American Women," *Review of Black Political Economy* 40 (March 2013): 39–52; Bruce Western and Christopher Wildeman, "The Black Family and Mass Incarceration," *Annals of the American Academy of Political and Social Science* 621 (January 2009): 221–242.

2. Devah Pager, "The Mark of a Criminal Record," *American Journal of Sociology* 108 (March 2003): 937–975.

3. See, for instance, Department of Corrections websites for Missouri, Arkansas, and Colorado, as well as the Federal Bureau of Prisons website.

4. Interviews with respondents who had been incarcerated in state prisons in Missouri, Texas, and New York, as well as those who had spent time in federal facilities.

5. Upton Sinclair, *I, Candidate for Governor: And How I Got Licked* (1935; reprinted in Berkeley: University of California Press, 1994), 109.

6. Amanda Chicago Lewis, "The Prisoners Fighting California's Wildfires," *Buzzfeed*, October 30, 2014.

7. Ibid.

8. Brooke Shelby Biggs, "Solitary Confinement: A Brief History," *Mother Jones*, March 2, 2009.

9. Rachael Kamel and Bonnie Kerness, *The Prison Inside the Prison: Control Units, Supermax Prisons, and Devices of Torture*, a Justice Visions Briefing Paper, American Friends Service Committee, 2003.

10. Ibid.

11. Human Rights Watch, *Statement to the U.S. Senate Committee on the Judiciary, Subcommittee on the Constitution, Civil Rights, and Human Rights,* June 18, 2012.

12. Kamel and Kerness, *The Prison Inside the Prison.*

13. *Madrid v. Gomez,* 889 F. Supp. 1146 (N.D. Cal. 1995), quoted in Human Rights Watch, Statement to the U.S. Senate Committee on the Judiciary.

14. "Solitary Nation," *Frontline,* April 22, 2014.

15. Randall G. Shelden and Daniel Macallair, *Juvenile Justice in America: Problems and Prospects* (Long Grove, IL: Waveland, 2007).

16. E. Fuller Torrey et al., "The Treatment of Persons with Mental Illness in Prisons and Jails: A State Survey," Treatment Advocacy Center, April 8, 2014; http://www.tacreports.org/treatment-behind-bars.

17. Human Rights Watch, Statement to the U.S. Senate Committee on the Judiciary.

4. "Prison's Just Like the Street—with a Different Color of Chips"

1. Edwin Sutherland, *The Professional Thief* (Chicago: University of Chicago Press, 1937).

2. Robert K. Merton, "Social Structure and Anomie," *American Sociological Review* 3, no. 5 (1938): 672–682.

3. Richard Cloward and Lloyd Ohlin, *Delinquency and Opportunity* (New York: Free Press, 1960).

4. William J. Baumol, "Entrepreneurship: Productive, Unproductive, and Destructive," *Journal of Political Economy* 98, no. 5 (1990): 893–921.

5. J. A. Price, "Private Enterprise in a Prison: The Free Market Economy of La Mesa Penitenciara," *Crime and Delinquency* 19, no. 2 (1973): 218–227.

6. M. Sonfield and R. Barbato, "Testing Prison Inmates for Entrepreneurial Aptitude," *Journal of Small Business Strategy* 5, no. 2 (1994): 45–51.

7. R. W. Fairlie, "Drug Dealing and Legitimate Self-Employment," *Journal of Labor Economics* 20, no. 3 (2002): 538–563.

8. A. Reiple, "Offenders and Entrepreneurship," *European Journal on Criminal Policy and Research* 6, no. 2 (June 1998): 235–256.

9. M. Sonfield, R. Lussier, and R. Barbato, "The Entrepreneurial Aptitude of Prison Inmates and the Potential Benefit of Self-Employment Programs," *Academy of Entrepreneurship Journal* 17, no. 2 (2001): 85–94.

10. S. Goodman, "Prisoners as Entrepreneurs: Developing a Model for Prisoner-Run Industry," *Boston University Law Review* 62 (1982): 1163–1195.

11. Mathew Sonfield, "Entrepreneurship and Prisoner Re-entry: The Development of a Concept," *Small Business Institute Research Review* 35 (2008): 193–200.

12. Robert W. Fairlie, "Drug Dealing and Legitimate Self-Employment," *Journal of Labor Economics* 20, no. 3 (2002): 538–567.

13. Robert Smith, "Entrepreneurship: A Divergent Pathway out of Crime," in ed. K. Jaishankar, *International Perspectives on Crime and Justice* (Newcastle upon Tyne: Cambridge Scholars Publishing, 2009), 162–184.

14. Drew Kukorowski, Peter Wagner, and Leah Sakala, "Please Deposit All of Your Money: Kickbacks, Rates, and Hidden Fees in the Jail Phone Industry," *Prison Policy Initiative,* May 8, 2013.

15. Liliana Segura, "With 2.3 Million People Incarcerated in the U.S., Prisons Are Big Business," *The Nation*, October 1, 2013.

16. R. Parke and K. A. Clarke-Stewart, "Effects of Parental Incarceration on Young Children," U.S. Department of Health and Human Services, 2002.

17. Creasie Finney Hairston, "Prisoners and Their Families: Parenting Issues During Incarceration," in eds. Jeremy Travis and Michelle Waul, *Prisoners Once Removed: The Impact of Incarceration and Reentry on Children, Families and Communities* (Washington, D.C.: Urban Institute Press, 2003), 260–282; D. Derksen, R. Gobeil, and J. Gileno, *Visitation and Post-Release Outcomes Among Federally Sentenced Offenders* (Ottawa, Ontario: Correctional Service of Canada, 2009); Minnesota Department of Corrections, *The Effects of Prisoner Visitation on Offender Recidivism*, 2011.

18. Tim Murphy, "Prison Phone Companies Have Found Yet Another Way to Squeeze Families for Cash," *Mother Jones*, February 24, 2015.

19. Ibid.

20. Kukorowski, Wagner, and Sakala, "Please Deposit All of Your Money."

21. Murphy, "Prison Phone Companies Have Found Yet Another Way."

22. Ibid.

23. Report of the Sentencing Project to the United Nations Human Rights Committee Regarding Racial Disparities in the United States Criminal Justice System, August 2013, http://sentencingproject.org/doc/publications/rd_ICCPR%20Race%20and%20Justice%20Shadow%20Report.pdf.

24. Marie Gottschalk, *Caught* (Princeton, NJ: Princeton University Press, 2009), Chapter 3.

25. Mona Lynch, *Sunbelt Justice: Arizona and the Transformation of American Punishment* (Stanford, CA: Stanford University Press, 2010).

26. Gottschalk, *Caught*, 39; Public Safety Performance Project, "Public Safety, Public Spending: Forecasting America's Prison Population, 2007–2011" (Washington, D.C.: Pew Charitable Trusts, 2007), 27.

27. Commission on Safety and Abuse in America's Prisons, "Confronting Confinement" (New York: Vera Institute of Justice, June 2006), 5.

28. Gottschalk, *Caught*, 39–43; National Research Council, "Ensuring the Quality, Credibility, and Relevance of U.S. Justice Statistics" (Washington, D.C.: National Academy of Sciences, 2009), 253; Caitlin Dewey, "With Few Other Outlets, Inmates Review Prisons on Yelp," *Washington Post*, April 27, 2013.

29. Report of the Sentencing Project to the United Nations Human Rights Committee Regarding Racial Disparities in the United States Criminal Justice System, August 2013, http://sentencingproject.org/doc/publications /rd_ICCPR%20Race%20and%20Justice%20Shadow%20Report.pdf.

30. Sonfield, "Entrepreneurship and Prisoner Re-entry."

31. Devah Pager, *Marked: Race, Crime, and Finding Work in an Era of Mass Incarceration* (Chicago: University of Chicago Press, 2008).

32. For a national directory of prison entrepreneurship programs, see http://www.inc.com/articles/2009/02/prison-entrepreneurship.html.

33. See New York Small Business Development Center, http://www.nyssbdc .org.

34. Less than 1 percent of the nation's prisoners receive postsecondary education; the federal government eliminated funding for postsecondary education in 1995. See "Maximum Security Education," *60 Minutes*; http:// www.cbsnews.com/news/maximum-security-education/.

35. Lois M. Davis et al., "Evaluating the Effectiveness of Correctional Education: A Meta-Analysis of Programs That Provide Education to Incarcerated Adults," *Rand Corporation*, 2013, http://www.rand.org/pubs/research _reports/RR266.html.

36. Ibid.

37. Bard Prison Initiative, "What We Do," http://bpi.bard.edu/what-we -do/; Prison Studies Project, "Hudson Link for Higher Education in Prison," http://prisonstudiesproject.org/2011/08/hudson-link-for-higher-education-in -prison/.

38. Jake Cronin, "The Path to Successful Reentry: The Relationship Between Correctional Education, Employment and Recidivism," Institute of

Public Policy, Harry S. Truman School of Public Affairs, Report 15-2011, September 2011.

39. Aaron Wildavsky, *Implementation: How Great Expectations in Washington Are Dashed in Oakland; or, Why It's Amazing That Federal Programs Work at All, This Being a Saga of the Economic Development Administration, As Told by Two Sympathetic Observers Who Seek to Build Morals on a Foundation of Ruined Hopes* (Berkeley: University of California Press, 1973).

40. Michael Lipsky, *Street-Level Bureaucracy: Dilemmas of the Individual in the Public Services* (New York: Russell Sage Foundation, 1980).

5. "This Is Jail, Not Yale"

1. Luke Mullins, "Enter a 'Hellish Place,'" *The American*, May/June 2007.

2. John Carney, "Is Raj Rajaratnam Really Living Like a Prison King?" *CNBC.com*, August 27, 2013.

3. Mullins, "Enter a 'Hellish Place.'"

4. Carney, "Is Raj Rajaratnam Really Living Like a Prison King?"

5. Mullins, "Enter a 'Hellish Place.'"

6. Lisa DePaulo, "The Secrets of White Collar Prisons," *DuJour*, n.d.; http://dujour.com/news/inside-white-collar-prisons-bernie-kerik-jack-abramoff/.

7. Adapted in part from Jeff Smith, "Twelve Tips for Blago," *Chicago Tribune*, March 15, 2012.

6. "You Best Not Go to Sleep Tonight, Cellie"

1. Alex Tepperman, "We Will NOT Pump You Up: Punishment & Prison Weightlifting in the 1990s," http://www.academia.edu/552799/We _Will_NOT_Pump_You_Up_Punishment_and_Prison_Weightlifting_in _the_1990s.

2. Bill Misner, "The Importance of Sleep for Muscle Growth," *Elite Fitness*, July 11, 2009.

3. Tepperman, "We Will NOT Pump You Up."

4. Christopher Wildeman, "Parental Imprisonment, the Prison Boom, and the Concentration of Childhood Disadvantage," *Demography* 46 (2009): 265–280; Susan Phillips, Alaattin Erkanli, Gordon P. Keeler, E. Jane Costello, and Adrian Angold, "Disentangling the Risks: Parent Criminal Justice Involvement and Children's Exposure to Family Risks," *Criminology and Public Policy* 5, no. 4 (November 2006): 677–702.

5. Christopher Wildeman, "Paternal Incarceration and Children's Physically Aggressive Behaviors: Evidence from the Fragile Families and

Child Wellbeing Study," *Social Forces* 89 (2010): 285–310; also see Center for Research on Child Well-Being, *Fragile Families Research Brief, Parental Incarceration and Child Wellbeing in Fragile Families* (Princeton, N.J.: Princeton University, 2008).

6. Joseph Murray and David Farrington, "Effects of Parental Imprisonment on Children," *Crime and Justice: A Review of Research*, vol. 37 (Chicago: University of Chicago Press, 2008).

7. Steve Christian, "Children of Incarcerated Parents," National Conference of State Legislatures, March 2009.

8. Ibid.

9. Daniel Genis, "Barbells Behind Bars," *T-Nation,* July 30, 2014.

10. Ibid.

7. "You Don't Wanna Get a Cellie with Boobs"

1. Stephen Donaldson, "The Rape Crisis Behind Bars," *New York Times*, December 29, 1993.

2. Ibid.

3. Alan J. Davis, "Sexual Assaults in the Philadelphia Prison System and Sheriff's Vans," *Trans-Action* 6, no. 2 (December 1968): 8–16.

4. W. S. Wooden and J. Parker, *Men Behind Bars: Sexual Exploitation in Prison* (New York: Plenum, 1982).

5. Chandra Bozelko, "Why We Let Prison Rape Go On," *New York Times*, April 17, 2015; United States Department of Justice, Regulatory Impact Assessment for Prison Rape Elimination Act Final Rule (May 17, 2012), available at http://www.ojp.usdoj.gov/programs/pdfs/prea_ria.pdf.

6. Submission to the United Nations Committee Against Torture, During its Consideration of the Third to Fifth Periodic Reports of the United States of America CAT 53rd Session, October 20, 2014.

7. David Kaiser and Lovisa Stannow, "Prison Rape: Obama's Program to Stop It," *New York Review of Books*, October 12, 2012.

8. Elizabeth Stoker Bruenig, "Why Americans Don't Care About Prison Rape," *The Nation*, March 2, 2015.

9. Donaldson, "The Rape Crisis Behind Bars."

10. Sheryl Pimlott Kubiak, "The Effects of PTSD on Treatment Adherence, Drug Relapse, and Criminal Recidivism in a Sample of Incarcerated Men and Women," *Research on Social Work Practice*, 14, no. 6 (2004), 424–433.

11. John Irwin, *Prisons in Turmoil* (Boston: Little, Brown, 1980); see

also Kubiak, "The Effects of PTSD on Treatment Adherence, Drug Relapse, and Criminal Recidivism in a Sample of Incarcerated Men and Women."

12. Donaldson, "The Rape Crisis Behind Bars."

13. Ibid.

14. Matthew Silberman, "Resource Mobilization and the Reduction of Prison Violence." Paper presented at the annual meeting of the American Sociological Association, Los Angeles, August 1994.

15. Regina G. Kunzel, "Situating Sex: Prison Sexual Culture in the Mid-Twentieth Century United States," *GLQ: A Journal of Lesbian and Gay Studies* 8, no. 3 (2002): 253–270.

9. "You'll Be Back, Shitbird"

1. Annie Lowrey, "What's the Matter with Eastern Kentucky?" *New York Times Magazine*, June 26, 2014.

2. Bill Estep, "Chapter 12: A Drug-Addled City Hits Bottom, Strives to Get Clean," *Lexington Herald-Leader*, November 30, 2013.

3. Lowrey, "What's the Matter with Eastern Kentucky?"

4. Rich Johnston, "When Spider-Man Invented Electronic Tagging," *Bleeding Cool*, June 24, 2012.

5. Daniel Carson, "Electronic Guard for Felons," *Lodi News-Sentinel*, June 19, 1984.

6. Ibid.

7. Johnston, "When Spider-Man Invented Electronic Tagging."

8. Christian Henrichson and Ruth Delaney, *The Price of Prisons: What Incarceration Costs Taxpayers*, Vera Institute, Center on Sentencing and Corrections, February 29, 2012.

9. Henrichson and Delaney, *The Price of Prisons*.

10. Nancy La Vigne and Julie Samuels, "The Growth and Increasing Cost of the Federal Prison System: Drivers and Potential Solutions," Urban Institute Justice Policy Center, December 2012.

11. The Women's Prison Association and Home, Inc., "Family to Family; Partnerships Between Corrections and Child Welfare: Collaboration for Change, Part Two," Annie E. Casey Foundation, Baltimore, 2001.

Epilogue

1. Paul Steinhauser, Ashley Killough, and Greg Clary, "Rand Paul: 'Fight for Justice Now' on Unfair Sentencing," *CNN*, July 25, 2014.

2. Blacks voted 93 percent to 6 percent for Barack Obama over Mitt Romney in 2012.

3. Naomi Murakawa, *The First Civil Right: How Liberals Built Prison America* (New York: Oxford University Press, 2015), Chapter 4.

4. Ibid., 110.

5. Ibid., Chapter 3.

6. Ibid., Chapter 3.

7. Adam Serwer, "California AG 'Shocked' to Learn Her Office Wanted to Keep Eligible Parolees in Jail to Work," *Buzzfeed,* November 18, 2014.

8. V. O. Key, *Southern Politics in State and Nation* (New York: Knopf, 1949).

9. Edwards Carmines and James Stimson, *Issue Evolution: Race and Transformation of American Politics* (Princeton, NJ: Princeton University Press, 1989).

10. Gottschalk, *Caught,* 53.

11. Evan McMorris-Santoro, "The Big, New Bipartisan, Well-Funded Effort to Change the U.S. Criminal Justice System," *Buzzfeed,* February 19, 2015.

12. Evan McMorris-Santoro, "Inside The Weirdly Bipartisan, Very Optimistic World of Prison Reform," *Buzzfeed,* March 9, 2014.

13. Ibid.

14. Dr. Oliver Roeder, Lauren-Brooke Eisen, and Julia Bowling, *What Caused the Crime Decline?* (New York: Brennan Center for Justice, 2015).

15. Dana Goldstein, "How to Cut the Prison Population by 50 Percent," *The Marshall Project,* March 4, 2015.

16. Ibid.

INDEX